The
Contemporary American Comic Epic

Humor in Life and Letters

SARAH BLACHER COHEN, *General Editor*

Advisory Editors

JOSEPH BOSKIN
Boston University
History and American Studies

ALAN DUNDES
University of California, Berkeley
Folklore and Anthropology

WILLIAM F. FRY, JR.
Stanford University Medical School
Psychiatry

GERALD GARDNER
Author and lecturer
Politics and Government

JEFFREY H. GOLDSTEIN
Temple University and London University
Psychology

GERALD MAST
University of Chicago
Film Studies

DON L. F. NILSEN
Arizona State University
Linguistics

JUNE SOCHEN
Northeastern Illinois University
Women's Studies

LARRY WILDE
Comedian and author

Elaine B. Safer

The Contemporary American Comic Epic

The Novels of Barth, Pynchon, Gaddis, and Kesey

WAYNE STATE UNIVERSITY PRESS   DETROIT 1989

92   91   90   89   5   4   3   2   1

Library of Congress Cataloging-in-Publication Data

Safer, Elaine B.
    The contemporary American comic epic : the novels of Barth,
Pynchon, Gaddis, and Kesey / Elaine B. Safer.
        p.   cm.—(Humor in life and letters)
    Bibliography: p.
    Includes index.
    ISBN 0-8143-2050-3 (alk. paper)
    1. American fiction—20th century—History and criticism.
2. Humorous stories, American—History and criticism.   3. Epic
literature, American—History and criticism.   4. Comic, The, in
literature.   5. Barth, John—Criticism and interpretation.
6. Pynchon, Thomas—Criticism and interpretation.   7. Gaddis,
William, 1922–   —Criticism and interpretation.   8. Kesey, Ken—
Criticism and interpretation.   I. Title.   II. Series.
PS374.H86S23 1988
813'.54'0917—dc19   88–17264
                                                        CIP

*Elaine Berkman Safer is Professor of English at
the University of Delaware. She earned her M.A. and
Ph.D. degrees from Case Western Reserve University. A
specialist in the American comic novel and in the poetry
and prose of John Milton, she has published essays on the
contemporary novel in such journals and books as* Studies in the Novel, Critique, Studies in American Fiction,
Studies in American Humor, Renascence, *and* Critical
Essays on Thomas Pynchon; *she has also edited* John
Milton: L'Allegro and Il Penseroso *(1970) and has published essays on Milton in* Milton Studies, Milton Quarterly, Ariel, *and* A Milton Encyclopedia.
    *The manuscript was edited by Lois Krieger. The
typeface for the text is Sabon and the display faces are
Clarendon Bold and Sabon. The book is printed on
55-lb. Glatfelter text paper and bound in Holliston Mills'
Roxite Vellum.*
    Manufactured in the United States of America.

For my students
at the University of Delaware

CONTENTS

ACKNOWLEDGMENTS

I am grateful for the advice and generosity of a number of friends and colleagues who truly have shown me the benefit of being part of the academic community. I especially thank Sarah Blacher Cohen, editor of Wayne State University Press's Humor in Life and Letters series. Her suggestions for the manuscript have been invaluable. Others who graciously have shared their expertise with me by commenting on chapters of the book include Jerry C. Beasley, Richard A. Davison, J. A. Leo Lemay, Ronald E. Martin, Donald C. Mell, and Linda P. Miller. I wish to thank Margaret P. Hassert and Wayne State University Press's Lois Krieger for their fine editorial assistance. In addition, Margaret Hassert helped with the index. Erin M. Everson and Moira A. Owens also reviewed the manuscript, checked references, and gave useful suggestions. Moira, in addition, helped with the typing. I also wish to thank my students Susan Brizzolara, Diane Frick, A. Thomas Bozzo, and Donald M. Brown for their research assistance. Steven Moore, of Rutgers University, kindly aided me in locating materials on William Gaddis.

Acknowledgments

While writing the book, I enjoyed discussions of this material with enthusiastic students in my graduate seminars on the modern and postmodern American novel. These dialogues clarified my thinking. I also thank the editors of *Studies in the Novel, Studies in American Humor, Critique, Studies in American Fiction,* and *Renascence* for their permission to use material from my published essays.

I wish to express my gratitude to the National Endowment for the Humanities for a grant that helped support my work. So, too, I thank the University of Delaware for two summer faculty fellowships, and I thank Dean Helen Gouldner and her committee for arranging a grant-in-aid to help defray the expenses of manuscript preparation.

Finally, thanks go to my children—Debra, Alan, and Judy—for their patience and concern. And thanks go to my husband, Dan, for his encouragement and for his sound critical judgments on the manuscript.

ABBREVIATIONS

The following works by John Barth, Thomas Pynchon, William Gaddis, and Ken Kesey have shortened titles placed parenthetically in the text.

John Barth

Chimera	*Chimera*. New York: Random House, 1972.
End of the Road	*The End of the Road*. New York: Doubleday, 1958. Revised edition, 1967. Reprint. New York: Bantam, 1969.
Friday	*The Friday Book: Essays and Other Nonfiction*. New York: Putnam, 1984.
Goat-Boy	*Giles Goat-Boy or, The Revised New Syllabus*. New York: Doubleday, 1966. Reprint. Greenwich, Conn.: Fawcett Crest, 1968.
Letters	*Letters: A Novel*. New York: Putnam, 1979.
"Exhaustion"	"The Literature of Exhaustion." *Atlantic Monthly* (August 1967): 29–34.
"Replenishment"	"The Literature of Replenishment." *Atlantic Monthly* (January 1980): 65–71.
Funhouse	*Lost in the Funhouse*. New York: Doubleday, 1968. Reprint. New York: Bantam, 1969.
Sabbatical	*Sabbatical: A Romance*. New York: Putnam, 1982.
Sot-Weed	*The Sot-Weed Factor*. New York: Doubleday, 1960. Revised edition, 1967. Reprint. New York: Bantam, 1975.

11

Thomas Pynchon

Lot 49   *The Crying of Lot 49.* Philadelphia: Lippin-
                     cott, 1966.
Gravity's Rainbow   *Gravity's Rainbow.* New York: Viking, 1973.
V.   *V.* Philadelphia: Lippincott, 1963. Reprint.
                     New York: Bantam, 1968.

William Gaddis

JR   *JR.* New York: Knopf, 1975.
Recognitions   *The Recognitions.* New York: Harcourt,
                     1955.
"Rush"   "The Rush for Second Place." *Harper's* (April
                     1981): 31–39.

Ken Kesey

Cuckoo's Nest   *One Flew Over the Cuckoo's Nest.* New York:
                     Viking, 1962. Reprint. New York: Signet,
                     1962.
Notion   *Sometimes a Great Notion.* New York: Vi-
                     king, 1964. Reprint. New York: Bantam,
                     1969.

CHAPTER ONE

Introduction: An Overview

The epic traditionally has been lauded as a heroic poem, advancing "men to the quality of Gods,"[1] a narrative that records the moral vision of a righteous nation and the honorable exploits of its great warriors, and a work that is "elaborate above all others," exhibiting a grandeur of effect as it selects for objects of imitation that which "ought to be."[2] Because of its depth and breadth, John Milton used the form to "justify the ways of God to men" in a manner that would be "doctrinal and exemplary to a nation"; Cotton Mather employed it to reveal the *"Wonderful Displays"* of Christ's work in America;[3] and Walt Whitman used the genre to celebrate and sing of himself and all mankind, as well as of the transcendent meaning in all of nature. Epics customarily focus on events of great magnitude, exalting the heroic quest and placing it in the larger cosmic order.

This study focuses on the comic use of epic patterns in selected contemporary American novels of John Barth, Thomas Pynchon, William Gaddis, and Ken Kesey. A number of postmodern novels of these writers are encyclopedic in scope, allude to grand themes in history, and often employ epic devices such as epithets, similes, catalogues, and multiple cross-references. They incorporate themes, myths, and structural patterns that are found in traditional epics such as Milton's *Paradise Lost,* Mather's *Magnalia Christi Americana,* and Whitman's "Song of Myself." Unlike the traditional works, however, the new epics offer an absurd hero's ironic quest instead of a holy mission; they build to disorder rather than unity, and use exaggeration to satirize all institutions and systems of knowledge—instead of celebrating a nationalistic or religious vision.

The postmodern narratives refer to revered American values and then disappoint reader expectation for the restatement of these customary themes, creating instead an absurdist vision. They allude to traditional conventions and then deploy these against themselves to present lively parodies of twentieth-century American society.

Epic Novels

The Sot-Weed Factor, Giles Goat-Boy, V., Gravity's Rainbow, The Recognitions, and *Sometimes a Great Notion* have roots in the traditional epic and also in wide-ranging comic narratives. The role of their postmodern American authors seems to be burlesqued by Barth's Ebenezer Cooke, who intends to write an epic poem—"An epic to out-epic epics: the history of the princely house of Charles Calvert, Lord Baltimore and Lord Proprietary of the Province of Maryland, relating the heroic founding of that province" (*Sot-Weed* 83–84). Ebenezer Cooke ultimately lampoons the heroic much as the postmodernists Barth, Pynchon, Gaddis, and Kesey satirize rather than extol the people of their province (America). They, like Eben, reveal that they know *Paradise Lost* "inside out" and "*Hudibras* upside down" (*Sot-Weed* 11). And they, like Eben, draw upon works such as "the volumes of Milton and Samuel Butler . . . as references" (*Sot-Weed* 250) to reinforce their comic-ironic message.

In addition to such allusions, the postmodernists frequently use literary devices and themes that are prevalent in Rabelais's *Gargantua and Pantagruel,* Cervantes's *Don Quixote,* and Fielding's *Joseph Andrews,* comic narratives that Northrop Frye includes in "the anatomy."[4] For example, all contain encyclopedic listings. In *The Sot-Weed Factor,* the comic catalogue of twins and those regarded as twins in history and legend includes Castor and Pollux ("the sons of light and thunder"), Helen and Clytemnestra from Leda's egg, Romulus and Remus in Rome, saints who were thought of as twins, and also "Heavenly Twins, revered by sundry salvages [*sic*]" (*Sot-Weed* 534–35). The Rabelaisian catalogue includes strange births in mythology and legend—Bacchus "begotten by Jupiter's thigh," Minerva "born from Jupiter's brain . . . Castor and Pollux from the shell of an egg laid and hatched by Leda,"[5] as well as the birth of Gargantua. Both Barth and Rabelais also revel in synonyms. In *Sot-Weed*, for example, two prostitutes verbally fling at each other a list of terms for whoring (for example, "Fastfanny," "Furrowbutt," "Tart," "Poxbox," "Trollop" [477–82]). In Rabelais, similarly, many synonyms for excrement are used (for example, "shit, turds, crots, ordure").[6]

Pynchon's detailed description in *V.* of the freewheeling activity of the "folk" of Manhattan—who go from one bar to another, ride in the subways, create paintings like Slab's danishes, and shoot alligators in the sewers—calls to mind Rabelais's panoramic depiction of the lower classes and their free-flowing bawdy laughter. Pynchon's listing of items in *Gravity's Rainbow*, ranging from rockets and weapons to songs, films, and items on Tyrone Slothrop's desk (18), resembles the encyclopedic catalogues in Rabelais that include stores in the Parisian marketplace ("the druggists' shops, the herbalists, and the apothecaries"),[7] the food Gargantua eats ("hams, smoked ox-tongues, botargos, sausages"),[8] the 216 games he plays (including "Flushes," "Beggar-my-neighbor," "Cuckold," "Scare," and "Flip-finger"),[9] and the variety of oaths and curses aimed at Gargantua—"some in a fury and others in sport (*par ris*)"[10]—by those who escaped his "piss-flood," which drowned over 260,000 (for example, "Carymary, Carymara! My holy tart, we've been drenched in sport! We've been drenched *par ris*").[11]

The cataloguing in Barth and Pynchon, as well as in Gaddis and Kesey, also has roots in Cervantes. The elaborate listing of legendary details about twins in *Sot-Weed* is similar to the listing in *Don Quixote* of the legendary chivalrous romances, including the well-known ones of King Arthur and those of Tristram and Yseult and Guinevere and Lancelot, who, the hero insists, were real persons. The mixing of historical characters in *Sot-Weed* (for example, Lord Baltimore and John Coode) with fictional ones (like Burlingame) echoes the "medley of truth and fiction" uttered by Cervantes's Don Quixote.[12] So, too, Ebenezer Cooke's foolish idealism calls to mind the early model of Don Quixote, whose heroic illusions and grand imagination are treated ironically as he engages in bizarre adventures, complex journeys, and hilarious battles such as those with windmills (envisioned as giants) and sheep (envisioned as armies).

The postmodern comic narratives have roots in the "comic Epic-Poem in Prose" described by Fielding in his Prefaces to *Joseph Andrews* and to his sister's novel *The Adventures of David Simple*.[13] This form, according to Fielding, is a narrative of great magnitude that differs "from Comedy, as the serious Epic from Tragedy: its Action being more extended and comprehensive; containing a much larger Circle of Incidents, and introducing a greater Variety of Characters." Fielding stresses that this form "differs from the serious Romance in its Fable and Action," which in the romance are "grave and solemn," compared to the comic epic, which is "light and ridiculous"; and "it differs in its Characters, by introducing Persons of inferiour Rank, and consequently of inferiour Manners, whereas the grave Romance, sets the highest before us; lastly in its Sentiments and Diction, by preserving the Ludicrous instead of the Sublime."[14]

This epic form is "truly of the Comic kind," following nature, and thus is distinguished by Fielding from burlesque, which exhibits "what is monstrous and unnatural."[15] This form may use burlesque to arouse laughter but this would be done without distorting nature. In the preface to *David Simple* (1744), Fielding emphasizes the "extended and comprehensive" scope of the comic epic, as distinguished from drama, and also its *"main End or Scope,"* which is to *"be at once amiable, ridiculous, and natural."*[16] The contemporary novels appear to be new adaptations of Fielding's comic epic.

In *Joseph Andrews*, Fielding used the comic to attack "the true Ridiculous": the vain and hypocritical members of society, people whose vices and folly are judged against the ideals of those who exhibit good-natured simplicity, chastity, and charity. The good Parson Abraham Adams and Joseph are placed at the epic novel's moral center—connecting them to biblical characters: Joseph, who rejects the sexual overtures of Potiphar's wife; and the faithful Abraham, who is ready to sacrifice his son Isaac to carry out God's will. Fielding also makes the innocence and idealism of Parson Adams and Joseph the subject of light humor—casting Joseph as a footman, resisting Lady Booby's advances, and Abraham Adams as a forgetful country clergyman, journeying among people whose hypocrisy and hardheartedness are alien to his innocent goodness. The innocence and humanity of Joseph and the parson establish the pattern of Christian heroism in the novel.[17]

Like Fielding, Barth uses innocents and their corresponding contrast with an immoral world as the basis of his ironic comedy in *The*

Sot-Weed Factor and *Giles Goat-Boy.* Ebenezer Cooke's concern over his chastity and George/Giles's naïve belief that he can revise a syllabus of education for mankind are cleverly burlesqued. With a heavier tone and less slapstick, Gaddis uses Wyatt Gwyon's innocence as a means to develop an ironic vision of the cheating, fraud, and selfishness he witnesses.

Like Fielding, the postmodern epic writers expose the follies of society and its vices, vices ranging from hypocrisy and vanity to cold-heartedness and materialism. These authors differ from Fielding, however, by presenting no obvious moral basis for their novels, no clear-cut answers or ordering principles for society. They offer no specific remedies for the contemporary world but instead use man's frustrated pursuit of virtue in the face of societal vice as part of their absurdist comedy.

The contemporary comic epic novels also are related to the nineteenth-century American epic novel *Moby-Dick.* Their references to the Bible, Shakespeare, and folklore, and their use of encyclopedic details from philosophy, geography, mathematics, history, religion, and different forms of literature, call to mind the massive compilations of names, places, and facts in *Moby-Dick:* an encyclopedia of cetology with details of various types of whales, their history, their anatomy, and their use as products by the whaling industry; a reference book of folklore and stories about the sea; a rich supply of details from the Bible and Shakespeare.

Similarly encyclopedic, Pynchon's *Gravity's Rainbow* documents rocketry rather than whales. It presents a new kind of technological tale of scientific achievements instead of folklore about whaling. In addition, it, like other contemporary American epic novels, is different from the great American prose epic *Moby-Dick* in terms of its handling of the comic. Comedy in Melville's novel is used sporadically in scenes (as in Shakespearean comedy) to emphasize, by contrast, the tragic sense. For example, Stubb, the undeveloped man who "hath more of joy than sorrow in him,"[18] stands in contrast to Ahab, who is filled with woe and despair. Stubb's comic vision of the doubloon draws attention to Ahab's painful realization of its being "stout stuff for woe to work on."[19] Comic scenes with Queequeg, like those with Stubb, develop the other side of the power of blackness. For example, Ishmael's fear of Queequeg, the "head-peddling" harpooner who is to be his "bedfellow" at the Spouter-Inn, is juxtaposed with Ishmael's observation: "Better

17

sleep with a sober cannibal than a drunken Christian." Comic scenes with Queequeg balance lightness with the novel's underlying tragic sense, which is accentuated by a quarreling with God, as in Ahab's cry against the world: "I am madness maddened. . . . I will dismember my dismemberer."[20] The comedy contrasts with the anguish and despair of a novel by an author who "can neither believe, nor be comfortable in his unbelief."[21]

In *Moby-Dick* Ishmael says, "There are certain queer times and occasions . . . when a man takes this whole universe for a vast practical joke" (195). This statement sounds similar to what we find in the twentieth-century novels where humor and pain coexist. Ishmael, however, despite statements of this type, does not greet death and decay with bizarre humor, as do the speakers in the contemporary American novel.

The tone of the postmodern epic novel is closer to the comic tone of the absurd in Melville's *The Confidence-Man* (1857), a novel that underlines man's inability to reason successfully in an unreasonable world, a novel whose title character appeals to the reasonable desire of the passengers on the steamboat to trust their fellowman and then tricks them into giving him their money. That *The Confidence-Man* has this absurdist tone may account for its growing popularity in twentieth-century America.

The contemporary American novels, particularly in terms of their encyclopedic scope, are related to the modern exemplar of the epic novel, Joyce's *Ulysses*. Joyce's novel draws connections to linguistics (the evolution of English literature from Old English to that of the twentieth century, in the "Oxen of the Sun" chapter), the sciences (a summary of embryology in "Oxen of the Sun"), sociology (the range of people of Dublin exhibiting their different voices), and classical literature (the *Odyssey*). It also is an encyclopedia of literary types, including narrative, drama, and farce.

Ulysses, however, does not have the underlying sense of anguish and anger of the novels of America's postmodern humorists. In the "Cyclops" chapter there is a fascination with the brutality of hanging in some hangmen's letters and a gallows account of the last movements of the hanged Joe Brady "the invincible,"[22] but the humor throughout *Ulysses* has a clear-cut buoyancy. Bloom is not ultimately defeated by his countrymen's anti-Semitism or the loss of his son or his wife's infidelity. Though Bloom occasionally broods on Molly's infidelity, he never becomes depressed. And though what Molly says yes to is ambiguous, as is the comic resolution of the book, the overall effect of *Ulysses* is positive.[23]

The positive tone of *Ulysses* springs in no small measure from Joyce's underlying tie to religion. Joyce rejects tyrannical aspects of church practice, but he is close to his religious past. He uses his Irish Catholic background to provide the ritual-laden passages that develop parodies of religious ritual. Establishing this parodic method is the first passage of the novel, in which Buck Mulligan solemnly comes forward holding a shaving bowl and gives a mock blessing of his surroundings, starting with "*Introibo ad altare Dei*," the opening phrase of the Mass. Mulligan, with his "shaking gurgling face," notices with delight that the white corpuscles of the shaving cream fail to transubstantiate even though the "mirror and a razor lay crossed": "For this, O dearly beloved, is the genuine christine: body and soul and blood and ouns. . . . One moment. A little trouble about those white corpuscles."[24]

Similarly religiously imbued are two passages in the "Cyclops" chapter. In Barney Kiernan's pub, the discussion of the British navy (in whom the people trust) and its cruel punishment (which represents official brutality) is presented in a phrase-by-phrase parody of the Apostles' Creed. The navy creed substitutes "They believe in rod" for God, "creator of hell upon earth" for "creator of heaven and earth," "conceived of unholy boast" for "conceived by the Holy Spirit," and so forth.[25] This irreverence for religion becomes "yoked to reverence" as the chapter implies a need for profound human values.[26]

Such a blending of the irreverent and reverent is also evident later at the bar when the drinking ritual becomes a mock prayer and its "blessed company" is comically metamorphosed into monks and friars. The ritual moves from the sacred to the profane as names of legendary saints are mixed with names of those present at the bar—S. Leopold (Bloom), S. Martin of Tours (Cunningham)—and also with such absurdities as S. Anonymous (the narrator), S. Homonymous, and S. Synonymous. Reference is made to prayers from the Mass—"the introit *in Epiphania Domini*."[27] This produces a comic sense of elevation and desecration as the men's eating and drinking at the pub are connected to congregants' partaking of the consecrated elements, bread and wine, in the Sacrament of Holy Communion.

In the American comic epic novels, references to religion also generate laughter. But the novels lack the intrinsic religious character that exists in *Ulysses,* a pattern that is naturally part of the intellectual outlook of Irish Catholics and is commonly absent in the twentieth-century American world.

Contemporary American epics ridicule those who relentlessly look for meaning in an absurd world. They exchange the comfort of an optimistic and unified world view for the vision of a universe that exhibits the randomness posited by the Second Law of Thermo-dynamics.[28] They present an absurd portrayal of the times, absurd in Camus's view, which focuses on the "confrontation between the human need [for meaning] and the unreasonable silence of the world."[29]

Black Humor and the Absurd

The perception of the world in the contemporary American epic novel is similar to that of writers of the Theater of the Absurd, a vision most eloquently presented in the plays of Eugène Ionesco, Jean-Paul Sartre, Jean Anouilh, and Edward Albee. This view also is evident in novels of the absurd that are not epic: *Catch-22, One Flew Over the Cuckoo's Nest,* and *Slaughterhouse-Five.* The comic epic novels discussed in this book are labyrinthine developments of such absurdist works. Their tone is a mixture of the comic and tragic, farce and horror.

The conflict between the quest for meaning and the upset at finding none is used by humorists of the absurd to disorient readers and to cause them to experience black humor. The black humorist employs diverse means to disorient readers: (1) he moves quickly between darkness and laughter, horror and farce—as does Barth in *The End of the Road* when Joe Morgan insists that his wife, Rennie, continue her love affair with Jake so that Joe and Rennie can face "the facts squarely" and better understand what went wrong in their marriage (*End of the Road* 122). (2) He presents situations that appear bizarre—such as the action in the mental institution in Kesey's *One Flew Over the Cuckoo's Nest*—and then makes us aware that we are really looking at a microcosm of our own world and thus share the dilemma of the characters at whom we have been laughing. (3) He gets readers emotionally involved in the tension of a story and then reminds them of the work's artifice—as when Humbert, pained at seeing the pregnant Lolita, exclaims: "Then I pulled out my automatic—I mean, this is the kind of a fool thing a reader might suppose I did. It never even occurred to me to do it."[30] (4) He inverts the traditional allusive mode, exploiting the incongruity between the original work and its reversal in the postmodern text. Readers apply the " 'normal' system of expectations . . . [and] enjoy the way in which [their] expectations are frustrated." As Umberto Eco explains, the "critical spectator . . . appreciates the ironic ploy of the [original] quotation and enjoys its desired incongruity."[31]

The Inverse Allusive Mode

The assimilation of epic themes, myths, and patterns in the contemporary novels is a complex process, resulting in a highly allusive texture more akin to poetry than to prose. John Milton's *Paradise Lost* can serve as a paradigm for discussing the traditional allusive mode. Milton opens his Puritan epic by indicating that he "intends to soar / Above th' Aonian Mount,"[32] sacred to the Muses, to whom Homer and Virgil appealed for inspiration. The epic voice connects the guidance of the classical Muse to that of the Holy Spirit: "The meaning, not the Name I call."[33] Milton's Puritan epic seeks correspondences between temporality and the eternal, between biblical history and Apocalypse. *Paradise Lost* uses a strategy of allusiveness, emphasized by the appeal to inspiration, unlocking visionary meanings of promise and fulfillment.

Like traditional epics, all the postmodern comic epic novels discussed are notably allusive. However, these epics use materials from the past in "a half-farcical, half-passionate spirit."[34] Their allusiveness mocks the present and is often ambivalent about the past.[35] The novels form allusions to traditional values that literature depicts as part of our American and Western heritage, and then they make the pursuit of these values the subject of farce. For them, as for Camus, all systems are suspect. The use of reasonable systems to understand a chaotic universe is absurd.

Mythology and Postmodernism

These comic epics reveal their authors' interest in mythology. Like other postmodern works, they—through an ironic allusiveness— reimagine and revitalize all kinds of myths and legends. While Cotton Mather devoted Book Six of his *Magnalia* to explain divine causes for happenings in folklore so as to underline "DEMONSTRATIONS of THE DIVINE PROVIDENCE,"[36] twentieth-century writers cite new legends to reflect a disorganized world that is comic and absurd, a world that is neither divinely controlled nor revealing of man's heroism. Rather than showing connections between heroes and their biblical

21

counterparts, as in *Magnalia* or *Joseph Andrews,* and between America and the Garden of Eden, as in "Song of Myself," contemporary epics alter legends and create a new mythology that reflects the randomness and entropic decline of the twentieth century.

The Sot-Weed Factor remakes tales of colonial American history; *Giles Goat-Boy or, The Revised New Syllabus* redoes the Bible; *Gravity's Rainbow* reshapes stories used in the American tall tale to illuminate the fantastic nature of the contemporary mechanical world; *The Recognitions* recycles the Faust legend; and *Sometimes a Great Notion* gives the Oedipus myth a satiric twist. It is of interest, in this regard, that such varied re-creations occur in other postmodern novels: Barth's *Chimera* reinvents classical mythology; Joseph Heller's *God Knows* reinterprets Old Testament stories; and Donald Barthelme's *Snow White* reuses the fairy tale.

The comic epics (like a number of other postmodern novels) also experiment with language, employ imagery that forms structural patterns—as does poetry—employ narrative comments that continually draw attention to their artifice, and convey the sense of a fragmented world.

To help clarify the American mythic dream that the postmodern epic writers call upon for their comic reversals, the next chapter returns historically to Cotton Mather's prose epic history, *Magnalia Christi Americana,* which has been called the "greatest effort in the century to organize the experience of this [American] people."[37] *Magnalia* is a repository for genres and themes found in the traditional epic. Such genres are history, saints' lives, and the jeremiad; themes include the Garden, the *translatio* motif, and traditional heroism.

Following this is a discussion of Walt Whitman's *Leaves of Grass,* which, like *Magnalia,* is a source for major American myths and themes that the contemporary novels lampoon: America as new Eden, the American Adam, the grand celebration of a nation, and the transcendental vision. *Leaves of Grass* rejoices in the infinite possibilities for the individual, the wonder at the magnificence of the self, and the innocent excitement in exploring the beauty of the American terrain and its people. Such grand and optimistic concepts become the subject of comedy in the contemporary American epic novel.

Patterns in Traditional and Absurdist Comedy

This book, as a whole, investigates the use of an ironic allusive mode to generate absurd comedy in the contemporary epic novel. Traditional comedy advances from disorder to order, from illusion to an affirmation of the customary moral and social norms of society.[38] Absurdist comedy, by contrast, mocks man's quest for order and for the reasonable, concluding that firm reality is a deceptive fiction.

Traditional comedy usually moves toward reconciliation. As Dante observes, comedy "introduces a situation of adversity, but ends its matter in prosperity."[39] If the comedy has a theological base, repentance and forgiveness form the completion of the ordering pattern. If the comedy has a social base, it unmasks our weaknesses and "cures folly by folly"[40] as it progresses from disorder to an order established by the moral norms of society.

Comedy progresses toward a happy ending, a sense that "this should be." "Its opposite," explains Northrop Frye, "is not the villainous but the absurd" or irrational. The comedic movement is from illusion to reality. "Hence," as Frye states, there is "the importance of the theme of creating and dispelling illusion in comedy: the illusions caused by disguise, obsession, hypocrisy, or unknown parentage."[41] This pattern is found in Chaucer's *The Canterbury Tales,* in Shakespeare's plays, in the writings of Ben Jonson and Molière, to cite a few examples.

At the end of "The Miller's Tale," disorderly elements are brought into harmony, and characters get what they "deserve" when the older husband, John the foolish carpenter, is ridiculed and Alison's lover, *hende* Nicholas, is burned appropriately. In Shakespearean comedy, fallible laws of society, such as the mandate for executing Syracusans in the *Comedy of Errors* and the law of compulsory marriage in *A Midsummer Night's Dream,* are eventually disregarded or clarified. Similarly, there are correctives to change foolish or misdirected characters such as Claudio, in *Much Ado about Nothing,* and Angelo, in *Measure for Measure.* The curative progression also is seen in the plays of Ben Jonson and Molière—for example, in *Volpone* and *The Misanthrope.* Volpone and Alceste get what they "deserve" according to a rational scheme of justice, and the dramas advance toward endings that reflect social standards. Traditional comedy gauges behavior in terms of a norm, stressing what author and audience hold to be of value.[42] This "shared" belief often, as in *Joseph Andrews,* is "the design of Providence" rewarding the good in this world and in the eternal.[43]

In works that have a theological base like *Paradise Lost,* divine comedy operates through the perspective of eternity. Within the absolutist time frame, the continual contrast between the confusion of hell and the harmonious peace of heaven achieves an urgent immediacy. There is a progression from the disorder of the fall of Adam and Eve to man's repentance and forgiveness through Jesus Christ. This culminates in hope for the everlasting future when mankind will be redeemed, when all will be purged and refined: "New Heav'ns, new Earth, . . . / To bring forth fruits Joy and eternal Bliss."[44]

The contemporary epic novels of Barth, Pynchon, Gaddis, and Kesey invert the structure of traditional comedy. The movement toward normative and redemptive order is rejected, and a sense of chaos is affirmed, as in George/Giles Goat-Boy's revelation of nothingness at the close of his quest. Absurdist comedy ridicules man's quest for order and meaning, determining that what "should be" is a deceptive fiction in our irrational world.

Theirs is a world in which the myth of the American dream has been destroyed: the Garden transformed into the Street of the twentieth-century; the hero as American Adam turned into the schlemihl;[45] the hope for a nation transformed into the sense of entropic decline; and religious fervor metamorphosed into the sardonic humor of the absurd.

This book considers what kind of absurd affirmation develops in postmodern epic novels whose characters yearn for meaning but achieve neither deep insight nor happiness. Longing is reflected in all the major characters of these novels: in Burlingame's quest for freedom from societal restraints in *Sot-Weed;* George/Giles's desire for understanding and learning in *Giles Goat-Böy;* Stencil's pursuit of *V.;* Slothrop's quest for information in *Gravity's Rainbow;* Wyatt's desire to achieve the beauty of the Flemish painters in *The Recognitions;* and Hank's and Lee's perseverance as they jump from log to log on the Wakonda Auga River at the conclusion of *Sometimes a Great Notion.*

Some contend that love creates affirmation in Barth and Pynchon, that art is expiation in Gaddis, and that the heroic energy of the struggle itself rectifies the absurdities in Kesey's world.[46] My position is that affirmation for readers involves a tripartite process: first, realization of the exposure of false ordering systems; second, the readers' disorientation when they cannot find meaning; and, finally, the comic awakening to and acceptance of the sheer absurdity of the human predicament, the acceptance of the Camusian exhortation to laugh with scorn at the absurd quest and try our best to meet disappointment with humor and strength.[47]

CHAPTER TWO

Twentieth-Century Comic Epic Novels and Cotton Mather's *Magnalia*

Magnalia *Christi Americana* (1702) is important in the study of the American epic novels of John Barth, Thomas Pynchon, William Gaddis, and Ken Kesey for three major reasons. It is an early example of a highly allusive American epic in prose, a form to which the twentieth-century epic novels develop an ironic counterpart. It contains themes that recur in American literature and are mocked in the contemporary American comic epic novel: the concept of America as a new Garden of Eden; America as a new Canaan; and America as the high point of the westward advancement of culture, the arts, and empire. It utilizes genres (in addition to the epic) that are parodied in the twentieth-century novel: the history or chronicle; saints' lives; and the jeremiad sermon, which encourages men to repent their evil and preaches God's forgiveness.

The Traditional Allusive Mode and Its Reversals

Magnalia can serve as a paradigm for the traditional allusive mode, the primary means by which epics have developed a sense of a legendary past. Mather comments extensively on his use of allusions: "I must, in a way of Writing, like that of *Plutarch,* prepare my Reader for the intended Relation, by first searching the Archives of Antiquity for a Parallel."[1] He enriches his depiction of the work of Christ in America by paraphrasing lines from the *Aeneid* at the opening of *Magnalia,* suggesting correspondences between the Puritan founders of America and those heroes of Rome who, with Aeneas, did "traverse so many perils . . . face so many trials" (Harvard 90).[2] Later on, these epic connections are strengthened by comparisons between the Indian wars with the Puritans and the battle in heaven in *Paradise Lost,* involving the good angels and the satanic host. Mather explains: "We . . . can scarce forbear taking the colours in the Sixth Book of Milton to describe our story" (2:566).

Mather appreciates that this elaborate method may cause people to criticize *Magnalia* for having a *"Style* Embellished with too much of *Ornament,* by the multiplied References . . . in almost every Paragraph" (Harvard 101). He insists, however, that the embellishments are "choice *Flowers"* (Harvard 101). The parallels prepare the reader for the relationships between the exemplary Puritan heroes and those of the classical and biblical past. They evoke traditional moral and aesthetic values in the later piece.

Mather's allusive method is primarily one of typological exegesis. He views persons, events, and narratives of the Old Testament as prophetic signs that foreshadow the persons and events in God's redemptive plan as it is revealed in the New Testament. For Cotton Mather, the heroes of both the Old and New Testament are "types" figuring forth the exemplary heroes in New England who carry out the wonderful work of Christ in America. This method represents a way of looking at persons and events in colonial America in relation to a theology of history that posits God's eternal presence at every moment. The "types" are essentially progressive images whose meaning becomes clear at the end of the process.[3] According to this process, New England becomes many things: a new Garden of Eden; a Canaan for the New Israelites' "errand into the Wilderness";[4] a place in which to combat the Devil as Christ did in the desert; and also a prefiguration or type for the New Jerusalem, "a new heaven and a new earth" (Rev. 21:1).[5]

In their portrayal of America and its settlers, Barth, Pynchon, Gaddis, and Kesey also employ a highly allusive method, but their works use the allusions for ironic deflation. These writers of the absurd virtually trap the reader who looks for correspondences of meaning and order. They set up traditional literary patterns, alter the message, and then laugh at the reader's disappointment. Desire for the clues and allusions to build an edifice of the eternal verities is ridiculed in these epic novels, which drop the clues and make the allusions, only to reverse the usual meaning associated with them.

The allusive strategy sets up a three-step process. On one level, the works present a vision of harmonious order residing in myth and literature from an earlier period. On another, they detail the chaotic imperfection of the twentieth-century world. The absence of customary insights aggravates the reader's desire for them, and the futile struggle for the unattainable creates the comedy of the absurd. On a third level, the comic-absurd is developed by the strong suggestion that the ordered universe posited in the revered literature of the past was deceptively idyllic and has always been unattainable for mankind.

Epic Conventions

Magnalia provides a model for the traditional American epic.[6] Its historical scope returns to Adam and his descendants (the leaders in biblical history) and moves forward to the future, when man will be redeemed. Typological associations connect first-generation heroes with these biblical leaders: Adam, Noah, and Nehemiah; John and Paul. The Puritans' battles with the Indians become grand confrontations between good and evil, as God's will is carried out on earth.

Magnalia is often referred to as "the first in a long line of distinctively American epics," to be followed by such as Barlow's *Columbiad* and Whitman's *Leaves of Grass*.[7] It alludes to *Paradise Lost* and paraphrases from it to give epic proportions to the exemplary heroes;[8] it also pays close attention to epic conventions.

The epic voice appeals to the muse, states the central action and its consequences, and reveals the moral points.[9] *Magnalia*, like *Paradise Lost*, Christianizes the poetic muse. In *Paradise Lost*, the epic voice asserts, "Sing Heav'nly Muse," and then connects the poetic muse with the Holy Spirit:

Thou from the first
Wast present, and with mighty wings outspread
Dove-like satst brooding on the vast Abyss
And mad'st it pregnant.[10]

In *Magnalia,* the epic voice states: "assisted by the Holy Author of that *Religion,* I do, with all Conscience of *Truth,* required therein by Him, who is the *Truth* it self, Report the *Wonderful Displays* of His Infinite Power, Wisdom, Goodness, and Faithfulness" (Harvard 89). The narrator again addresses the Divinity at the close of the Introduction to Book I: "Grant me thy Gracious Assistances, O my God; that in this my Undertaking I may be kept from every false way" (Harvard 116).[11]

In *Magnalia,* the narrator describes the central action as the *"Considerable Matters"* that "attended the First Settlement of COLONIES" (Harvard 89), the "History of these PROTESTANTS" (Harvard 91). The consequence of the action is a history that shows how "Divine Providence hath *Irradiated* an *Indian Wilderness"* (Harvard 89). Next the epic voice asks who started the action: "The Reader will doubtless desire to know, what it was that—*tot Volvere casus / Insignes Pietate Viros, tot adire Labores, / Impulerit"* [Did drive men of such wondrous goodness to traverse so many perils, to face so many trials] (Harvard 90).[12] The answer is clear: "a few powerful *Brethren* . . . [drove the settlers] to seek a place for the Exercise of the *Protestant Religion,* according to the Light of their Consciences, in the Desarts of *America"* (Harvard 91).

Magnalia employs another important component of the epic, the catalogue: "Take then a catalogue of New-England's first ministers" (I:235). Seeming to have taken the "colours" of Milton, the *Magnalia* reverses Milton's use of the catalogue for evil (the devils) and uses it to detail the types of ministers that settled churches in the wilderness. *Magnalia,* like *Paradise Lost,* departs from the English epic convention of being in rhyme. *Paradise Lost* uses English heroic verse without rhyme. *Magnalia,* going a step farther from convention, is in prose.

Traditional Genres and the Twentieth-Century Epic

Magnalia and other traditional epics are encyclopedic in scope, incorporating materials from history, mathematics, geography, religion, and literature. Also, like other epics, it is an encyclopedia of literary types, such as saints' lives, jeremiad, and history. Primarily, *Magnalia* is an ecclesiastical history, recounting the work of Christ in America through the actions of its Puritan leaders. It is linked to other important chronicles in colonial America, such as Captain John Smith's *Generall Historie of Virginia* and William Bradford's *History of Plymouth Plantation.*

28

Twentieth-century new epics also are encyclopedias of literary types, including some of those that Mather employs in his prose epic: history, saints' lives, and the jeremiad. The new epics use these forms but do so for parodic purposes. In *The Sot-Weed Factor*, Barth makes fun of the reader's nostalgia for American history by depicting the New World's first settlers as gamblers and debauchers instead of saintly heroes. He burlesques the mythic adventures of the national figures Captain John Smith and Pocahontas by indicating that the explorer was more concerned with "conquests and feats of love" (*Sot-Weed* 162) than expeditions, and that the Indian princess was motivated by her desire to lose her maidenhood rather than by her innocent love for the grand hero. William Gaddis, to similar ends, details the ecclesiastical history of New England ironically in the life of Reverend Gwyon, who leaves behind traditional Puritan concerns in his fascination with the ancient pagan rites of Mithraism. This pre-Christian minister is eventually replaced by a post-Puritan preacher, "Dick," who discards the esoteric books in the parish library and adopts instead popular books that focus on how to influence people. Dick is an ironic fulfillment of Cotton Mather's fears that the increasing materialism of his contemporaries in colonial America would destroy the faith.

Another genre important in *Magnalia* and travestied in the contemporary novel is saints' lives. *Magnalia* instructs the readers through the lives of Puritan heroes whose biographies are patterned after those in John Foxe's *Book of Martyrs:* ministers; many worthy leaders who graduated from Harvard College; and a multitude of pious Americans who fought valiantly in the "Wars of the Lord."[13] Mather advocates these Fathers of New England, the Puritan saints, as models for all to follow: "I hope the plain history of their lives will be a powerful way of propounding their fatherly counsels to their posterity" (I:234). Mather's heroes are Puritan leaders who have been chosen for salvation. They range from John Cotton, who all his life walked with God; to the adventurer William Phips, who rose through industry, honesty, and piety to be one of God's elect (Harvard 286); to John Winthrop, whose sermon on the *Arbella* emphasized that the new land "shall be as a city upon a hill,"[14] "the light of the world" (Matt. 5:14).

Giles Goat-Boy casts a comic light on saints' lives, particularly on the life of George/Giles Goat-Boy, who fights the computer WESCAC instead of Saint George's dragon and literally lives with the goats instead of being a wearer of goatskins like Saint Giles.[15] The connections between Giles and his prototypes create humorous reversals of exempla

29

described in *Magnalia* and in other saints' lives that were popular in colonial America. The idea of sainthood is deflated most blatantly in the popular maxim that Max Spielman proposes: "*Ontogeny recapitulates cosmogeny*—what is it but to say that proctoscopy repeats hagiography?" (43). This statement—with its scatological imagery— yokes together the mysteries of the spiritual and the riddle of the anal sphincter that is to be examined with a proctoscope. In *The Recognitions* chance occurrences rather than Christian heroism cause one to be made a saint. For example, the Church mistakes the body of Camilla, Wyatt's mother, for that of an eleven-year-old Spanish girl whom it has declared a saint and accidentally canonizes Camilla in her place (791–92).

A third major genre treated seriously in *Magnalia* and used ironically in twentieth-century absurdist literature is the jeremiad. Mather uses the jeremiad form with its stress on man's afflictions and the imminence of the Last Judgment to implore his "backsliding" contemporaries to repent their sins and ask God's forgiveness. He wishes to "stop, the turn of this degeneracy" and get the New Englanders to "*stand fast* in their *faith*." For this purpose he shows them "the graves of their dead fathers" (I:249).

The jeremiad narrative, as Bercovitch explains, is a lamentation of the imperfections of this world, while it also shows a vision for redemption.[16] This movement from *chronos,* or earthly time, to *kairos,* or the eternal, providential time,[17] anticipates "the holy city, new Jerusalem, coming down from God out of heaven" (Rev. 21:2). Mather uses the jeremiad form to affirm his belief in the covenant between God and the Puritans, his faith in redemption, and the importance of New England's mission in history. The contemporary prose epic *Gravity's Rainbow,* on the other hand, uses the jeremiad form to convey lamentation but not a hope for salvation. A hymn of lamentation is recalled at the close of the novel, just as the rocket lands on the roof of the theater:

> There is a Hand to turn the time,
> Though thy Glass today be run,
> Till the Light that hath brought the Towers low
> Find the last poor Pret'rite one. (760)

Pynchon's novel presents a world in which there is no covenant between man and God, no hope of redemption. The only way of lessening the torment is through the laughter of black humor.

30

The Garden and the *Translatio* Motif in Contemporary Literature

A major epic theme in *Magnalia* that twentieth-century writers draw upon for their satire is the concept of America as the new Garden of Eden and also the Promised Land. Puritan founders viewed America as the new Canaan, land of milk and honey, analogous to that which Moses saw from the top of Mount Pisgah: a new Eden filled with hills and valleys of "precious fruits" (Deut. 33:14), "vineyards and olive-yards" (Josh. 24:13), burgeoning trees, the "abundance of the seas" (Deut. 33:19), God's plantation in which all seed flowered. Mather describes the colonies as "Clusters of *Rich Grapes,* which had a *Blessing* in them" (Harvard 271). In New England live "Holy Souls, having been *ripened* for Heaven under the Ordinances of God" (Harvard 142). The people show a "wonderful Prayerfulness" and charity. In this locale, the *"Boughs . . .* [are] *like the goodly Cedars"* in Lebanon, the house of the Lord (Harvard 165). From Mather's description, America seems like a new Eden. Here the first generation New Englanders exhibit a prelapsarian "Thankfulness, . . . Piety, Charity . . . and Affection to the things that are above" (Harvard 142). Like their first parents in Eden, they pray to God "under op'n Sky" amidst the harmonious voices of the angelic choir "Singing thir great Creator."[18]

Pynchon's *V.* treats with humor the Puritan belief in America as the Promised Land, a new Garden. Its America is diametrically opposite to that in *Magnalia.* Its religious tale concerns Father Fairing and the inhabitants of the sewers below the streets rather than describing those in a land of milk and honey expecting an afterlife in heaven.

Another major theme in American literature, evident in *Magnalia,* is the *translatio* motif—the concept of the westward movement of culture and the arts (*translatio studii*) and also of empire (*translatio impereii*). The term defines a transferring of culture from east to west, stressing the westward progress of civilization from Asia to Europe and also from Europe to America. The motif is evident in Mather's opening statement: "I WRITE the *Wonders* of the CHRISTIAN RELIGION, flying from the Depravations of *Europe,* to the *American Strand"* (Harvard 89). Here Mather echoes lines from George Herbert's "Church Militant," the major seventeenth-century British example of the *translatio* theme applied to America: "Religion stands on tip-toe in our land, / Readie to passe to the *American* strand."[19]

Barth comically handles the idea of westward progression in *Sot-Weed.* Ebenezer Cooke travels from England to America (in 1694) with

31

the expectation of settling in a virgin land of infinite possibilities for growth. However, instead of meeting virtuous settlers, the new Adams of the Promised Land, he meets barbarous Americans who take his money, steal his clothes, and trick him into giving up his estate, Malden. And Pynchon, in *V.* and *Gravity's Rainbow,* shows the ultimate devastation of twentieth-century man's reversal of the *translatio* motif. For Pynchon's contemporaries, the westward movement of civilization is traced by the path of rockets screaming across the sky from Germany to England, aiming to annihilate rather than create, to destroy human civilization rather than to advance mankind.

Gaddis, in *The Recognitions,* also uses the belief in the westward progress of culture and civilization for satiric purposes. The main character, Wyatt, is brought up in a New England parsonage. For Wyatt, however, the Puritanism of Aunt May, who cares for him in his early years, is so stifling that he yearns to escape and move east, at least spiritually. He longs for the artistic beauty that existed in Holland, the land from which the *Mayflower* Pilgrims originally set forth for America. Wyatt desires to go east, not west, for culture and meaning and wishes to go back in time to the fifteenth century in order to be at one with the Netherlandish painters of the golden age of Flemish art. For Wyatt—in contrast to his forebears—America is no land of hope and opportunity.

The *translatio* motif is used ironically in *Sometimes a Great Notion,* where the Stamper family's westward migration to Oregon from Kansas ends not with the sense of having arrived in a land with new possibilities but rather with the realization that the earth in Oregon is so saturated with rain that grandfather Jonas must go back east for firmer ground. Mocking the traditional hope for westward progress, Kesey also has protagonist Hank Stamper, who returns from Korea to Wakonda, Oregon, ponder the significance of his grand progression. Hank observes that he "had almost completed a circle," sailing west from San Francisco and eventually arriving on the eastern seaboard and finally returning to the west. Hank waits for an epiphany to make "all things clear forever. . . . He waited" (150–51).

Exemplary Heroes and the Hero of the Absurd

There are four major qualities of early American heroes, described by Cotton Mather, that are treated ironically in the fiction of

Barth, Pynchon, Gaddis, and Kesey. These are: (1) a recognition of living in a divinely ordered universe, in which man's actions become part of sacred history; (2) a sense of destiny as founders of a new nation, in which the work of Christ is made manifest; (3) a concern for community and continuity, assuming that the next generation will carry on the life-style of the founders; (4) a reverence for tradition—the acts of ancestors and their relation to events in biblical times.

In the world of *Magnalia*, the universe is meaningful and unified. The characters draw from it a sense of significance. John Winthrop, governor of the Massachusetts Bay Colony, had the noble design of founding a nation. His sermon "A Model of Christian Charity" (1630) set the groundwork for the Puritan American ideal: a vision of establishing a people who will form a society under God for all to emulate, a society that will exhibit the wonderful work of Christ in the world. Mather emphasizes Winthrop's destiny as leader of the Puritans by connecting him to the biblical lawgivers Moses and Nehemiah. He explains that Winthrop is a *"New-English Nehemiah,"* trying to build an *"American Jerusalem"* (Harvard 216). Just as Nehemiah, in the fifth century B.C., organized the repairs of the wall of Jerusalem and devoted himself to having the people of Judah follow God's law, so Winthrop, in the seventeenth century A.D., aims to build an "American Jerusalem" and give these people a law of piety to follow.

The characters in *Magnalia* carry out a destiny of Christian heroism. This is evident in the life of Sir William Phips, the adventurer who rises from poverty to become governor of Massachusetts. On one level, Phips is an early example of the American ideal of rising from rags to riches. For Mather, he primarily is *"One Raised by God"* (Harvard 286), a man chosen for success because of his patience, humility, honesty, and piety (Harvard 287). Mather describes Governor Phips as a magnificent hero, larger than life: "He was one *Tall,* beyond the common Set of Men, and *Thick* as well as *Tall,* and *Strong* as well as *Thick*" (Harvard 341).

Mather expands on Phips's adventures at sea: when Captain Phips outwits knaves who plot to seize him and leave him to die on an island (Harvard 281); when he, with a fleet of ships, sets out on an expedition against Quebec, "chief Source of *New-England's* Miseries" (Harvard 300); and—most memorable—when he discovers the splendid riches of a Spanish galleon, containing thirty-two tons of silver, bushels of jewels, gold and pearls, and exclaims: *"Thanks be to God! We are made"* (Harvard 284).

33

Magnalia's idealized depiction of the nation's early settlers reveals Mather's highly optimistic vision of America and her destiny, a vision similar to that of the first-generation Puritans.[20] Twentieth-century authors use this great vision and the heroes who developed it (whether Puritan or not) as a subject for comic deflation in their novels of the absurd. *Sot-Weed,* in addition to reinterpreting the story of Captain John Smith and Pocahontas, comically intermingles such historic figures as William Claiborne, John Coode, and Lord Baltimore with fictional characters. The plots and swindles perpetrated by characters such as Coode and Lord Baltimore reverse the traditional image of the God-fearing colonial hero and his prophetic role in America. The virgin land of our forebears is reduced to "poor shitten Maryland" (*Sot-Weed* 318). Barth explains that he "found colonial history so fantastic" that it had to be toned down for his "farcical" novel.[21]

Gravity's Rainbow depicts Slothrop, the protagonist, as a twentieth-century deflation of a hero of America's Puritan past. It is of historic interest that Slothrop's Puritan ancestor William—like Thomas Pynchon's own forefather William Pynchon—[22] came to America on the fleet that accompanied John Winthrop in the *Arbella.* Also, like the author's ancestor, William Slothrop wrote a heretical tract, *On Preterition,* which was "among the first books to've been not only banned but also ceremonially burned in Boston" (*Gravity's Rainbow* 555). For the twentieth-century Slothrop, Puritan concerns about the Elect and other of God's mysteries have been reduced to an involvement with the mystery stimulus in the descent of the V-2 rocket. Slothrop is "last of his line, and how far fallen" (*Gravity's Rainbow* 569).

Sometimes a Great Notion also uses America's history and its dreams as a means to develop the absurd. Hank, the hero, compares his acts to those of his ancestors, the early settlers in America (150–51), but—as the narrator stresses—Hank is barred from the exciting opportunity of exploring a virgin land with limitless opportunities. In a nuclear age no one "*played at Dan'l Boone in a forest full of fallout*" (116).

The contrast between the twentieth-century hero's desire to believe in a meaningful universe and his perception of the randomness of a chaotic world creates the absurd. The absurd hero, like Camus's Sisyphus, believes that action is important, but the action is unfortunately fruitless. Man wishes "to put 'a scar on the map,' . . . [but] he becomes dubious about the value of inflicting scars and is not sure he can even locate the map."[23] Unlike the Puritan champion who is sure of

34

his place in the universe, the absurd man awakens to a world that is characterized by chaos.[24] He lacks a sense of destiny and of a meaningful self. He feels estranged from the universe and from a community. Man's "awakening" to a discovery of nothingness is an inversion of the Puritans' spiritual revelation of God's ways.

In *Magnalia*, man's affirmation of faith in a heroic destiny is exhibited by William Bradford and his companions who arrived at Cape Cod in 1620. Mather conveys Bradford's religious conviction with a tale portraying the courage of these Separatists, who have left England to go to Holland and who, after suffering hardships in the Netherlands, leave for America (Harvard 201).[25] Aboard ship, the mariners cry out, "*We Sink! We Sink,*" but "the Passengers . . . even while the Water was running into their Mouths and Ears, would chearfully Shout, *Yet, Lord, thou canst save! Yet Lord, thou canst save!*" The narrator observes, "the Lord accordingly brought them at last safe unto their *Desired Haven*" (Harvard 202).[26] The passage emphasizes a basic pattern in *Magnalia* as a whole: the movement from persecution, suffering, and separation from loved ones to the eventual reunification of the Pilgrims, who have a sense of destiny and who rejoice in a prophetic vision of God's mercy and goodness.

The disembarkation from the *Mayflower* of Bradford and the other Pilgrims in Cape Cod is a memorable introduction to "great and honourable actions" (Ford 1:60) that are part of the Pilgrims' forthcoming experience in America. It is a description that has reverberations in later American literature. The ultimate faith of the Puritans in God's ways is stressed: "If they looked behind them, ther was the mighty ocean which they had passed, and was now as a maine barr and goulfe to seperate them from all the civill parts of the world." And in front of them was "a hidious and desolate wilderness, full of wild beasts and willd men," a vast desert through which to journey. Wherever they turned their eyes, there was no solace "save upward to the heavens." What sustained the people was "the spirite of God and his grace" (Ford 1:156) and the conviction of the importance of their destiny.[27] The Pilgrims prayed to the Lord, and as in their earlier adventure at sea, He heard their voices and gave these new Israelites strength in their journey and in their forthcoming trials with the Tempter in the desert.[28]

Instead of believing, as did the colonial hero, that God "canst save," the hero of the absurd feels alienated and alone in a world that reveals no divine structure, no meaningful destiny for man. Unlike the colonial hero in *Magnalia,* who believes that his entreaties are heard, the absurd hero in the comic American epic novel realizes that he lives *"without appeal"* to a God.[29]

In *The End of the Road,* Barth's early novel, Jake Horner is a humorous example of a man without a sense of meaningful destiny. Jake is the comic antithesis to the goal-oriented Puritan heroes of the past. He cannot choose among alternatives and has no reference system with which to align himself. He is bereft of orientation and feels that only "IN A SENSE" is he Jacob Horner (1).

In this respect, he is like Ebenezer Cooke, in *Sot-Weed,* who several times experiences "cosmopsis"—a world view of nothingness. Eben reveals this feeling of emptiness in a letter to his sister, Anna: *"All Trades, all Crafts, all Professions are wondrous, but none is finer than the rest together. I cannot choose"* (11–12). Eben withdraws from all activities: "Finally one day he did not deign even to dress himself or eat, but sat immobile in the window seat . . . unable to choose a motion at all even when . . . his untutored bladder suggested one" (12). When Ebenezer asks his friend and teacher, Burlingame, to help him "think things through" so he can find some significance in his experiences, Burlingame only laughs and tells Eben that man "is Chance's fool, the toy of aimless Nature" (372).

In *Gravity's Rainbow,* another example of deflation of meaningful destiny is Slothrop's bizarre fate to react sexually to the fall of the V-2. His "destiny" is mechanically controlled, not divinely ordained. Dr. Jamf conditions him in infancy to respond to a mysterious stimulus. Most people know this, but not Slothrop, who is unaware of his own motivation and also bewildered by the actions of others who wish to exploit his affinity with the rocket so that they can predict its falls. Slothrop, the New England Puritan protagonist, futilely traces mysterious clues about "Them"—the controlling agents during World War II—but is unable to understand the forces that influence him.

A loss of direction in life is humorously exemplified in *The Recognitions,* where people repeatedly wander aimlessly from one party to the next and also drift from one topic of conversation to the next. They retell stories like that of a man who, when asked if it is all right to kiss a nun, responds with the banal pun: "As long as you don't get into the habit" (103). Such trivial pursuits show how far removed are the characters in the contemporary American novel from Mather's purposeful heroes of colonial America.

Another aspect of the absurd hero is his awareness of man's alienation not only in a meaningless universe but also in a society where there is no communal feeling, no place where virtuous leaders prevail. These experiences are in direct contrast to those of the early American heroes in *Magnalia*. For example, in *Magnalia*, leaders like John Winthrop are successfully involved with their community. The following anecdote is a simple revelation of the leader's sensitivity to his people's basic needs and his somewhat humorous handling of those who have a false and selfish sense of justice. Mather's story details Winthrop's reaction to a complaint about a needy man who had been stealing from his woodpile. The governor, aware that the man did this out of dire necessity, not meanness, tells those who wish to see the man punished that he will cure the man of stealing. To the poor man, he says: *"Friend, It is a severe Winter, and I doubt you are but meanly provided for Wood; wherefore I would have you supply your self at my Wood-Pile till this cold Season be over."* Then Winthrop asked everyone *"Whether he had not effectually cured this Man of Stealing his Wood?"* (Harvard 218).

Another representative hero who shows love of community and of God is William Bradford, governor of Plymouth Plantation. Bradford, Mather explains, has mastered many languages, including Dutch, French, Latin, Greek, and finally Hebrew, so that *"he would see with his own Eyes the Ancient Oracles of God in their Native Beauty"* (Harvard 207). Throughout his life, Bradford was concerned about the communal spirit of Plymouth Colony.[30] In the Christmas game episode, he shows great moderation in his treatment of young men who, appealing to liberty of conscience, refuse the governor's order to do work for the public good on Christmas Day. Bradford excuses the men but then finds them playing games in the street. He has their games taken away and chastises them for being at play while others have to work. Bradford's "gentle [but firm] Reproof put a final stop to all such Disorders for the future" (Harvard 205). Bradford shows the Christian virtues of patience, prudence, justice, and moderation in handling these unruly men. He accepts their pretense that working on Christmas is against their consciences but then judges them strongly on their own terms and criticizes them for not following out their religious convictions by failing to show *"Devotion to the Day."* He also has the courage to emphasize *"That it was against his Conscience that they should play whilst others were at Work"* (Harvard 205).

The acquisition of the first land patent to all freemen illustrates the governor's concern for the financial stability of the community. Bradford stresses the importance of growing corn, fishing, increasing the fur trade with the Indians, and selling corn and cattle to people in the Massachusetts Bay Company. The governor's sense of communal spirit contributes to the growth of the colony.[31] Bradford's concern for his people is reflected throughout *Plymouth Plantation*, which, in manuscript, was used extensively by Cotton Mather in his *Magnalia*, as well as by other colonial historians (Nathanial Morton, Increase Mather, William Hubbard, and Thomas Prince).[32]

Heroes of the absurd long for a communal spirit and for religious values such as those stressed in *Magnalia*. This longing is most ironic for Ebenezer Cooke in *Sot-Weed* and Wyatt Gwyon, in *The Recognitions*. Eben leaves England with the expectation of finding a harmonious spirit in America and an Edenic existence on his father's estate, Malden. Wyatt, a twentieth-century American, harkens back to the Flemish artists who dedicate themselves to serving God and to working for a guild that would look after all their needs. Eben and Wyatt experience a conflict between their desire for a communal life in a meaningful world and the alienation they experience in their everyday lives in America. Their frustrations, a satiric inversion of the fulfilled aspirations of the historic American settlers, contribute to the biting humor of the comic epics that mock the American dream.

Because of its traditional colonial themes and use of various genres, *Magnalia* is a good touchstone for illuminating the system of expectations that twentieth-century comic epic novelists employ as subject matter for farce: Barth's burlesque of the John Smith–Pocahontas legend in *The Sot-Weed Factor;* Pynchon's humorous allusions to his ancestor William Pynchon; Gaddis's depiction, in *The Recognitions,* of protagonist Wyatt Gwyon, who longs to reverse the journey of his New England ancestors and travel back to Europe; and Ken Kesey's observation, in *Sometimes a Great Notion*, that early members of the Stamper family forged westward across wild America "not as pioneers doing the Lord's work in a heathen land . . . but simply as a clan of skinny men . . . [engaged in] foolish roaming" (16). The disparity that these novels stress between the colonial American dream and the meaninglessness of twentieth-century life takes the form of burlesque, irony, and parody and so transforms the despair of loss into the vigor of comedy.

CHAPTER THREE

Whitman's *Leaves of Grass* and the Twentieth-Century Comic Epic

Walt Whitman, in "Song of Myself," chooses to sound his "barbaric yawp over the roofs of the world."[1] "Not a bit tamed," he swoops like a hawk over the rooftops and, like a meteor, shakes his "white locks at the runaway sun" (52.1332, 1337). He fuses primitive feelings of sheer physical pleasure with intimations of transcendent meaning. He proclaims the joyous freedom and optimism of an innocent Adam in a new world filled with opportunity. America is a new Eden whose nature the poet invokes "without check with original energy" ("Song" 1.13).[2]

Though a transcendental and not a Puritan work, Whitman's epic *Leaves of Grass*, like *Magnalia*, is a repository of the themes that twentieth-century novels of the absurd use ironically: America as new Eden, land of abundance and natural fruitfulness; the view of man as innocent Adam, who reaches out to all aspects of nature; the grand celebration of the nation with infinite possibilities for perfection; the transcendent vision that affirms the "Over-Soul" in all of creation.

By recalling the optimism and enthusiasm exuded in the Garden of Whitman's nineteenth-century world, one may see more clearly the

39

American dream turned nightmare in the world of the twentieth-century novel. The contemporary novels of John Barth, Thomas Pynchon, and William Gaddis depict America as a wasteland:[3] where the natural declines toward the artificial and the mechanical; where the concept of entropy suggests that there is no transcendental reality, no such thing as a soul. Even Ken Kesey, who advocates living closely with nature, points out how different the twentieth-century world is from the past. The contemporary world has no "limitless supply of tomorrows to work with" (*Notion* 415). "The little red button," explains Lee Stamper, "and *zap*. Right? And this little button makes a definite difference in our world; in our generation, ever since we've been old enough to read, our tomorrows have been at the mercy of this button" (*Notion* 416).

The Garden and the Street

Whitman's innocent enthusiasm for America and its potential is representative of the optimism of the traditional American dream, which is mocked repeatedly in the twentieth-century novel. Whitman celebrates America and specifically "his own Manhattan and Long Island as no other poet has ever done."[4] Barth, Pynchon, and Gaddis also focus on the urban scene, often centering on Manhattan, as in *V.* and *The Recognitions,* but their attitude toward the city and its people is ironic and satiric rather than venerating.

For Whitman, "chanter of Adamic songs" ("Ages and Ages" 4 in "Children of Adam" 107), all of Manhattan participates in an Edenic dance of life: the conductor beating time for the band; the peddler sweating with his pack on his back; the bride unrumpling her white dress; the prostitute dragging her shawl; the crowd laughing; the men jeering and winking ("Song" 15.298–306). The poet's interest and love for all rejuvenates and transforms the city. Whitman describes his journey through the streets of Manhattan, as well as through different parts of the country, as that of "Adam early in the morning, / Walking forth from the bower refresh'd with sleep" ("As Adam" 1–2 in "Children of Adam" 111). He, like prelapsarian Adam in the Garden, has "an air of adventurousness, a sense of promise and possibility."[5] Whitman wants people to behold him and take joy with him in the new Garden, America.

"I am afoot with my vision" ("Song" 33.716), exclaims the poet as he encourages the reader to join him in watching the people and listening to the "Sounds of the city" (26.587):

> The blab of the pave, tires of carts, sluff of boot-soles, talk of the promenaders,
> The heavy omnibus, the driver with his interrogating thumb, the clank of the shod horses on the granite floor,
> The snow-sleighs, clinking, shouted jokes, pelts of snow-balls. (8.154–56)

Whitman's joy in the present grows from achievements in the past. In "Song of the Universal," he points out: "In this broad earth of ours . . . / Nestles the seed perfection" (4–7). Health and joy continually emerge from "guile and tears." America and all creation are spiraling to perfection: "America . . . . / thou too by pathways broad and new, / To the ideal tendest" (42–47). Whitman has belief in "Health, peace, salvation universal" (61). For him, evil is discounted; "only the good is universal" (28). In Whitman's optimistic view, the United States is expanding spiritually and territorially.[6]

The celebrative, enthusiastic tone of Whitman's *Leaves of Grass* sharply contrasts with the derisive, satiric quality in the novels of the twentieth-century writers of the absurd. For these writers, the streets of Manhattan are part of a wasteland. For them, the Garden, land of milk and honey, has become the Street, home of the Whole Sick Crew. While Whitman exclaims "behold" and "love" as he describes his walk through Manhattan, Pynchon, in *V.*, writes of travels through a desolate land. On the twentieth-century street, people roam from one gathering to another. Their purposeless movements are recapitulated by those in subway trains below: the antiheroes, like Benny Profane, schlemihls of the city, riding aimlessly back and forth on the Forty-second Street shuttle from Grand Central to Times Square (*V.* 27).[7] Labyrinthine Manhattan and its inhabitants become a metaphor for unproductive movement in the absurd world of the twentieth century.

In *V.*, Fausto Maijstral, in the "confessions" about his life during World War II, discusses people on the street in Malta: "their compulsion to gather together, their pathological fear of loneliness extends on past the threshold of sleep. [. . .] You know the street I mean, child. The street of the 20th Century [. . . .] a street we must walk" (303).[8] On the street, explains Fausto, the people, because of their loneliness, follow shallow dreams that help them to disguise the truth of their situation, to avoid the "desert, or a row of false shop fronts; a slag pile" (303).

American Adam versus Alienated Man

Twentieth-century novelists mock the conception of man as American Adam, Whitman's archetypal hero who "radiates a kind of primal innocence in an innocent world."[9] Whitman's poetry is steeped in the concept of the nation as a new Paradise in which all people can relive the experiences of prelapsarian Adam. Whitman envisions himself as an Adamic chanter of songs. His terrain is "the new garden the West, the great cities" of the nation ("Ages and Ages" 5 in "Children of Adam" 107). "Song of Myself" celebrates man's limitless possibilities, the grandeur of the self, and the joy in being at one with all of mankind in a newly created world: America. The poem's hero is an individual who is to develop his great potential in a new land.

The Adamic poet of "Song of Myself" names and responds to different aspects of creation. He ascends to the nest of the "razor-bill'd auk" (31.682–83), wonders about the animals, embraces the stallion with his heels, and then outgallops him as he soars to the sky in his vision. He travels on land and sea, in the solitude of the country and the crowd of the cities.[10] All before him is the world. It is a world in which the poet-hero always moves ahead in the community of his fellowmen:

> Myself moving forward then and now and forever,
> Gathering and showing more always and with velocity,
> Infinite and omnigenous. (32.696–98)

The hero is "Walt Whitman, a kosmos, of Manhattan the son, / Turbulent, fleshy, sensual, eating, drinking and breeding" (24.497–98).[11] He is the man that Whitman, in an anonymous review, portrays as author of *Leaves of Grass:* "Of pure American breed, large and lusty—age thirty-six years" ("Walt Whitman" 778).

Contemporary writers Barth, Pynchon, and Gaddis deflate these Adamic traits in order to develop their comedies of the absurd. The subject of Barth's novel *Giles Goat-Boy* is the education of the innocent hero who looks at American society from the vantage point of one who is brought up close to nature, literally at the goat farm of the university. The innocent George/Giles looks to the university—New Tammany—

as a place that will lead him toward the Truth. The novel's humor is developed by means of the futile confrontation between George/Giles's serious desire to learn and then educate others as opposed to the frivolous attitude of the student body and the faculty.

Contemporary writers show the disparity between the optimistic Whitmanesque concept of innocent man and the more cynical modern perspective. They transform the American Adam into the naïve bumbler: for example, Barth's George/Giles Goat-Boy and Ebenezer Cooke; Pynchon's Benny Profane, who feels more comfortable chatting with a computer than with a person; Gaddis's Wyatt Gwyon, whose superior intelligence is of little help in his adjustment to a world where money and getting ahead in the marketplace are most important. Contemporary novelists, with humor and wit, change the hero as optimistic Adam—with all the world to explore—to the hero as *schlimmazel:* comic victim of bad luck like Pynchon's Benny Profane.[12] Yet there remains a nostalgia for the myth, particularly the Whitmanesque vision of innocence, which, when sought after to no avail, informs the absurd vision of contemporary American novels.

Celebration of America: Its Past, Present, and Future

A third theme that contemporary novelists satirize is the traditional celebration of country: America's past, present, and future. For the Whitman of the 1855 Preface, man radiates innocence in a New World filled with possibilities: "The United States themselves are essentially the greatest poem" ("Preface 1855" 711). Whitman's America is "a teeming nation of nations," exuding the "hospitality which forever indicates heroes" (711); Whitman, as Parrington explains, was an "embodiment of American aspiration . . . and his songs were defiant chants in praise of life."[13]

Whitman appreciates the richness of America, which "need never be bankrupt while corn grows from the ground or the orchards drop apples or the bays contain fish or men beget children upon women" ("Preface 1855" 711–12). He praises the fullness of America and exhorts his countrymen to have a magnanimity that would equal the grand resources of America. He celebrates the democracy's "common people" and the divine immanence in all ("Preface 1855" 712). And he conveys a sense of the vivacity of an American people, who, in their infinite variety of occupations, give forth limitless energy: "the pure contralto sings in the organ loft, / The carpenter dresses his plank . . . / The squaw wrapt in her yellow-hemm'd cloth" ("Song" 15.264–90). These are the people who make America great. They, like the natural elements, shower riches on America, a grand and expansive country, "more rich and free, to be evidenced by original authors and poets to come, by American personalities" (*Democratic Vistas* 410).

For Whitman, America is a nation of plenitude, one that in 1855 is *"expanding* in every sense of the term, geographically, economically, politically, culturally."[14] Whitman's journey to different parts of the country becomes an archetypal sojourn, revealing the limitless possibilities of an American Adam in the New World:

> Sprouts take and accumulate, stand by the curb prolific and vital,
> Landscapes projected masculine, full-sized and golden.
> ("Song" 29.646–47)

America is the land that the poet journeys afoot: "By the city's quadrangular houses . . . / Along the ruts of the turnpike . . . / Scaling mountains . . . / Walking . . . / Where the she-whale swims with her calf . . . / Where the steam-ship trails hind-ways its long pennant of smoke" ("Song" 33.717–43).

In his letter to Emerson (1856), Whitman writes of his prophetic vision of America and its people, who "dilate, a larger, brawnier, more candid, more democratic, lawless, positive native to The States" and are a "new race of men" ("To Emerson" 733). He exults in the turbulent and agitated nature of America, its "screaming, wrestling, boiling-hot days" ("To Emerson" 740), and rejoices in the growing "national character," the "identity" of America: that "character, strong, limber, just, open-mouthed, American-blooded, full of pride" ("To Emerson" 740–41). Whitman cherishes the common man in a free nation that reveres the "word Democratic, the word En-Masse" ("One's Self I Sing" 2).[15]

Celebrations of a nation such as Whitman's provide contemporary novelists with material for their satire, most notably the deflation of Captain John Smith, whose adventures Ebenezer Cooke reads in "The Privie Journall" of Burlingame I. The reader measures Barth's Smith—who has a reputation for having romantic "conquests" (162)—against Whitman's American hero, who innocently and expansively revels in sharing the beautiful physicality of the body and its passions in "I Sing the Body Electric" and "Song of Myself."

Barth not only brings into question notions of America's heroic past but also holds up to ridicule the dream that in America's future lies the humanistic progress of mankind. In *Giles Goat-Boy,* the leaders of twentieth-century America—the teachers at Tammany—show little humanistic concern. The scientist Eblis Eierkopf thinks only of the intricate variety of his optic lenses and ignores everyday matters (481–82). He cannot even take care of his own bodily functions without the aid of a servant, Croaker. Another scholar, Dr. Kennard Sear, is distracted by his scientific instruments. His wife is concerned that he has lost interest in ordinary coupling and prefers to watch others: she "could interest him only by masturbating before the fluoroscope" (399).

Drs. Sear and Eierkopf accomplish little of worth with their complex scientific equipment. Their speculative obsessions ironically reverse the Whitmanesque concern that man broadly pursue his mental and physical development in order to celebrate himself and mankind as a whole. Barth's scholars, by contrast, primarily give unquestioning respect to narrow scientific concepts; they eagerly accept theories that are "dogmatized by the Chancellor, taped by the Chief Programmer, and devoured by [the computer] WESCAC" (43–44).

More biting reversals of Whitman's epic celebration of country and its potential are evident in the novels of Kesey, Pynchon, and Gaddis. Instead of revealing "a cheerful nihilism" (*End of the Road* 47), as in the works of Barth, novels by these authors satirize the destructive nature of twentieth-century society. In particular, they point to repression of individual freedom: repression by the union over the independent Stamper clan in Kesey's *Sometimes a Great Notion;* by the "elect" in *Gravity's Rainbow;* by power-hungry nations over natives in South-West Africa in *V.;* and by those who determine society's values, be they religious or artistic, in *The Recognitions.* These include the fanatically Puritan Aunt May, who warps Wyatt's childhood years, and the art critic Cremer, who offers to sell Wyatt a favorable "review" of his work.

Transcendentalism versus Entropy

Whitman, like other transcendentalists, envisions the world "as it should be." Like them, he exhibits a prophetic vision that is achieved through "inspirations from the world of soul."[16] Whitman perceives the operations of divine energy in all the physical world, including phenomena such as gravitation and magnetism: "Does the earth gravitate? does not all matter, aching, attract all matter?" ("I Am He" 2 in

"Children of Adam" 109). Throughout nature, Whitman sees an infusion of divine energy: "Through Space and Time fused in a chant, and the flowing eternal identity" ("As They Draw to a Close" 7 in "Songs of Parting" 501). For Whitman, there is no conflict between the laws of science and a transcendent reality.

Whitman uses his prophetic vision to encourage others to see into the deeper meaning of things. For him, eyesight "foreruns the identities of the spiritual world. A single glance of it mocks all the investigations of man . . . all reasoning" ("Preface 1855" 716).[17] Whitman believes that the poet's vision enables him to transcend mere reason so as to perceive the mystery of life. "The greatest poet," affirms Whitman, "knows the *soul*" (718; italics added). As he begins "Song of Myself," Whitman pronounces: "I loafe and invite my soul" (1.4).

Whitman exults in the power of an eternal force, the "mystery" that unfolds as "the unseen is proved by the seen, / Till that becomes unseen and receives proof in its turn" ("Song" 3.51–54). He asserts the symbiosis between body and soul, man and nature, and man and his fellowman. He proclaims: "I am large, I contain multitudes" ("Song" 51.1326). His epic emphasizes that the soul, this eternal energy, is in all human beings and things, that the grass "is the handkerchief of the Lord, / A scented gift" ("Song" 6.102–3), that there is a connection between a blade of grass and the stars, that "the nearest gnat is an explanation, and a drop or motion of waves a key" ("Song" 47.1253), and that a single person is connected to the universal spirit in all.

Whitman's transcendentalism is similar to that of Thoreau, who speaks of time as a stream to "go a-fishing in. . . . Its thin current slides away, but eternity remains."[18] This focus also resembles that of Emerson, who sees "the world . . . in a drop of dew."[19] Like Emerson, Whitman stresses that "every natural fact is a symbol of some spiritual fact."[20] Whitman also celebrates the "doctrine of omnipresence," the idea that "the value of the universe contrives to throw itself into every point."[21] Whitman explains: "I hear and behold God in every object" ("Song" 48.1281). He believes that all things are invested with a deeper reality, what Emerson calls "that Unity, that Over-Soul, within which every man's particular being is contained and made one with all other."[22] For Whitman, there is no death:

> I bequeath myself to the dirt to grow from the grass I love,
> If you want me again look for me under your boot-soles.
> ("Song" 52.1339–40).

46

Whitman's transcendentalism is freewheeling and differs from that of Emerson and Thoreau in that, for him, the spirit is not superior to the flesh. In "Nature," Emerson explains his concept of hierarchy: "the universe becomes transparent, and the light of *higher* laws than its own, shines through it."[23] Thoreau also refers to the "higher" or "spiritual life" as being above the physical, the fact that "man flows at once to God when the channel of purity is open" and that "he is blessed who is assured that the animal is dying out in him day by day, and the divine being established."[24] For Whitman, however, the physical and the spiritual are indistinguishable.[25] The "bright suns" and "dark suns," the palpable and the impalpable, are in their place ("Song" 16.353–54) and partake in the "untranslatable" wonder of mankind and of the universe. God and His creation are inseparable:

I have said that the soul is not more than the body,
And I have said that the body is not more than the soul,
And nothing, not God, is greater to one than one's self is.
    ("Song" 48.1269–71)

Comic epic novelists of the absurd use reversals of Whitman's transcendental themes as a means to aid the reader in recognizing not only that the present twentieth-century world is a spiritual wasteland but also that people in past ages were nothing like their celebrative depictions in traditional literature such as "Song of Myself." *Gravity's Rainbow* turns Whitman's transcendental vision of man's natural goodness on its head.[26] Its description of war and destruction, of plots and counterplots, reveals emptiness and annihilation rather than a heavenly paradise on earth.[27]

In *Gravity's Rainbow*, Pynchon chooses as epigraph a statement by the German scientist Wernher von Braun. The epigraph and the image of the rocket in the novel's first line help define the lack of spiritual meaning in the nightmare world of *Gravity's Rainbow*, a world that is vastly different from the Eden of "Song of Myself." Von Braun states: "Nature does not know extinction; all it knows is transformation. Everything science has taught me, and continues to teach me, strengthens my belief in the continuity of our spiritual existence after death." At first glance, this remark seems positive. It alludes to a law of physics, the Conservation of Energy, with the added Christian connection between transformations from this life to the eternal. Pynchon, however, uses the epigraph as an ironic statement in his war-torn twentieth-century world, for he depends on the reader's knowledge of the following: that von Braun, who considered himself a devout Christian, designed—for the Germans—the V-2 rocket, which was used to blitz England; and that von Braun, after the war, had no qualms about helping his country's former enemy, the United States, build new rockets.[28]

The opening paragraph of *Gravity's Rainbow*, describing a V-2 rocket and the devastation it leaves behind, is an ironic counterpart to Whitman's "barbaric yawp," which exudes life and enthusiasm: "A screaming comes across the sky. It has happened before, but there is nothing to compare it to now" (3).[29] Pynchon's words point to a constrained twentieth-century world—one in which technological power is substituted for natural energy: the natural force of Whitman's innocent Adam. The twentieth century in the comic epic novel is a destructive age that has intensified cynicism about the spiritual nature of life, an age in which scientists speak of the entropic decline of the universe and novelists discuss the loss of humanistic values and meaning.

In place of Whitman's vision, which affirms the operation of a divine force in nature, twentieth-century absurdist writers stress the force of entropy, as stated in the Second Law of Thermodynamics. This law affirms that, in a closed system, molecules move from an orderly structure toward separation and randomness. There is a decline of structures and systems, leading to a lack of energy. The most chilling aspect of the concept of entropy suggests the lack of a soul: the notion that man—like all matter—will decay and the organization of his tissues will disappear, becoming nothing but random bits of molecules, deteriorating into formless dust.[30]

Popular views of the Second Law of Thermodynamics have led people to claim that "dissipation and degradation" are the ultimate fate of the universe.[31] Such pessimistic statements have been used metaphorically to point to the decay in physical, social, and spiritual aspects of our lives. In *V.*, the narrator relates that "the world started to run more and more afoul of the inanimate" as people were killed because of train wrecks, ice avalanches, drownings. "The same week a gas explosion in Monticello, Utah, killed fifteen and a typhoon through Japan and Okinawa killed thirty" (*V.* 270).

William Gaddis, in his essay "The Rush for Second Place," also presents an ironic contrast to the transcendental meaning evident in Whitman. He criticizes twentieth-century American society for placing materialistic concerns over spiritual ones, for being a society that values popularity and getting along well with people over spiritual interests. For the American people, "in the absence of a 'calling' and in place of the soul's stance in God's presence," there is a focus "on the shabby temporal alternative of 'being liked.' "[32] In such a society there is "a rush for second place."

This concern with the loss of spiritual meaning is shared by Barth and Kesey. Barth has Burlingame comment on the movement toward disorder in the universe: " 'Tis our fate to search, Eben, and do we seek our soul, what we find is a piece of that same black Cosmos whence we sprang and through which we fall: the infinite wind of space" (*Sot-Weed* 373). Ken Kesey points to the loss of meaning in our world, one tarnished by the annihilation caused by the atom bomb: *"Suburban survivors of Hiroshima described the blast as a 'mighty first boom'. . . . that mighty first boom was only the first faintest murmur of an explosion that is still roaring down on us, and always will be"* (*Notion* 505). These novelists all agree that entropy is a "central preoccupation of our time."[33]

Barth, Pynchon, Gaddis, and Kesey are very troubled about people's lack of meaningful values, their longing for a lost homeland, and for a God to whom to appeal. That these contemporary epic novelists use black humor to convey the absurdity of a twentieth-century nation does not mean that they "dismiss themselves with a joke" or ignore "the mystery of mankind," as Saul Bellow complains; nor that these novelists use laughter as a means to avoid crucial issues, as Robert Alter asserts; nor that they merely show interest in "newfangledness" or morbid fascination with "the ugly, the disgusting," as John Gardner maintains.[34] In direct contrast to the euphoric tone of Whitman, these writers combine laughter and pain, farce and horror, causing the reader to recognize the ideal and confront its absence.[35]

CHAPTER FOUR

Comic Retrospection in John Barth's *The Sot-Weed Factor* and *Giles Goat-Boy*

Barth builds on traditional literature and the values that form its context as the basis for his Rabelaisian comedy. With rollicking good humor, he transforms historic themes and conventions and deploys these "against themselves to generate new and lively work."[1] The American dream of the colonial settlers and the theme of the hero as American Adam—serious concerns of Cotton Mather and Walt Whitman—become the subject of comedy in Barth's novels. Also reshaped are patterns of the traditional epic.

This kind of revitalization is most evident in the novels published after *The Floating Opera* (1956) and *The End of the Road* (1958). In *The Sot-Weed Factor* (1960), Barth imaginatively re-creates the eighteenth-century novel (with Fieldingesque chapter headings and authorial intrusions) as well as the life of an eighteenth-century poet, Ebenezer Cook. The comic epic novel also satirizes the concept of America as new Eden and the hero as American Adam. In *Giles Goat-Boy* (1966), he writes a mock epic, as well as a parody of saints' lives, that reflects on the cold war between East and West Campus in the twentieth century. In *Chimera* (1972), he gives new vigor to the myths of Scheherazade, Perseus, and Bellerophon. In *Letters* (1979), he adapts the form of the epistolary novel of the eighteenth century to continue the tales of characters who appeared in his previous fiction, as well as to detail the adventures of a new character, Germaine G. Pitt. In *Sabbatical* (1982), he writes a romance that calls attention to contemporary events, ranging from CIA activities to those in academia. Throughout, Barth adapts old forms to new purposes and thus gives them new life.

"The Literature of Exhaustion" (1967) and "The Literature of Replenishment" (1980) clarify Barth's intention to use ironic allusions to the literature of earlier centuries. Barth points out that a writer who is "aware of where we've been and where we are" can turn to writing works "with ironic intent" ("Exhaustion" 31). In "The Literature of Exhaustion," he focuses on the writing of Jorge Luis Borges. He discusses the story "Pierre Menard," about a twentieth-century French symbolist writer who successfully and independently composes several chapters that are identical to those of Cervantes's *Don Quixote*. Because Cervantes's novel is shaped by a seventeenth-century sensibility and Menard's by a twentieth-century perspective, the passages take on different meaning. In his story, Borges comments on the contrast in style of Cervantes and Menard: "The archaic style of Menard—quite foreign, after all—suffers from a certain affectation. Not so that of his forerunner [Cervantes], who handles with ease the current Spanish of his time" (*Labyrinths* 43). Borges's transformation, explains Barth, results in "a remarkable and original work of literature." His artistic achievement "is that he confronts an intellectual dead end and employs it against itself to accomplish new human work" ("Exhaustion" 31).

This explanation of Borges's contribution elucidates Barth's own accomplishment when he incorporates Ebenezer Cook's 1708 poem "The Sot-Weed Factor" into his novel and uses the poem's title for his work, combining a seventeenth- and eighteenth-century setting with a twentieth-century sensibility. Barth fictionalizes the historic Ebenezer Cook, poet laureate of Maryland and author of the original 1708 poem. Barth's aspiring poet, however, is different from the Ebenezer Cook of 1708, who satirizes a foolish greenhorn persona in his poem. In Barth's *Sot-Weed*, the British emigré poet Eben is himself a greenhorn who evokes laughter.[2] Barth employs "a flavor of the antique"[3] as a means to emphasize the "fictive nature of 'reality.' "[4] In this way, he becomes "a creative mythographer,"[5] handling old literary and historical materials in a new way and broadening their scope in a manner that rivals Borges's treatment in "Pierre Menard."

Barth repeatedly applauds the innovative techniques to develop comic irony in Borges's fiction. The story "Tlon, Uqbar, Orbis Tertius" is a tale about the hypothetical world of Tlon and a secret society of scholars who write down their fictional data in the forty volumes of the *First Encyclopaedia of Tlon*. In the story, the hypothetical world begins to intrude into the world of reality. "The contact and the habit of Tlon," explains the narrator, "have disintegrated this world." The teaching of its history, continues the narrator, "has wiped out the one which governed in my childhood; already a fictitious past occupies in our memories the place of another" (Borges 18). Borges, Barth explains, who "merely *alludes* to the fascinating *Encyclopaedia, is* an artist ... [who combines an] intellectually profound vision with great human insight, poetic power, and consummate mastery" ("Exhaustion" 32).

Barth's enthusiasm for Borges's fictional *Encyclopaedia of Tlon* and its effects on people's notions of history reflects obliquely on Barth's own use—in *The Sot-Weed Factor*—of the "Privie Journall," the fictional Burlingame I's account of the actions of the historical personage Captain John Smith.[6] The details in Burlingame's journal begin to intrude upon the readers' notions of history, which may have governed them since childhood.

Barth observes, "If you were the author of this paper ["The Literature of Exhaustion"], you'd have written something like *The Sot-Weed Factor* or *Giles Goat-Boy:* novels which imitate the form of the Novel, by an author who imitates the role of Author" ("Exhaustion" 33). Thus he writes *The Sot-Weed Factor* in an old literary form, calling attention to his adaptation of an eighteenth-century Fieldingesque style (with digressive stories and mock-epic devices) and to the depiction of Ebenezer as a naïve and gullible innocent (resembling Fielding's Parson Abraham Adams).

Barth also draws upon themes from earlier comic epic works—Rabelais's *Gargantua and Pantagruel* and Cervantes's *Don Quixote*. Like Rabelais, Barth ironically focuses on the diverse pursuits of the multitude, cataloging details of the scene—whether an eating contest, an epic feast, a listing of twins from myth and legend, or extraordinary births. Barth also connects *Sot-Weed* to Cervantes's *Don Quixote*, particularly in the similarity between Eben and Don Quixote—two ideal-

ists who expatiate over their beloved, Eben over the prostitute Joan
Toast and Don Quixote over the farm girl on whom he confers the title
"Lady of his Thoughts."[7]

Barth is very conscious of the continuity of literature, that literature goes back so as to provide depth. The adaptation of old forms to
new purposes, he explains, opens up infinite possibilities for the novel.
Writers need to recognize literary tradition and be aware of and therefore responsible for its technical innovation ("Exhaustion" 33), innovation such as is evident in the works of postmodern authors.

Barth emphasizes that his "ideal postmodernist author neither
merely repudiates nor merely imitates either his twentieth-century modernist parents or his nineteenth-century premodernist grandparents."
There should be what he calls a "postmodern synthesis" that comes
from the realization that such premodern devices as "linearity" and
"cause and effect . . . are not the whole story." Their modernist opposites, he adds—"disjunction, simultaneity, irrationalism . . .—
these are not the whole story either" ("Replenishment" 70). In "The
Literature of Exhaustion," Barth states that Borges, by using the concept of a labyrinth, is able to move beyond linearity and cause and
effect. Explains Barth: "A labyrinth, after all, is a place in which,
ideally, all the possibilities of choice . . . are embodied and—barring
special dispensation like Theseus's [who, having a ball of thread, was
able to get out of the maze]—must be exhausted before one reaches the
heart" (34). In Barth's short story "Lost in the Funhouse," the title
work for his collection of short stories, the amusement park is like a
labyrinth. Outside the funhouse is Fat May, who laughs as everyone
goes through the maze. Barth's method, throughout his fiction, like that
of Borges's *Labyrinths,* is to "construct funhouses for others."[8] He
chooses not to provide the clue that allows one to get out of the maze,
not to provide the cause-and-effect relationships that develop the plot of
traditional novels. He wants the reader to go through the labyrinth
without a string. For Barth, the process of questing is the treasure:
"The *key* to the treasure may *be* the treasure."[9]

Again, Barth's *Sot-Weed Factor* seems to fulfill this postmodernist ideal of having the reader go through a labyrinth. It is linear but
based on a sketchy history of Eben's life, for there are no birth records.
In addition, at the end of this very complicated plot, the narrator
presents an overview of the persistent difficulties in Eben's life. As
Richard Hauck points out, Eben's "quest goes backward as well as
forward, down as well as up. . . . Ebenezer dies confused."[10] This calls

to mind the labyrinthine nature of the funhouse as structure for a work of art.

In "The Literature of Replenishment," Barth pays tribute to the work of Italo Calvino and Gabriel García Márquez. He praises Calvino's *Cosmicomics* (1965) for keeping "one foot always in the narrative past . . . of Boccaccio, Marco Polo, or Italian fairy tales—and one foot in, one might say, the Parisian structuralist present" (70). He celebrates *One Hundred Years of Solitude* (1967) for its "realism and magic and myth, political passion and nonpolitical artistry, characterization and caricature, humor and terror" (71). He speaks highly of Calvino's and García Márquez's ability to rewrite traditional myths: Calvino in fables of Italian reality and García Márquez in magical tales of the legendary past of the Latin American village of Macondo.

Like Calvino and García Márquez, Barth gives new comic life to traditional myths and tales. In *Chimera*, a twentieth-century Barthian-looking genie (balding and with glasses) travels back in time to the palace of the shah. There he tells Dunyazade, Scheherazade's sister, the tales that will cause the shah to spare Scheherazade's life. These are from *The Arabian Nights*, which the professor—a twentieth-century lover of past literature—has already read. The genie plays the role of tutor and gives Dunyazade the famous tales. The author does not discuss the tales themselves, just as Borges does not discuss the *Encyclopaedia of Tlon*, but the action suggests the complex nature of the imagination, and, therefore, of the writing process. *The Thousand and One Nights* is viewed as yet another tragicomic version of the academic publish-or-perish situation, a problem of Scheherazade for many years. As the genie explains: "My project . . . is to learn where to go by discovering where I am by reviewing where I've been—where we've *all* been" (*Chimera* 10).[11]

Barth's next novel, *Letters* (1979), also goes back in order to move forward. In *Letters*, Barth connects pasts to the present: the literary past, the historical past, and particularly the personal past of Barth's fiction, bringing up to date the humorous predicaments of such absurd heroes as Jacob Horner and Ebenezer Cooke, by their own letters or those of their descendants. Barth uses the form of the epistolary novel, made famous by Samuel Richardson in the eighteenth century, to describe his characters, who, like the form, are given new opportunities for comedy. *Letters* also shows Barth's interest in patterns, particularly the pattern of seven. The novel, published seven years after *Chimera*, also is Barth's seventh work of fiction. The book is divided into seven sections. Its seven characters—in seven different rhetorical styles of prose—write to the author, to one another, and to themselves during seven months (March through September). Comic incongruity is developed through repeated references to series of sevens, ranging from the Deadly Sins to the lists of groups of seven things in Jerome Bray's last letter (*Letters* 755–58).

Criticism of *Letters* itself ranges from witty statements such as that of John Leonard, who says that *Letters* "seems to have been written for graduate students and other masochists";[12] to the serious and reverential praise of Max Schulz, who calls it a "literary milestone" that fuses "the American experience and the . . . epistolary and confessional novel tradition";[13] and Charles Harris's praise of its excellent synthesis of "premodernist and modernist modes of writing."[14]

In what could be construed as a critique of his own writing, Barth discusses the need for postmodernist fiction to be more accessible to the reader, a literature that will not require the "priestly industry of explicators, annotators, allusion-chasers to mediate between the text and the reader" ("Replenishment" 69). "We really don't *need* more *Finnegans Wakes* and *Pisan Cantos*," he continues, "each with its staff of tenured professors to explain it to us" (70). Barth wants postmodernist novels to be accessible, but not simplistic. He advises that the author "may not hope to teach and move the devotees of James Michener and Irving Wallace. . . . But he *should* hope to reach and delight . . . beyond the circle of [the] . . . professional devotees of high art" ("Replenishment" 70).

This concern with accessibility may be another of Barth's put-ons, for, with the exception of *Sabbatical* and the early works *The Floating Opera* and *The End of the Road,* his own novels are not easily understood. They have the complexity of what has been termed the "academic novel," the highly allusive novel that is an epic in prose. These works are characterized by "multiplied References . . . in almost every Paragraph."[15] They are twentieth-century comic adaptations of the embellished style of traditional epics.

Readers have found fault with Barth's parodic novels for being "intellectual gymnastic[s],"[16] for subordinating human problems to "aesthetic implications of the basic form."[17] Others have criticized his glib statements—"I'm not very responsible in the Social Problems way, I guess."[18] Nevertheless, most continue to reread Barth's novels; also, most probably persist in their quest for ordering patterns even though the conflict between the quest for "enlightenment" and the "exasperation"[19] at finding none is disorienting and humorous in the absurd sense.

The Allusive Mode and Black Humor in
Barth's *Sot-Weed Factor*

The black humorist essentially disorients the reader by evoking conflicting responses: horror and laughter, involvement and detachment, and a longing for traditions versus an ironic appreciation of their loss in twentieth-century society. In *Sot-Weed*, Barth develops an ironic sense of loss by inverting the allusive mode. Examples of traditional frames of reference parodied by Barth are: the historic John Smith–Pocahontas story; the American Adam; the Socratic dialogue; traditional romance that contains conventions of chastity and love at first sight; and Aristophanes' famous explanation of love as a desire for one's other half (in Plato's *Symposium*).

Captain Smith in *Sot-Weed* is the diametric opposite of the legendary hero, the savior of the Virginia Colony, who (like Aeneas) was the "bearer of an old civilization to a new and better land."[20] While Captain Smith of the *Generall Historie* mainly was interested in explorations and expeditions and described the "blessed" Pocahontas who saved his life as "a childe of twelve or thirteene,"[21] Barth's Smith "taketh inordinate pride in his virilitie" and does "boast openlie, and in lewdest terms, of his conquests and feats of love." He, according to the record of Burlingame I, "fancieth him selfe a Master of Venereall Arts" (162–63), though he fools "him selfe as regards his comeliness to the faire sex." Barth's Smith has the "eyes of profligates and other dissolute old persons" (166, 165), and what is worse, he is a clumsy coward, an object of derision. When confronted by Indians, he pulls his "Guide before him for a shield," trips on a tree root, and falls into mud and ice (163).[22] Then, like Swift's Gulliver with the Yahoos, Smith is urinated upon by the Indians and "beshitt" by his countryman Burlingame: "I cd by no meanes see out of my eyes, or speake out of my mowth" (403). Scatological imagery prevails throughout the descriptions in Burlingame I's "Privie" account and Smith's "Secret Historie," making the revered hero a ridiculous, bawdy, Rabelaisian character, literally befouling the pristine romantic hero of legend.

Also deflated is the saintlike Pocahontas, renowned as the guardian angel of the Jamestown colony, the noble princess who "hazarded the beating out of her owne braines to save" Smith's life.[23] From

Smith's account in the *Generall Historie,* we can speculate that the saintly Pocahontas is moved by admiration and pity for the great adventurer: "Pocahontas the Kings dearest daughter, when no intreaty could prevaile, got his head in her armes and laid her owne upon his to save him from death."[24] This episode of bravery, nobility, and love has become a commonplace of American literature and lore. The famous scene recapitulates patterns in myth and folklore where the captor (Powhatan) would be a god or sorcerer and the hero (Smith) would be released through the love of the captor's daughter.[25] For Barth the absurdist, the name Pocahontas means *"she of the smallnesse and impenetrabilitie."* Barth's Pocahontas suffers the physical shortcoming of being impenetrable, a girl of "sixteene, who was yet a maide" (168–69), a maid who takes delight in pornographic pictures (167). Burlingame's "Privie Journall" indicates that Pocahontas, a sexually excitable girl of sixteen, intercedes to save Smith's life ("declar'd to Powhatan, that rather wd she loose her owne head, then that they shd dash in his" [168]) because she sees the captain as a man who can penetrate her "gate to Venus grottoe," a man who can "relieve Pocahontas of her maidenhood" (169, 791). The climax of this scene is held off till near the end of *Sot-Weed,* when Burlingame I's journal describes the ritualistic ceremony of adulthood not as the testing of Smith's courage (head placed on a stone) but as the testing of his manhood as he relieves Pocahontas of her maidenhood. Captain John Smith, whose organ is enlarged by the mysterious eggplant recipe, can barely keep his legs together as he walks toward the princess. The comedy is slapstick, a kind of "joking turned theatrical,"[26] with exaggerated diametrically opposed actions that aim solely to entertain. The former suitors of Pocahontas drop to their knees in prayer, Emperor Powhatan rises in dismay, and Pocahontas swoons "dead away."[27] Burlingame I relates: "My Captains yard stood full erect, and what erst had been more cause for pity than for astonishment, was now in verie sooth a frightful engine . . . a weapon of the Gods!" (794). The scene elicits hearty laughter from us as we view the ribald details of farce, much as we view the comic actions of Gargantua when he undoes "his magnificent codpiece" and floods the villagers.[28]

Barth shifts from farce to a more serious tone after Joan Toast's admission that she stole the journal's pages describing Smith's mysterious eggplant recipe: "Look at me! . . . Behold the fruits of lustfulness! Swived in my twelfth year, poxed in my twentieth, and dead in my twenty-first! Ravaged, ruined, raped, and betrayed! Woman's lot is wretched enough at best; d'ye think I'll pass on that murtherous receipt to make it worse?" (796). The tone changes from bawdy humor to grim horror at Joan's deterioration from pox and her imminent death, causing the formerly detached readers to contemplate Joan's unfortunate history. We recall Joan aboard the ship *Cyprian,* traveling to the New World. Pirates are raping helpless women, and Eben, who so values his virginity, is on the verge of raping Joan Toast without knowing who she is (286). Pain collides with humor and we are disoriented and strangely affected by the lust and exploitation that are reflected in the history of Joan Toast and of our early settlers. We begin to wonder whether gamblers, whores, and debauchers may indeed have been the New World's first settlers, and also whether Barth's demythologized Captain John Smith and Pocahontas are more accurate representations than the venerated characters of legitimate history.[29]

The Whitmanesque American Adam

In rewriting the Maryland colonial experience, Barth also parodies what R.W.B. Lewis terms the myth of the American Adam: the Whitmanesque character who is "the hero of the new adventure"; the New Adam, "undefiled by the usual inheritances of family and race"; the character who sees the world as lying before him; "the type of creator, the poet par excellence, creating language itself by naming the elements of the scene about him";[30] the hero who, like Whitman, presents the word of the "one complete lover" of the universe, "the greatest poet" ("Preface 1855" 717).

Eben, like the poet of "Song of Myself," wants to sing the praises of America in an epic (*Sot-Weed* 83). Whitman, however, wrote what he set out to; Barth's Eben is not able to. Eben leaves England for the New World, where—on his father's tobacco plantation, Malden—he hopes to lead a contemplative Edenic existence like Thoreau's at Walden Pond. His expectations are perverted when he comes in contact with tricksters, debauchers, and gamblers: America's early settlers. After he is swindled by a lawyer (because of his innocence) and loses the rights to his estate, Eben ironically becomes, in the Adamic sense, "undefiled" by inheritance.

Ebenezer also is a parody of Adam as poet; instead of creating language by naming the things he comes across in the world, he starts writing idealistically about the American scene before he even lands there. He originally wishes to write "an epic to out-epic epics" on the "courage and perseverance" of the settlers of Maryland, "a province, an entire people—all unsung!" (83–84). In America, however, he is disappointed by the contrast between his ideal vision and the actual world. His outpouring becomes a satire, *The Sot-Weed Factor* (495–98), an ironic counterpart to great celebrations of America such as "Song of Myself."

In contrast to epic extollers of the nation and its people, Barth's Eben is a loner. He can picture many kinds of men—"the bold as well as the bashful," the young boy and the tottering lecher—but he feels estranged from all: "no more one of these than another" (*Sot-Weed* 50). He is an ironic reversal of Whitman's speaker in "Song of Myself," who encompasses "multitudes" (51.1326). Also, unlike Whitman's speaker, who strongly believes in and sings of his self, Eben has no firm sense of self. He often feels that he is "no person at all" (*Sot-Weed* 50) and, for this reason, takes on the idealistic role of poet and virgin: Eben rejects all possibilities of physical love and substitutes a pursuit of the ideal. This is another ironic contrast to the sensuousness of Whitman's American Adam persona, who is the "one complete lover" ("Preface 1855" 717).

Ebenezer's rejection of bodily desires is made the butt of ridicule when Burlingame, who has described himself as "Suitor of Totality, Embracer of Contradictories, Husband to all Creation, the Cosmic Lover" (*Sot-Weed* 536), disguises himself as Tim Mitchell, lover of beasts. Burlingame's rhapsody gains much of its satiric humor because it burlesques the stance of one who has enthusiastic love for all things, a lover like the hero in Whitman's "Song of Myself," who exclaims, "I believe in the flesh and the appetites," a lover who is "Turbulent, fleshy, sensual, eating, drinking and breeding" ("Song" 24.522, 498). Burlingame, stroking the sow Portia, says: "How comely is a well-formed man! That handsome cage of ribs, and the blocky muscles of his calves and thighs. . . . Marry, sometimes I wish I had a gift with words, sir, or some poet had my soul: what lines I would make about the bodies of men and women! And the rest of creation as well" (*Sot-Weed* 354–55).

Burlingame is a comic exaggeration of Whitmanesque expansiveness and, as such, accentuates the contrast between an all-embracing poetic nature and a straitened one, flexibility versus rigidity, greatness versus meanness of mind, the exuberance of a Walt Whitman versus the growing cynicism of an Ebenezer Cooke. The comedy is heightened when Eben rigidly responds: "*Perversity*, Mr. Mitchell! [. . .] You've parted company now with Plato and Shakespeare, and with every other *gentleman* as well!'" (355; second italics added). The encounter between Eben and Burlingame emphasizes how Eben's innocence is viewed as incredibly naïve in Barth's world and so becomes an object of laughter. Burlingame criticizes this innocence: "My good man, is't that you were born yesterday?" (85). Eben's ignorance of worldly experience is without virtue. He lacks the open-mindedness and love for mankind that are part of Whitman's conception of innocence.[31]

Eben's expectations, unlike those of Whitman's persona, are continually thwarted whether the cause is the tobacco plantation Malden, which houses debauchers and gamblers; or Burlingame's Whitman-esque expansiveness (as "cosmic lover"),[32] which contrasts with Eben's rigid withdrawal from sexual encounters. It is because of Eben's incredible innocence (not his fall from it) that he loses his "earthly paradise." "Your father," states Burlingame, "will not lose this chance to turn ye out o' the Garden" (434). Barth, in such farcical episodes, takes the reader off guard and troubles him with the implausibility of his national literature and its myths. Barth's depiction of Eben as the American innocent and his description of the new Eden as "the scene of all human ills" are part of his design to illustrate "an irony of epic proportions."[33]

The Platonic-Socratic Dialogue

Barth's third use of the allusive mode inverts the Platonic- Socratic dialectic to develop the incommunicative dialogue of the absurd. In the Platonic Dialogues, Socrates employs his dialectic to reveal falsehood and advance toward truth. He questions people who claim knowledge of moral entities such as virtue, justice, love. The overall pattern of the dialectic is similar to the upward movement in "The Allegory of the Cave":[34] a movement from the darkness of a topsy-turvy world toward the light of ultimate truth. Socrates' quest was to bring about "the speediest and most effective shifting or conversion of the soul"[35] to an intimation of universal truth. The interchanges between Eben and his instructor, Burlingame, form and collapse connections with the Socratic dialectic, as the debate moves toward uncertainty. Henry Burlingame, the instructor, takes an anti-Socratic stance throughout. He uses contraries to support rather than refute absurdities. He insists that contradictions are the *norm* in discourse and in random nature. For Burlingame it is laughable to assume that one can advance toward metaphysical truths or clarity or meaning in a world where human nature and the cosmos are in flux. Ebenezer, pointing to logical contrarieties, implores Burlingame for clarification: "Is't Burlingame that stands before me now, or was't Burlingame I left in Plymouth? . . . In sooth you are the man I knew in London. Yet I cannot believe Peter Sayer was a fraud!" (357). The anti-Socratic teacher explains: "Your true and constant Burlingame lives only in your fancy, as doth the pointed order of the world. In fact you see a Heraclitean flux" (357). For Burlingame it is nonsensical to speak of constancy or order in regard to man or the universe: "There is no *dome of heaven* yonder," Burlingame asserts (374). Man's soul, he explains, is part of "that same black Cosmos whence we sprang and through which we fall." Eben responds: "But there is so much unanswered and unresolved! It dizzies me!" (373).

Barth's laughter ranges from the sharp-edged almost Juvenalian tone of Burlingame's words (which stress randomness in contrast to the ideal of unity and order) to the lighter Rabelaisian tone elicited by Eben's exaggerated farcical reaction to contradictions between a senseless world and his own desire for a Platonic progression toward clarity and absolute significance. Burlingame emphasizes that in this world "one must choose his gods and devils on the run" (373). Eben, responding to such description of blind nature and a meaningless universe, follows his instructor's gaze, searches the vast vacuity of space, and becomes "bereft of orientation" (374). He loses his balance in the saddle and barely keeps from dropping headlong:

> he swayed in the saddle and covered his eyes. For a swooning moment before he turned away it seemed that he was heels over head on the bottom of the planet, looking *down* on the stars instead of up, and that only by dint of . . . holding fast to the saddlebow with both his hands did he keep from dropping headlong into those vasty reaches! (375)

The focus quickly shifts from the metaphysical to the physical and from there to the purely mechanical. The rigid Eben, unable to right himself in the saddle, becomes a caricature of a Bergsonian mechanical man,[36] a comic buffoon. As the farcical tone relaxes readers, they become vulnerable to the disruption of Burlingame's anti-Socratic dialectic, which focuses on man as "the toy of aimless Nature" (372). In the

Platonic-Socratic dialogue there is expectation for gradual clarity and meaning on the part of the characters and the reader. The conversations between Eben and Burlingame, on the other hand, move toward incommunicative dialogue, a reversal of the Socratic progression toward clarity and meaning.

Incommunicative dialogue of the absurd is pushed to the extreme in Ebenezer's early discussions with Joan Toast. Such dialogue is best understood as an inversion of the Socratic dialogical process. In Socratic dialogues the characters' moral aspect, or *ethos,* and their reasoning faculty, or *dianoia,* are clearly exposed. The *ethos* is clarified by what they choose and avoid, and the *dianoia* by how they prove or disprove arguments.[37] In *Sot-Weed,* Eben takes pride in his virginity, Joan in her occupation; he is a gentleman, she a prostitute. He is a poet, using literary allusions; she an uncultured woman, using street language.[38] Their debates—unlike Socratic dialogues—show no progression toward understanding. With incongruous moralities and opposing "reasoning," Eben and Joan jostle against each other like farcical clowns.

Traditional Romance

Barth's fourth inversion of the allusive mode is based on traditional romance. Eben, lacking flexibility, reacts to all he sees in terms of the ideal: virgin and poet. His seriousness, literary language, and romantic orientation conflict with the expectations and behavior of the whore Joan Toast. Joan, following the momentous wager in the tavern, enters Eben's room ready to do his bidding for five guineas. "Out with thy money . . . and off with thy breeches," she cries. But Ebenezer, like a Renaissance love poet, only wants to rhapsodize. For Eben the question is, "But how price the priceless? How buy Heaven with simple gold?" He compares their situation to that of the great lovers in literature: "Think thee Venus and Anchises did their amorous work on consideration of five guineas?" Joan Toast replies: "Let foreign bawds run their business as't please 'em" (59). Eben idealizes Joan, while she sees him as a customer who has reneged in paying five guineas. "I despise ye for a knave and fool," she yells. "I love thee for my savior and inspiration," he retorts. "May ye suffer French pox, ye great ass!" Joan replies. That Eben and Joan do not communicate does not bother Ebenezer, who, like an Elizabethan sonneteer, takes up a quill to write a love song and then proceeds to affirm his identity as virgin and poet (64–66).[39]

This farcical incommunicative dialogue between Eben and Joan is part of the continuum of black humor. One laughs at Eben for his Quixotism, or self-deception, as he persists in being blind to all signposts. One laughs at Eben for writing a love poem to a woman who, like Quixote's Dulcinea, lacks the education necessary to understand his wealth of literary references. One laughs at Eben for affirming his identity as virgin and poet when he is surrounded by prostitutes and profligates and for offering his love to a woman who ridicules his romantic notions. Yet, concomitantly, the reader appreciates that sonneteers *did* solemnly write poems in praise of the beloved, even when spurned, and epic poets such as John Milton *did* talk seriously about a poet's need to be virtuous and chaste, to be "himself . . . a true poem."[40] This sharpens the grim contrast between the cynical views expressed in literature of the twentieth century, such as *The Sot-Weed Factor*, and the positive attitude toward love and virtue that existed in earlier works, such as the Renaissance sonnet and the epic. Thus, once again, we recognize the ruefully comic contrast.

The inversion of the reader's longing for the pure love at first sight of traditional romance and romantic comedy is best exemplified in the ironic Mary Mungummory–Charley Mattassin vignette. The whore Mary Mungummory explains that her lover Charley had an unusually small sexual organ. To compensate for this he and she worked out a special love technique that became their shared secret pleasure. The following summarizes her tale: Mary's sister Kate marries an old man, Mynheer Wilhelm Tick, to inherit his fortune and deprive his two sons of it. Charley, Mary's lover, plays a role in this enterprise by pitting the two sons against each other. Willi kills the father, Peter slays Willi with a knife, and then Kate shoots Peter. Charley then pretends to be romantically happy with Kate but quickly knifes her after making love and returns to Mary—his true beloved. In the midst of his secret sexual activity with Mary, Charley laughs uproariously, and Mary later relates, "I wept like a bride for the first time in my life!" (455). Charley apologizes and gives an account of the above knavery, including his lovemaking with Kate. He thinks Mary will cherish him all the more for his cunning, but she is enraged that he has shared their sexual secret with Kate. "This trick of ours was the entire world o' love" (456), she later explains to Eben. Mary tells the sheriff of Kate's murder, and Charley is executed by the authorities. Mary does not turn Charley in for murder but "for love," because he has shared their special love technique with Kate. The fact that she clearly treasures his charms causes her to have him killed.

The Mary-Charley vignette builds its incongruities from the stockpile of romantic love. The whore falls in love at "first swive" rather than at "first sight"; Mary and Charley's love culminates in death at the gallows rather than, as in romantic comedy, in marital happiness; in addition, the woman, instead of the man, is the victim of cuckoldry. The tone fluctuates between sharp gravity and hearty laughter at the incongruities and stylized actions (such as Charley's "chuckling when they led him to the gallows" [456]). The black humor often has Juvenalian sharpness, but it lacks the satirical focus on reform of folly, vice, and corruption. Instead, laughter seems to act as a means of coping with comic absurdity, of facing the Heraclitean flux. Thus, the memory of Charley's laugh "sours the food in . . . [Mary's] belly" (457), yet also causes her to laugh. One is moved by Mary's and Charley's hysterical efforts to see themselves as "comedians" in the absurd game of life, the tough resiliency of their despair that does not let the pain blot out the humor. Pain and humor continually collide for the reader and for Mary, who laughs while "the tears coursed down her cheeks" (456). The laughter is the same that Mary experiences when Ebenezer signs away his property (Malden) at the Cambridge court: " 'Tis a disease, little poet, like pox or clap! Where Charley took it, God only knows, but yesterday showed me, for the first time, I've caught it from him!" The narrator relates, "She whipped up the horse and drove away, her head flung back in mute hilarity" (458).

The Fusion of Halves in Plato's *Symposium*

The fifth example of an inverse allusiveness in *Sot-Weed* is Barth's development of a negative counterpart to Aristophanes' famous explanation of the origin and nature of love in Plato's *Symposium*. Aristophanes explains that primeval man was round ("there was one head to the two faces, which looked opposite ways"), that he was sliced in two by Zeus, and that subsequently, when one half would meet with his other half, both would be "thrilled with affection and intimacy and love." Were the two to be asked, "Do you desire to be joined in the closest possible union," each would indeed wish to be fused. "The cause of it all," explains Aristophanes, "is this, that our original form was as I have described, and we were entire; and the craving and pursuit of that entirety is called Love."[41] In *Sot-Weed,* Burlingame inverts the Platonic emphasis on a fusion of halves, a progression toward wholeness, by focusing on it as a *futile* desire: "Aristophanes maintained that male and female are displaced moieties of an ancient whole, and wooing but their *vain* attempt at union" (528; italics added).

The pursuit of one's other half often is described in legend and literature as the quest for the double or the twin. "The twin," Otto Rank explains, "stands out as one who was capable of bringing with him into earthly existence his living double."[42] The intricate tapestry of twins and doubles on which the plot of *Sot-Weed* is built accentuates the gap between man's desire for unity, of twin halves, as explained in the *Symposium,* and "the world that disappoints,"[43] the desire for meaning confronting the randomness of the universe and the irrationality of human nature. At the center of *Sot-Weed* are the twins Anna and Eben. They are of similar *ethos;* they yearn for each other. Each, however, has chosen a mate who is the opposite of the twin's other half: Henry Burlingame and Joan Toast are mirror images for Eben and Anna. Henry, with ease, assumes many roles; Ebenezer adapts a fixed identity as virgin and poet. Henry is worldly; Eben is a greenhorn Englishman, in many ways similar to the persona in the original "Sot-Weed Factor" of 1708:[44] the fearful city man who mistakes the buzz of mosquitoes for the hiss of rattlesnakes (lines 221–31), is robbed of clothes at an inn (lines 442–47), not a corncrib, and exploited by an unscrupulous lawyer (lines 639–42), like the lying Richard Sowter. Similarly, Joan is a girl of the streets, in contrast to sister Anna, a gentlewoman; Joan is experienced, Anna innocent; Joan is unread, while Anna's reading includes the world's myths, legends, and epics (6–7). John Barth, as Robert Rogers points out, "has parodied the virginal maiden–temptress prostitute dichotomy out of existence in the characters of Anna Cooke and Joan Toast."[45] Barth exaggerates the futility of this search for a double by emphasizing that each person (each half) is self-contradictory in nature: Eben, the idealist, searches for identity as virgin and poet but experiences an incestuous desire for his twin sister, Anna, and (on the ship *Cyprian*) nearly rapes Joan Toast. As poet laureate, he wishes to write a celebrative poem on Maryland but instead writes the satiric *Sot-Weed Factor.* Burlingame, the absurdist, claims that history is a fiction yet feels compelled to search out his own history in the diaries of Captain Smith and Burlingame I (his grandfather); he (like Jake Horner in Barth's earlier novel *The End of the Road*) professes that continual change of roles is necessary for survival yet journeys to Bloodsworth Island to find his father, king of the Ahatchwhoops, whose strong desire is to place Burlingame in the fixed role of Indian prince (809–10).[46]

Barth alludes to the Platonic notion of wholeness, the desire of twin halves to form an entirety of ideal love, and then develops ominous references to multiplicity and chaos. Burlingame observes to Eben: "Of all the things our rustic forebears feared, the three that most alarmed them were thunder, lightning, and twins. . . . the most enlightened sages have seen in you the embodiment of dualism, polarity, and compensation. . . . the double face of Nature" (532). He frightens Eben by equating his Platonic yearning for unity and meaning with the dark desire for "coalescence" with twin sister Anna (528), a remark that foreshadows Anna's observation to Eben: " 'Tis the universal doubt of salvages [sic] and peasants, whether twins of different sexes have not sinned together in the womb" (811). One laughs at the irrational foolishness of such a bizarre comment, but the laughter wavers as one contemplates the "double face" of the twin motif. Similarly, the reader laughs at the deprecation of the nostalgia for unity of twin halves held dear by the rigid Eben, but then he realizes that this desire for wholeness and completeness is only aggravated in a world where randomness and duality prevail.

Twins have been the source of slapstick in much traditional comedy. In Shakespeare's *Comedy of Errors*, two pairs of twins and the multiple entanglements they cause create confusion for all, including the Duke who complains:

> One of these men is Genius to the other;
> And so of these. Which is the natural man.
> And which the spirit? Who deciphers them?[47]

In *Twelfth Night*, Viola, disguised as a man, is repeatedly mistaken for her twin brother, Sebastian. Side by side, their resemblance is astonishing:

> One face, one voice, one habit, and two persons,
> A natural perspective, that is and is not![48]

Such confusion accentuates—in traditional comedy—the illusion and disorder from which the drama must eventually progress to reach a happy ending, a sense of unity and meaning. In these works, the unraveling of mistaken identities eventually replaces the irrational or absurd as the dramas progress toward a sense of unity and clarity. In Barth's black humor comedy, on the other hand, the complicated ramifications of the twin motif are never resolved. Instead of "dispelling illusion" and the "irrational,"[49] as in traditional comedy, *Sot-Weed* emphasizes the existence of both. At the close, most people still think that Eben has fathered twin sister Anna's child, and it is indicated that people continue to hold the irrational belief that twins coalesce in the womb (811).

Shakespeare's *Comedy of Errors* and *Twelfth Night* have implicit allusions to the farcical handling of twins in Plautus's *Menaechmi*. Barth employs the allusive mode but in a way that rather than affirming meaning through precedents of tradition, dissolves correspondences as it drains them of significance. He alludes to the Platonic notion of wholeness and perfection of twin halves and then has Eben experience the fear of breaking the incest taboo. He alludes to the romantic tradition of falling in love at first sight with an innocent maiden and then has the virgin protagonist place his affection on the whore Joan Toast. He alludes to the Platonic-Socratic notion of a dialectic that advances from darkness to light and contrasts it with the incommunicative dialogue of his fiction. He points to historical records that value the John Smith–Pocahontas tale, and then he makes a travesty of it all. He sharpens his statement by parodying the complicated sentence structure and pretentious phrases that academicians would use to criticize his untraditional presentation: "LEST IT BE OBJECTED by a certain stodgy variety of squint-minded antiquarians that he has in this lengthy history played more fast and loose with Clio, the chronicler's muse, than ever Captain John Smith dared." He continues, "The happenings of former times are a clay in the present moment that will-we, nill-we, the lot of us must sculpt" (805).[50]

"The Sot-Weed Factor" of 1708

Indeed Barth's "history" is an extravaganza, similar in many respects to Ebenezer Cook's "Sot-Weed" of 1708. Cook's satirical account of the men and manners of the New World had two audiences: the credulous British readers who believed the exaggerated description of barbarous Americans so unschooled that most of their judges could not write or read;[51] and the American readers, familiar with the rough conditions of pioneer life, who could laugh at the fearful greenhorn narrator and the prejudiced English readers as well.[52] Readers laugh at the greenhorn Eben, who writes a satire, *The Sot-Weed Factor* (495–98). Readers are well aware that all of the poem's lines are from the 1708 satire and that, though specific circumstances differ, Eben's reactions are virtually identical to those of Cook's gullible narrator. This is what gives rise to particular glee, for Barth's aspiring poet is unlike the original poet Ebenezer Cook and all good satirists who have the wit necessary to separate themselves as poet from an ignorant persona.[53] Readers laugh at Eben's naïveté and optimism, his trust in what he takes for facts. However, when Barth turns upside down romantic beliefs about history and genealogy, readers find that in laughing at Eben they also have been laughing at themselves. There is a loss of distance from the situation and the laughter develops a nervous, brittle edge.[54] Barth anticipates the readers' expectations and then makes troublesome assertions that collapse valued notions about history, philosophy, and literature.[55] He jostles the readers when they are laughing and off guard and then eases them back to the picaresque antics of *The Sot-Weed Factor*. The picaresque episodes amuse readers and lessen their discomfort over the bizarre quality of Barth's world and their own.

The Allusive Mode and the Absurd in *Giles Goat-Boy*

In quest literature, the traditional hero is a protector of mankind, a destroyer of evil, the epitome of temperance, wisdom, and altruism; he aims to restore a kingdom to his people. The protagonist leaves the known—the homeland—is tested by a series of adventures, and returns home, where his perfection is rewarded. He thus completes a monomythic pattern of separation, initiation, and return.[56] According to Joseph Campbell, *"a hero ventures forth from the world of common day into a region of supernatural wonder: fabulous forces are there encountered and a decisive victory is won; the hero comes back from this mysterious adventure with the power to bestow boons on his fellow man."*[57]

John Barth, master of the absurd and black humor, inverts the usual patterns of quest literature and, instead of describing actions of great heroes, presents the adventures of a deformed protagonist, the gimping George, who is brought up with the goats (not the sheep).[58] He writes a book that handles the hero and salvation comically, a book that Robert Scholes calls "a tract for our times, an epic to end all epics, and a sacred book to end all sacred books." Barth's comic novel points out that "in our time any sacred book must be a work of fiction."[59] The twentieth century has indeed turned all sacred books into fictions.

Like the Bible, *Goat-Boy* is divided into two volumes. As in the Bible, the numbers three and seven appear often, three calling to mind the doctrine of the Trinity and seven the Sabbath, the seven Sacraments, the seven visions of the Apocalypse and their subdivision into a seven-fold representation of elements, and so forth. Barth divides each volume of *Goat-Boy* into three reels and seven subdivisions or chapters. George attempts three interpretations of his seven assignments, goes down into the belly of WESCAC three times, and completes the revision of the New Syllabus at the age of thirty-three and a third.[60]

Born of a virgin mother impregnated by a computer, George is a Barthian adaptation of a Christ figure; he spends his childhood, or unknown years, among the goats, later reinterprets the New Syllabus, and inspires his followers to set up a Gilesian kingdom. George comes to campus, collects a small following for his new religion, creates a new Bible, but finds that reason is inadequate to handle the complexities of his experience. His striving for perfection is reminiscent of the quest of Joe Morgan, in *The End of the Road*, who wants to be the superrationalist, and of Ebenezer Cooke, in *The Sot-Weed Factor*, who tries to be a great poet and an admirably good man. Barth wishes to show the hopelessness of such striving in an absurd universe, peopled not by great heroes such as Odysseus, Aeneas, Adam, or Christ but by antiheroes such as Ebenezer Cooke, Joe Morgan, and George/Giles Goat-Boy.

A parodic allusiveness is evident in George/Giles's first appearance at New Tammany's Spring Carnival, where candidates for registration casually celebrate ritual without any knowledge of the significance behind it. References to a past Christian age and its stress on a meaningfully ordered universe contrast with the irreverent attitudes of the students and professors. The scene ironically points toward apocalypse as students casually engage in "Trial by Turnstile," which theoretically would admit them to "the tiny gate somewhere beyond . . . [and] to the Final Examination" (297).[61]

For the students at the spring ritual, not only the *Last Judgment* and God's will but also mankind's education are irrelevant. The scene is described as a Mardi Gras, which for the devout catechumens—the early Christians—would culminate in the joyous Easter dawn celebration of Christ's triumph over death and His opening of heaven's gates for the baptized. Barth explains that the spring carnival originated "in ancient agronomical ceremonies and [was] modified by the Enochist Fraternity to celebrate the Expulsion of Enos Enoch, His promotion of the Old-Syllabus Emeritus Profs from the Nether Campus, and His triumphal Reinstatement" (297). At Tammany, however, the qualified and unqualified matriculate, graduate, and even go on for further study to become professors.

At spring registration, George receives his "assignment" on a computer printout just as he tries to charge through Scapegoat Grate. On it is the PAT phrase "Pass-All/Fail-All"[62] and the list of seven essentials for his assignment:

To Be Done At Once, In No Time

1) *Fix the Clock*
2) *End the Boundary Dispute*
3) *Overcome Your Infirmity*
4) *See Through Your Ladyship*
5) *Re-place the Founder's Scroll*
6) *Pass the Finals*
7) *Present Your ID-card, Appropriately Signed, to the Proper Authority* (428)

That the seven requisites of the assignment are allegorical is evident. The number seven is itself mystical, manifesting perfection; its components four and three are sacred numbers in Christian numerology. Where the allegory points, however, is questionable.[63] Charles Harris assumes that the novel moves toward synthesis; that, originally, George sees only the individual categories of the assignment, sections that are artificial and should not be approached separately.[64] At the close, George "arrives at an awareness of the unity of an apparently various universe."[65] Harris discusses the novel's tripartite nature—its dialectical structure of thesis, antithesis, and synthesis; its "three mythological components" (the hero, Satan, and "mythopoeic implications"); and George's three descents. All, he says, contribute to George's transcendence and to "synthesis." Harris asserts that George finally "transcends the disparate nature of things."[66]

However, it seems more probable that the allegorical possibilities here and in the rest of the novel move toward disparity rather than unity. In the contemporary world of the novel, the symbols are meaningless, "the stage sets collapse." This calls attention to what Camus terms the "awakening" to the absurd.[67]

For example, one could look at the theological implications of George/Giles's assignment. This method is encouraged by Barth, who calls the work a "souped-up Bible."[68] It also is underlined by the PAT-Card, with its circle-encased cross, symbolizing man's immortality in the Christian triumph over death. These allusions suggest that there may be a relationship between the seven requirements for graduation from the university and the seven Sacraments, which are considered the signposts on the Christian journey toward salvation: Baptism, the initiation into eternal life; Penance, the alleviation of moral ills; Eucharist, the sustenance of divine life; Confirmation, the growth to Christian maturity; Matrimony, the sanctification of procreation; Holy Orders, the sanctification of the priestly vocation; Extreme Unction, the preparation for the final, spiritual journey.[69] However, the seven aspects of George's assignment for graduation become signposts for an ironic, not a meaningful, journey: one that parodies the quest of the traditional Christian hero. At the conclusion of the quest George/Giles makes no distinction between passage and failure, truth and falsehood: "Unnamable! Unimaginable! Surely my mind must crack!" (709).

George/Giles's quest burlesques that of the traditional hero, as is exhibited in the quadrated circle (see figure) from Barth's "Bellerophoniad" novella in *Chimera* (261).[70] The diagram shows the multileveled structure that underlies heroic literature,[71] events such as George/Giles's extraordinary conception by Virginia Hector and WESCAC (542–44),[72] his Summons to Adventure by the mystical sound of the shofar (145), his pledge to fulfill the seven academic assignments of his PAT-Card with its PASS-ALL/FAIL-ALL mystery (428–29), his sacred marriage to Anastasia in the belly of WESCAC (731), and his extraordinary death on Founder's Hill (764) amid peals of thunder.

Barth exploits for comic purposes numerous patterns that are basic both to the Bible and to the epic. We grasp what seems to be a master plan of structures, get caught up in its intricacies, and long for the revelation of fundamental truths. However, readers repeatedly become aware that the allegorical subjects never move toward an anagogical level. After George's three trials, readers conclude that there are no final answers (709). At the close of *Goat-Boy*, it still is unclear whether or not George indeed is a Grand Tutor, a Christ figure. Tharpe explains that George "feels neither optimism, transcendentalism, nor innocence. . . . The result is existentialism in the fullest sense."[73] It is a "cosmic joke."[74] In fact, as Umberto Eco explains: the reader "appreciates the way in which he was tricked."[75] Readers, aware of traditional quest literature, enjoy the incongruity between expectations and their reversals and they take pleasure in the black humor of the absurd.

Figure 1

The gimping Giles, who views the world from the perspective of an innocent Adam, is an object of mirth, similar in many respects to Barth's earlier hero, Ebenezer Cooke, who holds the extremely naïve and rigid perspective of virgin and poet. For George and Ebenezer, the journey from innocence to experience is fraught with mishaps that obliquely illuminate man's continual attempts to use reason to unravel the complexities operating in a universe that is beyond comprehension and control. The heroic quests of George and Ebenezer lead to awareness of the irrational rather than to knowledge of significant truths. Reason tends to recoil upon itself and becomes the object of laughter. It is a laughter born of the confrontation between "the aspirations of the human mind and the world's incapacity to satisfy them."[76]

Goat-Boy is structured to move from an initially chaotic state (George with the goats) to a frustrating attempt at order or affirmation of values (his three trials) to a cyclical affirmation of the chaotic or absurd state: "Passage *was* Failure, and Failure Passage; yet Passage was Passage, Failure Failure! Equally true, none was the Answer" (708–9). This black humor novel shows the inversion of traditional comedy when disorder, not order, emerges at the end of the quest.

The frame of *Goat-Boy* compounds the dissolution of reader expectation. The certainty of the fictional world itself is brought into question by reports on the spurious nature of the comments of George, who records the tale, and J.B., who types and sends it to the publisher. The "professor and *quondam* novelist," J.B., believes that the posttape supposedly recorded by George is spurious. The footnote to the postscript to the posttape further eliminates certainties by pointing out that J.B.'s postscript itself may be spurious because "the type of the typescript pages . . . is not the same as that of the 'Cover-Letter to the Editors and Publisher' " (766). This novel of the absurd erects and then undermines the grounds for any truth whatsoever.

John Barth, the University, and the Absurd

Barth's *Giles Goat-Boy,* like other contemporary epic novels, has been criticized for being excessively allusive and, therefore, addressed to an exclusively academic audience.[77] Indeed, one of the novel's basic metaphors is the "universe as a university,"[78] and a major part of its plot revolves around the adventures of George Goat-Boy from matriculation to graduation.

Satiric comments on the fallen nature of the twentieth-century university permeate the novel. There is Harold Bray's orientation lecture, with its businesslike approach to learning: "*Not for nothing are 'Staff' and 'Faculty' equally privileged, so that groundskeepers and dormitory-cooks are affluent as new professors; . . . Was not Enos Enoch, the Founder's Boy . . . a do-it-Himselfer who chose as His original Tutees the first dozen people He met; who never took degree or published monograph or stood behind lectern, but gathered about Him whoever would listen . . . and taught them by simple fictions and maxims proof against time*" (448–49).

In a similar focus on the reward rather than the quest, Bray advises: *"Get the Answers, by any means at all: that is the undergraduate's one imperative! Don't speak to me of cheating—... To cheat can only mean to Pass in ignorance of the Answers, which is impossible"* (445). The deflation of the pursuit of knowledge is evident in what Bray terms the professor's prayer: *"Above all, Sir, stand by me at my lectern; be chalk and notes to me; ... be now and ever my visual aid, that upon the empty slate of these young minds I may inscribe, bold and squeaklessly, the Answers!"* (454–55). For him, there is no concern for intellectual excitement, no interest in learning itself. For him, success in the classroom and in the backseat of a car—learning and making love—are devoid of any spiritual or ethical meaning: *"Be with each co-ed at the evening's close: paw her with facts, make vain her protests against learning's advances; take her to Thy mind's backseat, strip off preconceptions, let down illusions, unharness her from error"* (454). Barth pokes fun at the "spectacle of these enormous universities,"[79] which frustrate both the pursuit of reason and the advancement of knowledge.

Barth, who has spent most of his adult years teaching at a university, manages to incorporate many of his own experiences as teacher and writer into his satiric novels. In this respect he is in the tradition of contemporary academic writers such as Mary McCarthy, in *The Groves of Academe*, Randall Jarrell, in *Pictures from an Institution*, Philip Roth, in *Letting Go,* and Saul Bellow, in *The Dean's December.*[80] Barth's novels, like the works of these authors, show a strong preoccupation with the frailties of university teachers and students. In two of his novels—*The End of the Road* and *Giles Goat-Boy*—the action takes place on a university campus. In all of the novels, Barth gives the academic background for the major characters and, in addition, draws upon his own experiences in the university for specific particulars. Largely, the setting for the novels is the Eastern Shore of Maryland, where he was brought up; Johns Hopkins, where he received B.A. and M.A. degrees and is now Alumni Centennial Professor of English and the Writing Seminars; and Penn State, where he taught for many years.

Barth's method ranges from using the university for the entire setting, as in *Giles Goat-Boy,*[81] with its East versus West Campus cold war, to employing merely the trappings of academia. In *Sabbatical* (1982), Susan Seckler, an associate professor of literature and creative writing at Washington College, is on leave for a year. Susan is unsure whether or not she will return to teaching and accept a tenured position at Swarthmore. Fenwick, her husband, likewise has to decide if he will accept an adjunct professorship at the University of Delaware. In Barth's first novel, *The Floating Opera,* the protagonist, Tod Andrews, was an undergraduate at Johns Hopkins; Jacob Horner, of *The End of the Road,* has completed his Master's examination at Johns Hopkins and immediately enters a state of gross motivational decline. Upon his recovery, he obtains a position as instructor of English at Wicomico State Teachers College, on Maryland's Eastern Shore. Ebenezer Cooke, of *The Sot-Weed Factor,* leaves Cambridge and then completes his education in the wilderness of Maryland. George/Giles Goat-Boy leaves his tutor Max to matriculate at New Tammany College, which has many topographical similarities to Penn State, including a goat farm.[82] Scheherazade, in *Chimera,* makes reference to her early training at Banu Sasan University. Later, in the palace of the Shahryar, she has her own special twentieth-century tutor in creative writing. In *Letters,* the principal new character—acting provost Germaine G. Pitt—and most of the characters from Barth's previous novels are involved in educational pursuits. Barth satirizes educational practices and the theoretical suppositions that lie behind them. Readers—particularly if they are academicians—recognize in the situations truths about the profession, the university community, and themselves.

Emersonian Traditions of Education and Their Contrast

In *Giles Goat-Boy,* Barth's comic vision is often developed by ironic allusions to traditional views of education such as those in Ralph Waldo Emerson's "The American Scholar," the Phi Beta Kappa address at Harvard in 1837. Barth does not allude to "The American Scholar" directly. Nevertheless, Emerson's work is a repository for many of the traditional notions of the American ideal of teacher and scholar.

In the oration, Emerson characterizes the scholar as "Man Thinking" and actively reasoning as he moves toward basic truths. He is an observer of nature, a reader of books of the past, as well as a creator of new books. He also is a man of action, who serves society as teacher and leader: "Him Nature solicits . . . Him the past instructs. Him the future invites."[83]

As an observer of nature, the scholar classifies phenomena, states that these "are not chaotic, and are not foreign," and reduces "all strange constitutions . . . to their class and their law,"a law that can be apprehended "by insight."[84] The scholar writes books that promote the progressive thinking of the others, who will brood on the material and actively create knowledge. The scholar also has duties in the world. He should not be a recluse, "a valetudinarian." "He is the world's eye" and "the world's heart."[85] He leads men toward the truth, away from the ephemeral dictates of society.

This conception of the scholar-teacher is of utmost importance to Emerson, evident in the Harvard oration and also in an "Address on Education," presented two months earlier in Providence, Rhode Island.[86] In the earlier speech, Emerson emphasizes the need to reform education so that instead of creating "accountants, attornies [*sic*], engineers," scholars will help to "form heroes and saints." The teachers and leaders of colleges, churches, and schools will foster the best in man. Teachers have to exert their vision to prevent a people from perishing.[87]

Emerson's celebration of the instructors and leaders in colleges is reminiscent of Cotton Mather's praise of the early Puritan divines who founded our country. In *Magnalia Christi Americana,* Mather devotes an entire book to the history of Harvard College and the exemplary Puritan divines who taught there. *Magnalia,* as a whole, educates the reader by presenting the lives of great Puritan teachers, such as John Winthrop, John Cotton, and Thomas Hooker. Their errand was to lead the people to God through sacred texts, through the Word. Before the arrival of these men, America was a "hell of darkness," but after their leadership was felt, it became "a place full of light and glory" that provided a model for all to follow.[88] Mather continually shows the esteem in which he holds the university and educational leaders.

It is such ideals of American education that satirist Barth deflates. The narrator signals the disparity between present practices at spring registration at New Tammany College and traditional ones when he explains: "Few who participated in these festivities were aware of their original significance, any more than they recognized *Carnival* as coming from the Remusian 'farewell to flesh' that preceded any period of fasting" (298). He indicates that these revelers on West Campus—at the outset of their university career—grasp eagerly the promises of easy graduation and will gladly accept a diploma with no work expected. They lack the educational and moral standards of early scholars.

The actions of the university's students and teachers contrast with the three major roles that Emerson emphasizes for the scholar: an observer of nature; a reader and creator of books; and a thinker who has duties in the world. At New Tammany College, professors pursue abstract theories and talk nonsense. They are estranged from nature and from their fellowmen. For example, the scientist Eblis Eierkopf is preoccupied with measuring the exact points of tick and tock in a complicated clock project (481–82). He is so completely engrossed with his complex optical equipment—telescopes, binoculars, and his own gigantic eyeglass lenses—that he is blind to everyday concerns.[89] He distorts reality by "concentrating on portions of the Whole . . . producing scientific 'truths' that . . . [merely reflect] the mind which formulates them."[90] Dr. Kennard Sear, another academician, is absorbed wholly in using fluoroscopes, one-way mirrors, and optical prisms to investigate sexual activity.[91]

Barth uses scatological imagery, reminiscent of Rabelais, to deflate further the theorizing that exists in the university. He refers to Max Spielman's theory that "the 'sphincter's riddle' and the mystery of the University . . . [are] the same" (43). One could observe that the reduction of Oedipus's heroic solving of the Sphinx's riddle to the ribald and comic sphincter's riddle—to be examined with a proctoscope—typifies how far educational pursuits have fallen.[92] The statement also parodies the role of saints' lives as a model for instruction. Instead of Foxe's *Book of Martyrs,* so popular in seventeenth-century England and in colonial America, or Cotton Mather's *Magnalia,* there is Barth's *Giles Goat-Boy* with its ironic models: George/Giles, who is a rather confused Grand Tutor, and Max Spielman, who has left the university for the goat farm. In Barth's academic travesty, the heroes are "saints" of the absurd. They do not show the exemplary lives described by Foxe and Mather.

George looks to the university—New Tammany College[93]—as a place that will help him progress toward the Truth, in the Emersonian sense. The futile confrontation between George's serious desire to gain knowledge during his stay at college and the frivolous attitude of the student body creates a comic-ironic effect. Barth uses Emersonian values and ideas in *Goat-Boy,* just as he uses Plato's in *Sot-Weed,* to develop his sharp satire. However, as Gresham points out, Barth's method "differs from conventional satire in its norm, which is the Real rather than the Ideal."[94] He, like other twentieth-century comic epic novelists, refuses to advocate any transcendent or ideal organizing system in an absurd world. All systems, particularly that of the university, are subject to his ironic treatment.

Even though Barth satirizes academia, he gains his primary readership from university faculty and students. He himself puzzles over this: "Do you know what I think is interesting. . . . It's the spectacle of these enormous universities we have now, all over the place, teaching courses in *us*. . . . Now that means that a born loser like *The Sot-Weed Factor* might even be gotten away with, because 2,000 kids in northeast Nebraska or somewhere have to read it in a Modern Novel course. Alarming . . . God knows what we're up to."[95]

CHAPTER FIVE

The Tall Tale, the Absurd, and Black Humor in Thomas Pynchon's V. and *Gravity's Rainbow*

Thomas Pynchon's V. (1963), in a darker and more caustic vein than the "cheerful nihilism" of *The Sot-Weed Factor* and *Giles Goat-Boy*, satirizes man's quest for meaning in an absurd world. In V. characters attempt to pursue basic truths, but they never succeed. This frustrated yearning helps to set up an absurd perspective, absurd by Camus's definition, which focuses on a "divorce between the mind that desires and the world that disappoints, [the] nostalgia for unity, this fragmented universe and the contradiction that binds them together."[1]

Like Barth and other black humorists, Pynchon uses specific methods to disorient the reader who is searching for meaning in an absurd world: he shifts quickly between horror and farce; he develops episodes that appear fantastic—like those in a tall tale—but then brings the problem into a more likely modern perspective; he involves the reader emotionally in the tension of a story and then points out the work's artifice—as when the narrator in *Gravity's Rainbow* tells the reader who expects clarification of relationships: "You will want cause and effect. All right" (663); he emphasizes the disparity between customary religious values as expressed in early American Puritan works—like Cotton Mather's *Magnalia Christi Americana*—and their ironic presentation in the comic epic novel.[2]

Most of the scenes in *V.* have a humorous quality even though the novel has a very serious undercurrent. Humorous episodes exhibit such devices as slapstick, incongruity, verbal play, and puns. Slapstick humor usually involves the antics of Benny Profane, the schlemihl figure[3] whose simplicity is somewhat reminiscent of Singer's "Gimpel the fool," but who does not have Gimpel's genuine faith. Profane is a figure who resides "between the comedy of errors and a comedy of terrors,"[4] one who seeks fun, is usually without money, and threatens no one because he is so low on the "scale of competition."[5]

Slapstick humor is evident in the party episodes in which Mafia Winsome gets sexually involved with one man after another in her search for a man "fashioned for Heroic Love" (268), while her husband, finally angered by it all, attempts to commit suicide. The boisterous action increases as Winsome attempts jumping out the window, only to be grabbed by Pig Bodine, who then chases him down the fire escapes: "After a while they got dizzy and started to giggle. The audience cheered them on. So little happens in New York" (339).

To obtain a dramatic effect, Pynchon adapts to his own purposes the American tall tale with its extravagant description, adventurous yarns, and slapstick humor. Examples of such frontier tales are the newspaper accounts of gold growing "to the roots of the grass" in California, where the "grass is pulled up and the gold shaken off, as gardeners pull up the vines to shake off young potatoes";[6] recollections associated with Davy Crockett, who shoots a flock of geese flying in a line with one shot and then falls into the river, climbing out with his pockets full of fish;[7] stories of Mike Fink, who with quick wit and sharpshooting overcomes Indians, mountain men, and a steamboat captain; and exaggerated revelations about Daniel Boone, great Indian fighter and explorer of the wilderness.

The tales in *V.* differ from the comic frontier stories of heroes whose accomplishments are bigger than life. In the tall tales in *V.*, the protagonists are inept instead of successful, fearful and somewhat paranoid rather than bragging and confident. They are schlemihls instead of capable men with grand accomplishments.[8] The tales in *V.*, like those of the frontier, use exaggeration and fantasy, but in the novel these aspects are combined with the grotesque, and farce is combined with horror. Pynchon tells many tall tales that are presented as real (as in traditional tall tales). But in addition, he presents much of the horror of societal decline as a tall tale that cannot possibly be real even if it did happen. The German General Lothar von Trotha could not have ordered the extermination of thousands of natives in South-West Africa; the Holocaust could not have killed the six million; mankind cannot be destroying itself with machinelike precision.

While in traditional American tall tales real and surreal merge in the splendid exploits of the hero, in *V.* the swift intermingling of the real and surreal and of the farcical and the horrible troubles and disorients the reader. The mixing of reality levels and the shifts of mood create a turbulence similar to that found in the novels of Kafka and in the grotesque art of Bosch and Bruegel.[9] In Pynchon, a black humor tone emerges when distress and laughter, horror and farce collide.[10]

Black humor is evident in the pseudo-realistic description of Benny Profane as he attempts to shower in a Manhattan flophouse. His efforts are met with "handles [that] wouldn't turn. When he finally found a shower that worked, the water came out hot and cold in random patterns. He danced around, yowling and shivering, slipped on a bar of soap and nearly broke his neck. Drying off, he ripped a frayed towel in half, rendering it useless. He put on his skivvy shirt backwards, took ten minutes getting his fly zipped and another fifteen repairing a shoelace which had broken as he was tying it. [. . .][11] being a schlemihl, he'd known for years: inanimate objects and he could not live in peace" (*V.* 27–28).[12]

Benny is a buffoon, an inept figure who is the object of our mirth because he slips on soap and is too clumsy to cope with a simple act like dressing. At the same time that we laugh at him, however, we recognize a serious problem in the highly technological age of the twentieth century: when our modern mechanical devices fail, we are at a profound loss to cope with even simple things.

Another tall-tale-like episode is revealed through Benny's imaginary conversations with the robots SHROUD (synthetic human, radiation output determined) and SHOCK (synthetic human object, casualty kinematics), whom he meets during his job as a night watchman for Anthroresearch Associates:

Me and SHOCK are what you and everybody will be someday. (The skull seemed to be grinning at Profane.) [. . .]
"You don't even have a soul. How can you talk."

Since *when did you ever have one?* What are you doing,
getting religion? All I am is a dry run. [. . .]
After a while [Profane] got up and went over to SHROUD.
"What do you mean, we'll be like you and SHOCK someday? You
mean dead?"
Am I dead? If I am then that's what I mean.
"If you aren't then what are you?"
Nearly what you are. None of you have very far to go.
"I don't understand." [. . .]
To hell with it. Profane went back to the guardroom and busied
himself making coffee. (*V.* 266–67; italics added)

Despite the narrator's cautionary description of the "imaginary conversation" (274), the scientific details seem realistic and dupe the
reader, as they do in tall tales such as those of the nineteenth-century
George Horatio Derby, who described many plausible but bizarre scientific inventions. One such "scientific" invention was a tooth-pulling
machine that was so effective it inadvertently disfigured an old woman
when it "drew the old lady's skeleton completely and entirely from her
body, leaving her a mass of quivering jelly in her chair! . . . She had
suffered terribly with the rheumatism, but after this occurrence never
had a pain in her bones."[13]

At first we are somewhat tricked by Pynchon's yarn about the
robot and Benny, considering all the stories we have heard about artificial intelligence, but then we realize that one cannot have such a
conversation with a robot, which would have no more to say than what
is put into it. The letdown of expectation is funny. Benny's talk with the
robot also is humorous because it is a manifestation of Bergson's point
that "something mechanical encrusted on the living" evokes laughter.[14]
However, here too, there is a difference. Underlying Bergsonian humor
is the precept that human beings indeed are not mechanical, that they
are open, expansive, elastic. From Bergson's traditional vantage point,
one laughs at the metamorphosis from the natural to the mechanical. In
V., however, as one laughs at the interchange between Benny and the
robot, one realizes that Benny suspects he does not have a soul and feels
more comfortable talking to a robot than to a human being, and
indeed wishes to be a thing, not a person. He tries to do his best to
denude himself of humane traits, to be a thing because things "don't
change" (359).

The realistic and depressing incongruities in *V.* create the brittle laughter characteristic of black humor. The humor arises from a

shifting in distance between the reader and the text, ranging from the superior position of the reader who chuckles at the ineptitude of Benny (who thinks that he speaks with a robot) to the awareness that the reader who, despite apparent distance, is part of a world where man's social interactions often lose their humane qualities and are reduced to the mechanical.

To emphasize mankind's loss of humane concerns, the narrator lists the killings of natives by the Germans in South-West Africa in 1904 and connects it to the annihilation in the Holocaust during World War II: "The German forces were ordered to exterminate systematically every Herero man, woman and child. [. . .] Out of the estimated 80,000 Hereros living in the territory in 1904 [there was a] decrease of 64,870. Similarly the Hottentots were reduced in the same period by about 10,000, the Berg-Damaras by 17,000. . . . [von Trotha] is reckoned to have done away with about 60,000 people. This is only 1 percent of six million, but still pretty good" (227).[15]

The narrator, with his cynical closing comment, is letting the reader know that he is responding directly to the reader's calculations. This unexpected intrusion is somewhat disorienting and, in its own way, is on the leading edge of black humor: the gallows humor that ends with a laugh what would otherwise become a tirade or a feeling of depression or angst. Such commentary adds a touch of demonic humor to the twentieth-century world, an age in which the war machine relentlessly destroys.

The reader's perspective ranges from an unimpassioned view of the farcical "imaginary" dialogues between Benny and the robot to a painful response to the grotesque mingling of fantasy and horror, where laughter seems to be, in Wolfgang Kayser's terms, "an involuntary response to situations which cannot be handled in any other way." It is a response like that of E.T.A. Hoffman's characters, who are "shaken with laughter when they do not feel at all in the mood for laughing." Kayser points out that a grotesque "play with the absurd . . . may begin in a gay and carefree manner" but may end in one's being afraid of "the demonic aspects of the world."[16] Pynchon, at his lightest, is never totally "gay and carefree." Even his farcical scenes have a harsh element in them.

V.'s movement from farce to the grotesque is evident in the myths and legends at the novel's center, which inform the basic structure of the work. In Mather's *Magnalia*, connections between America and the Garden of Eden and between the exploits of colonial heroes and biblical ones help to convey the sense of America's Christian mission. The legends of the fragmented world of *V.* ironically invert such promise, stressing instead such themes as man's increasing vulnerability as he becomes more dependent on inanimate support systems. Reinforcing this point is the folk tale of a boy born with a golden screw where his navel should be. Desperate to remove it, he succeeds after twenty years. With joy, he "leaps up out of bed, and his ass falls off" (30). The boy's accomplishment, instead of leading to the rectification of his anatomy, leads to its disintegration. This farcical example, which employs Bergson's mechanical theory of laughter, emphasizes an underlying theme in the novel: the concept of a mechanically controlled body. Another example is a recurrent dream that the character Mélanie has, in which her father searches for and finds a small key in her back: " 'I got you in time,' he breathed. 'You would have stopped, had I not' " (377). The tall tales portray the concepts of a culture in which the energy of the mechanical, like that of the V-2 rocket, is exceedingly difficult to control. Pynchon deals with this by using bizarre humor.[17]

V. also has several "sewer legends" that comically point to the decline of American culture and gain additional humor from their resemblance to the American tall tale. One legend involves the development not of God's chosen people in a new Garden, but of alligators abandoned in the Manhattan sewers. Supposedly, children bought these young creatures as pets for fifty cents at Macy's and flushed them down the toilets when they tired of them. The alligators grew and reproduced under the streets and later are hunted by members of a sewer patrol (33). Another sewer legend involves Father Fairing and his parish of rats located in sewers near the East River in Manhattan (105). According to the tale, Father Fairing, in the 1930s, decided that Manhattan, with its "starved corpses," its breadlines and missions, would soon belong to the rats. With the optimism of a founding father, he leaves the city's streets for its sewers, hoping to convert the new rodent colonists. The legend recounts how Father Fairing blesses the waters flowing through sewers in that section of Manhattan where he planned to establish a "New City" (105–7).

Such tall tales blatantly parody the actions of the founding fathers who preached to eager congregants in a "Virgin Land." The several tales show how life in the Garden envisioned by America's first settlers has declined. In the twentieth-century world, where spiritual concerns are of low priority, attempts at salvation are delegated to subterranean areas and are reserved for rodents. The last entries in Fairing's journal indicate that he was aware that "his pale and sinuous parishioners might turn out no better than the animals whose estate they were succeeding to" (107).

For approximately twenty years, the sewer story was transmitted more or less underground. Its status was mythic; no one ever questioned its validity. The narrator explains, as though he were discussing legends of old, "It is this way with sewer stories. They just are. Truth or falsity don't apply" (108).

Puritan Themes

V. shows the comic deflation of the Puritan dream in twentieth-century society. In this novel, published ten years before *Gravity's Rainbow*, Pynchon seems more cautious about his Puritan past than in his later novel, where the terms "elect" and "preterite" clearly refer to the haves and the have-nots and where there are specific references to the author's ancestor William Pynchon, founder of the Springfield Colony.[18] In *V.* Pynchon makes connections to a Puritan past without drawing obvious biographical parallels. However, the novel does make satiric references to Puritanism, and these, like the allusions in *Gravity's Rainbow*, indicate a framework of ironic return to America's past.

On the lighter side, such deflation is evident in the name for a gathering place for the Whole Sick Crew—"Matilda Winthrop's" bar (326)—a name that creates the blatant black humor joke on how far fallen from the Garden of John Winthrop is the Street of the twentieth century. Decline is also evident in the name of one of the two protagonists—Benny Profane, indicating a desecration of the sacred; or possibly one who is " bene," that is, "thoroughly" or "properly" vulgar or profane—and in the description of Brenda Wigglesworth (a comic contrast to the devout Puritan poet Michael Wigglesworth).[19] Brenda will eventually mend her ways and become "the *inviolable Puritan* she'd show up as come marriage and the Good Life" (426; italics added). On the darker side is the narrator's rumination over how a youthful woman, Victoria Wrenn, becomes divested of all moral perspective, that is, of the "many controls over herself" that "we have come to call *Puritan*" (386; italics added).

The Sacred and the Profane

In the world of *V.*, twentieth-century American activities present an ironic counterpart to the subject of Cotton Mather's Puritan epic:

the wonderful workings of Christ in America. *V.* describes events that indicate a final fall into entropic deterioration instead of a progression toward the millennium. The novel's setting, the Street, presents a comically blatant contrast to the Garden of early America.

In *V.*, the metaphor of the Street defines the experiences of the antiheroes in relation to those of America's founding heroes and their new Eden. Characters traveling on the street, in the subways below, and also in the subterranean sewers have no direction or goal. They present an ironic counterpart to those founders who believed America to be a "city on a hill," a place to set an example of morality and religion for all.[20]

Instead of traveling in a land of natural fruitfulness, characters spend much time in the underground regions of subways. In the nether darkness, they travel back and forth on the Forty-second Street shuttle from Grand Central to Times Square (27). "There are nine million yo-yos in this town," says Slab, who "spent a weekend on the West Side express" (282). In this subterranean setting there seems to be an interchange between the inanimate and the human. The subway trains gain animation in contrast to the passengers, who lose theirs. The narrator relates: "The subway pulled in to Times Square, disgorged passengers, took more on, shut up its doors and shrieked away down the tunnel" (29), as though the riders—the city's poor—have become the food for the subway. The sleeping bums, old women on relief, vagrants, beggars, the "schlemihls of the city"[21] are ironic degenerations of pioneers in America's Garden. These inhabitants, like Camus's absurd man, seem "deprived of the memory of a lost home or the hope of a promised land."[22]

The artistic concerns of such modern travelers are satirized to convey further a reduction from the meaningful to the pathetically ridiculous. Slab shows off his paintings of cheese Danishes done in "every conceivable style, light and setting." He explains: "Monet spent his declining years at his home in Giverny, painting the water lilies. [. . .] These are my declining years. I like cheese Danishes, they have kept me alive" (262–63). The comic incongruity between Slab and Monet, as well as Slab's inability to appreciate the ironic contrast between the beauty of the water lilies and his mundane subject, provides a comic means of depicting the general deflation of the spiritual in art and also in religion.

The disparity between the myth of the new Eden, where mankind can prepare for salvation, and the legends and subterranean mysticism in *V.* creates dark humor. As the reader contemplates decay and mortality, there is a tone that "won't let the pain blot out the humor . . . [or] the humor blot out the pain."[23] This carefully balanced presentation makes tolerable the decline from the spiritual to the profane and from the Garden to the Street where the Whole Sick Crew wanders.

Benny Profane and Stencil as Heroes of the Absurd

In direct contrast to great Puritan heroes who had a sense of destiny is Benny Profane, the schlemihl, who sleeps a lot and shuns anything that would give him direction, such as a steady job or a girl friend. When Fina wants him to make love to her, he thinks, "Why did she have to behave like he was a human being. [. . .] What did Fina have to go pushing it for?" (123). When Rachel indicates that she cares for him, he tries to avoid responsibility for her feelings by saying: "All a schlemihl can do is take" (346).[24] Benny sees himself as an object and his "own disassembly plausible as that of any machine" (30). It is ironic that he cannot even conceptualize what it would mean to be heroic: "What was a hero? Randolph Scott, who could handle a six-gun" (268). Benny sees himself as a descendant not of heroes but of "schlemihls" (208).

Benny's given name calls to mind, in street language, the "upper" Benzedrine, and his surname denotes the downward progression toward the profane, in contrast to the sacred. His actions gain much of their humor from the fact that they expose the gulf between the sacred and the profane and are cast in a mock-religious form. Extending the comic irony is the fact that a schlemihl-like figure is set within the context of Christian mysticism as he travels in the area of Father Fairing's parish.[25]

Benny's experiences gain much of their humor from the fact that they contrast with the longing for unity and meaning, evoked in the reader by the details that typically accompany religious experiences. These proliferate in circumstances involving Benny, only to be deflated by what is funny and bawdy. Such elements include strange radiances of light, unusual landscapes, and the uncanny. For example, while pursuing an alligator in the sewers, Benny undergoes a mock version of a spiritual "awakening." He sees a dim light ahead of him in the waters of Father Fairing's parish. The narrator describes the scene: "a wide space like the nave of a church, an arched roof overhead, a phosphorescent light coming off walls whose exact arrangement was indistinct"

(110). On the walls, there are chalk-written words, including Latin quotations from the Gospels, which Father Fairing had written. "Wha," Benny says aloud, as he reacts to the frightening radiance. The alligator faces him and Profane waits for something to happen: "Something otherworldly, of course. [. . .] Surely the alligator would receive the gift of tongues" (110).

There is comic incongruity in this scene. On the one hand, there are spiritual suggestions of Benny's seeing a radiant, dim light in the darkness, indicative of an occurrence that is a "trigger" for a religious experience, one that "seems positively to communicate a message."[26] On the other hand, all is deflated by the banal language and gross details that follow. Benny exclaims: "Ah, schlemihl. [. . .] Accident prone, schlimazzel."[27] The deflation of the spiritual is completed with a final lazy gush of reptile blood and the failure of a flashlight. In Pynchon's words, "blood began to seep out amoebalike to form shifting patterns with the weak glow of the water. Abruptly, the *flashlight* went out" (110–11; italics added).

The last glimpse we have of Benny is in Malta, where he and Brenda Wigglesworth, whose "heroic" attribute is the possession of seventy-two pairs of Bermuda shorts, race into the dark streets of Valletta. This twentieth-century possible descendant of the Puritan poet Michael Wigglesworth laments the fact that her many experiences have taught her nothing. When she asks Benny what he has learned from his experiences, Benny responds: "I'd say I haven't learned a goddamn thing." They are quiet. Then, "hand in hand," they mindlessly run down the streets, "momentum alone carrying them toward the edge of Malta, and the Mediterranean beyond" (428).[28]

Just as absurd as Benny is Herbert Stencil, whose desire for order and connection provides the complementary antithesis to Benny's free-spirited attitude. Stencil's experiences are described in a way that develops a negative mirror image of the spiritual model. Stencil, at the beginning of his "heroic" quest, leafs through his father's Florentine journal "when the sentences on V. suddenly acquired a light of their own" (44). Stencil appears to undergo an epiphany like that had by Christian heroes. The epiphany is accompanied by the trappings of a spiritual "awakening" involving an enigmatic light, a "shining vision of the transcendent spiritual world," and an uncanny feeling of apprehending "another order of reality."[29] This epiphany, however, is a negation of any kind of spiritual revelation. The narrator sardonically explains: "Work, the chase—for it was V. he hunted—far from being a means to glorify God and one's own godliness (*as the Puritans believe*) was for Stencil grim, joyless; a conscious acceptance of the unpleasant for no other reason than that V. was there to track down" (44; italics added).

While the Puritans looked to examples from the Bible for patterns on which to model their lives, Stencil humorously gets his patterns from things he reads in the Parisian or Florentine journals, written by his secret agent father. For Stencil, opportunities for revelation reside in moments of vision, which can be said to resemble "a Puritan reflex of seeking other orders behind the visible" (*Gravity's Rainbow* 188). Seeking transcendent signs, Stencil focuses on these peculiar spiritual notions as a model for action but unintentionally gets involved in gross details of this world.[30] When he reads that his father, Sidney, had an interview with someone who worked in the main sewer lines in France and that the person recalled having seen a woman "who might have been V.," Herbert optimistically finds reason enough to investigate the activities of the Alligator Patrol in Manhattan. Herbert thinks: "Having been lucky with sewers once, [. . .there was] nothing wrong with trying again" (120). When someone in the Alligator Patrol misses his target and, instead, hits Stencil in the left buttock, his paranoid response appears comic: "How did they get on to you?" (119).

The paranoia continues as he tells this story to Eigenvalue, in the dentist/psychiatrist consultation chair. His friend observes: "In a world such as you inhabit, Mr. Stencil, any cluster of phenomena can be a conspiracy" (140). In talks with the dentist and with the Whole Sick Crew, Stencil always tries to find out how details fit into the "grand Gothic pile of inferences he was hard at work creating," the "leads" that would bring him closer to his goal (209).

For Stencil, the quest for V. takes on spiritual associations that invest all possible connections with pregnant significance. The reader laughs at the incongruity between Stencil's mundane experiences in Manhattan and Malta and the mystic significance he attaches to them because of their possible connection to V. Stencil's exaggerated reaction to details burlesques the experiences of a religious hero. His devotion to an "ultimate Plot Which Has No Name" (210) parodies the traditional quest. His search is a "travesty" of the quest of the traditional Christian hero "for some ultimate truth or goal—or grail."[31]

The last one hears about Herbert Stencil shows how reluctant he is to give up his search. In Malta, even though Fausto Maijstral is certain of V.'s demise, Stencil picks up a remote clue and leaves the country to track down the glass eye worn by the hypnotist, Mme. Viola: "It will do for the frayed end of another clue" (425), he tells Fausto, as he leaves for Stockholm. This is 1956; V., if alive, would be seventy-six!

The Whole Sick Crew

Deflation of the spiritual to the profane is a major means of developing ironic humor throughout *V.* This method emphasizes the absurd position of the novel's characters: for example, Esther expects Dr. Shoenmaker to do a nose job that will transform her life into one filled with love and happiness, but instead becomes a passive victim to his butchery and lust (91–98); Fina, the romantic Puerto Rican girl, tries to care for members of a New York street gang, only to become the object of their gang rape (137); McClintic Sphere desires to "keep cool but care" (343), in spite of the fact that he lives in Harlem, with its gang fights, and in America, with its constant threat of nuclear war; Rachel Owlglass yearns to find a soul mate but selects Benny Profane, who does not believe he has a soul (346).

Beyond the borders of the United States, there is a continuation of the same vain pursuits. Kurt Mondaugen, in South-West Africa (in 1922), is assigned by the German military to record and analyze atmospheric radio disturbances (213), which take on for him implications of another world. However, Lieutenant Weissmann (who returns, more fully developed, in *Gravity's Rainbow,* as does Mondaugen) breaks the code and reveals its real message: "Kurt Mondaugen. . . . The world is all that the case is" (258–59).[32]

Entropic Decline

Instead of the Puritan hope for the millennium, *V.* stresses the absurdist theme of entropic decline. Instead of the world growing in abundance and fertility, the opposite is emphasized. To get this idea across, Pynchon uses satiric pronouncements that are worded similarly to those of Henry Adams in *Education* (1907) and *Degradation of the Democratic Dogma* (1919).

Henry Adams, in his cynical treatise *The Degradation of the Democratic Dogma,* writes of the shrinking of the sun and the gradual cooling of the earth and gives details of decline described in French and German newspapers:[33]

social decrepitude;—falling off of the birthrate;—decline of rural population; . . .—multiplication of suicides;—increase of insanity or idiocy,—of cancer . . . "habits" of alcoholism and drugs . . . and so on, without end.[34]

Compare a similar list from Pynchon:

> Twenty days before the Dog Star moved into conjunction with the sun, the dog days began. [. . .] Fifteen were killed in a train wreck near Oaxaca, Mexico, on 1 July. The next day fifteen people died when an apartment house collapsed in Madrid. [. . .] Ice avalanches on Mont Blanc swept fifteen mountain climbers into the kingdom of death in the week 12 to 18 August. (*V.* 270)

The narrator caustically amasses examples of disasters that occur within days of one another: an apartment house collapses; a bus falls into a river and its passengers drown; lives are lost in tropical storms, earthquakes, tidal waves, plane crashes. The calamities are depicted by extravagant details reminiscent of the American tall tale. But these stories, instead of emphasizing a world burgeoning with crops, over-sized animals, and courageous hunters such as Davy Crockett and Mike Fink, accentuate examples of entropic decline. These tales, instead of being promotional literature for new territory, underscore the decline of nature and of man's powers as well.

This material reflects the author's fascination with the Second Law of Thermodynamics. The scientific law, describing entropy, is used metaphorically to point to the decay in the physical, social, and spiritual aspects of our lives.[35]

With grim humor the narrator gives as an example of entropy the tale of Evan Godolphin, Hugh's son, whose face is deformed in a plane accident during World War I. Like the frontier tale, this story convinces by revealing a somewhat plausible story in a realistic setting. The narrator relates that a British air force surgeon operates on Evan, using inert material instead of organic cartilage to rebuild his face. He makes "a nose bridge of ivory, a cheek-bone of silver and a paraffin and celluloid chin" (87). Within six months, the body rejects the foreign matter and his face becomes a misshapen blob: "The upper part of the nose seemed to have slid down, giving an exaggerated saddle-and-hump; the chin cut off at midpoint to slope concave back up the other side, pulling part of the lip up in a scarred half-smile" (447).

Momentarily, the reader is taken in by the tale. Its picture of bad medicine fits in with stereotypes of inadequacies in the military. Then, however, we realize that we have been tricked into believing a tall tale. No physician would build up a face with the metals ivory and silver; and the use of their opposites—paraffin and celluloid—completes the bizarre joke. Godolphin's deterioration reinforces the theme of entropy mentioned by an old seaman, Mehemet: "I am old, the world is old. [. . .] The only change is toward death. [. . .] Early and late we are in decay" (432–33).

The Dream of Annihilation

Another entropic tale of black humor that contrasts with the Puritan hope for the millennium is that of Hugh Godolphin (Evan's father), who unsuccessfully quests for an Edenic land, Vheissu. In his earlier years, Godolphin chances upon the mysterious Vheissu during an exploring expedition and is overwhelmed by its prelapsarian beauty, its many colors and its spider monkeys, which are "iridescent" and "change color in the sunlight" (155). Godolphin feels compelled to search again and again for the mysterious land and its message. Godolphin's quest ends in horror, at a lonely place: "Staring up at me through the ice, perfectly preserved, its fur still rainbow-colored, was the corpse of one of their spider monkeys [. . .] a mockery of life, planted where everything but Hugh Godolphin was inanimate." "If Eden was the creation of God," ponders Godolphin, "God only knows what evil created Vheissu" (189–90). Here, again, Pynchon develops an extravagant tale, one that stresses the loss of an Edenic wilderness and the estrangement of man from nature.

The tall tales about Davy Crockett, Mike Fink, and Jim Doggett ignore any possible frustration at the loss of nature's wild life by emphasizing humorous details such as those involving Jim Doggett in "The Big Bear of Arkansas." When the bear surprises Doggett, the hero is in the woods defecating: "Yes, the old varmint was within a hundred yards of me, and the way he walked *over that fence*—stranger, he loomed up like a *black mist*, he seemed so large, and he walked right towards me. I raised myself, took deliberate aim, and fired." Doggett, carried away by the fantastic story he is telling, expands on the bear's great strength and size: he "*walked through the fence* like a falling tree would through a cobweb."[36] This climactic scene exhibits the salient aspects of the tall tale: details exaggerating the size and power of the bear; use of the fantastic; and also the mixing of the earthy and the fantastic, an "incongruous coalescence,"[37] such that initially the grand hero is a "man, caught with his pants down."[38]

Pynchon adapts many devices of the tall tale—exaggeration, the fantastic, scatological details, and incongruities. But he differs from early American writers in his use of a bitter tone and a depressing outcome. Because of the seriousness of the subject matter in *V.*, the laughter elicited is often a helpless response rather than the carefree humor of the frontier tale.

The destruction of Vheissu acts as a symbol for entropic decline, what Pynchon calls the Twentieth-Century Nightmare: the "dream of annihilation" (190).[39] The incongruity between this "dream" and the hopes of early American settlers is upsetting, but Pynchon uses humor as a vehicle for retaining the reader's interest. He then compels the reader to peer at the demonic aspects of contemporary society, creating comedy alongside this terror as a helpless response. As Morris Dickstein observes, in such situations "things are so bad you might as well laugh."[40]

Godolphin's appreciation of the Dream of Annihilation foreshadows its more horrifying aspects, as expressed by Foppl. At this juncture, incongruities shock without creating laughter, and a grotesque quality is developed. Foppl, a former German trooper, dreams of reliving the joys he experienced when massacring the South-West African natives in 1904. He wishes to return to General Lothar von Trotha's leadership, under which the uprising of the natives (in 1904) was quelled by the "*Vernichtungs Befehl*" (227), the order to annihilate. "I loved the man," Foppl tells Mondaugen. "He taught us not to fear." With caustic use of incongruity, Pynchon has Foppl use uplifting language to express a downright monstrous act: "the sudden release; the comfort, the luxury; when you knew you could safely forget all the rote-lessons you'd had to learn about the value and dignity of human life" (234). Compounding the grotesque depiction of modern man as destroyer is a spiritual description of a trooper's epiphany as he kills a native: "Things seemed all at once to fall into a pattern: a great cosmic fluttering in the blank, bright sky." For the trooper, the act "meant something different." It "had only to do with the destroyer and the destroyed, and the act which united them." The trooper experiences "an odd sort of peace" (245), a sense of transcendence in the act of annihilation.[41] This ironic mystical experience obviously lacks the playful fulfillment experienced after reading a traditional tall tale. So, too, it lacks the comic irony exhibited in the tales of Benny's strange experiences with the alligators. Instead its grotesque details compel us to appreciate that what seems to be a tall tale actually is both real and terrifying.

V. and Twentieth-Century Society

Generally, *V.* uses tales to mix terror with imaginative satire. This is particularly true as we react to the character V., for whom the epic novel is named. On one level, the portrayal of this character shows an individual's loss of humanity. She is obsessed with "bodily incorporating little bits of inert matter" (459), as if that would draw her into the inanimate and divest her of all spiritual nature. She has a glass eye with the iris in the shape of a clock, false teeth, a wig, a star sapphire in her navel, and has exchanged her own feet for artificial ones (321–22). On another level, V. is Pynchon's vehicle for satirizing the dehumanization of the race of mankind. "Be like—the rock" (319), she advises, perhaps because it does not feel and it will last, though flesh will not. Her desire to incorporate inert material into her person is V.'s attempt to ward off her own dissolution. As a result, she becomes corporally lifeless and mechanical.[42]

V.'s preoccupation with dehumanization and with the inanimate is evident when she falls in love with fifteen-year-old Mélanie, who becomes a fetish for her.[43] In actions that mock the sacred, she, at the biblical age of thirty-three, takes on the inanimate rather than the spiritual, the "Kingdom of Death" (386) rather than eternal life, the destruction of mankind rather than its salvation. Her use of a human being as merely an object of pleasure, like a shoe or locket, is described in comic-grotesque terms: "V. [. . .] watching Mélanie on the bed; Mélanie watching herself in the mirror; the mirror-image perhaps contemplating V. from time to time" (385).[44]

Stencil observes that the horrifying change in V. is part of a phenomenon "for which the young century [in 1913] had *as yet* no name" (386; italics added). His comment shows how the novel ironically reverses Puritan heroism, which revealed the workings of Christ in this world. Instead the novel describes man's decay, the establishment of a wasteland rather than a new Eden. Pynchon uses "typological" associations to suggest a twentieth-century nightmare, the entropic experience of annihilation.[45]

Humor and the Absurd

The reader may wonder why it is not depressing to read *V.*, with its strong social criticism. Acting as a means of balancing the negative are the actions of frolicking characters such as Benny and the Whole Sick Crew. Benny has a certain loose, resilient vitality that one may yearn for. He views his life as meaningless; he dares not attempt responsibility, and he keeps asserting that he has learned nothing. His spontaneous, earthy responses arouse interest. In a major sense, Benny exemplifies freedom from restraints, something a Puritan background causes us to fear.

V. conveys this needed humor in sections that describe the behavior of the Whole Sick Crew—as they tell jokes, drink, and make merry—or in the antics of the sailors, when they go to bars such as the Sailor's Grave, where absurdist references are made to Dante's Beatrice as the model for the barmaids, and where irreverent humor is developed by means of linking the cherished Beatrice to the crude "Suck Hour" at the bar (4). Such scenes deflect from the novel's painful allusions to events like the massacres in South-West Africa in 1904 and in 1922, and to the novel's many references to entropy. Such scenes act as a "Counterforce," similar to that which is developed more fully in *Gravity's Rainbow*.

The Allusive Mode, the Tall Tale, and Black Humor in *Gravity's Rainbow*

Gravity's Rainbow (1973) begins with a rocket screaming across the sky during the last months of World War II and ends with a rocket about to destroy the observers in the theater. The narrator's last words, "Now everybody" (760), presents an ironic connection between those in a theater uneasy about waiting for the show to begin and all the readers who are waiting for the final annihilation. The scene exemplifies the black humor tone that is evident throughout the novel, a tone that mixes the comic and the horrific, causing people to laugh at the wit even while awaiting catastrophe.

As in *V.*, Pynchon continually juxtaposes scenes of disaster with blatantly humorous episodes that develop like a tall tale. In the midst of war torn London, Captain Geoffrey ("Pirate") Prentice is introduced.

Pirate has built a glass hothouse on a roof in order to grow bananas because of the shortage during wartime. Pirate, the narrator relates, "has become famous for his Banana Breakfasts. Messmates throng here from all over England, even some who are allergic or outright hostile to bananas, just to watch [. . . they] have seen the fruit thrive often to lengths of a foot and a half, yes amazing but true" (5–6). Incongruous with a war situation, Pynchon's ironic promotional literature depicts the captain's "giant bananas cluster, radiant yellow, humid green." Pirate's associates "dream drooling of a Banana Breakfast." Adding to the earthy humor, Pirate, in Rabelaisian style, stands in the lavatory "pissing, without a thought in his head." The scene ends with the bizarre statement that "this well-scrubbed day ought to be no worse than any" (6).

In the midst of this humorous description, Pynchon indicates another significant point: the "new sunlight"—in contrast to the winter scene of death and blind white light—sustains the vegetable compounds on the roof and tells Death "to fuck off." The tone is ironic and comic, but the message that plant cells and bacteria preserve life in the midst of death is clear. There is a biological structure that "allows this war morning's banana fragrance to meander, repossess, prevail" (10).

Developing another tall tale, the narrator describes the pleasures of the absurd hero, Lieutenant Slothrop, as he cavorts around London. In a mock-courtship scene with Darlene, he is encouraged to eat many bad-tasting English candies so as to endear himself to her. There are vile-tasting wine jellies, licorice drops, and hard candy that he has to choke down because of their terrible taste, which ranges from the flavor of nitric acid to menthol: "The Meggezone is like being belted in the head with a Swiss Alp. Menthol icicles immediately begin to grow from the roof of Slothrop's mouth. Polar bears seek toenail-holds up the freezing frosty-grape alveolar clusters in his lungs" (118). The incongruity between the traditional pleasure derived from eating candy and the shockingly awful taste this candy has for the optimistic lover creates humor. Even the lovemaking is subject to shocking incongruity. When the rocket blast fills the room, it seems to connect to the sexual union of Slothrop and Darlene. They reason: "Why shouldn't this stupid Blitz be good for something?" (120). Their innocent question is made sinister by the fact that the rocket actually may trigger Slothrop's erection. The ironic humor lies in the paradoxical point that the rocket (death) inspires sex (life). On a more sinister level, the scene emphasizes that sex and death are oddly connected.

In *Gravity's Rainbow* tall tales abound to convey much of the action and they are characterized by outrageous incongruities, puns, and farce. Depictions have similarities to Davy Crockett, who "kilt him a bar when he was only three,"[46] and the hero of Thomas Bangs Thorpe's "The Big Bear of Arkansas," who brags of Arkansas's great fertility, its continual harvests of huge corn, potatoes, beets,[47] its turkeys that weigh forty pounds, and its huge "creation bar," the "*unhuntable bar*" that "*died when his time come.*"[48] Pynchon, however, instead of using tall tales to aggrandize a locale or a person, employs them to describe a war-oriented society; he replaces the fortuitous good fortune of the frontiersman with the devastation caused by a high-powered V-2 rocket descending on people. The enormous expansion in weaponry is itself a tall tale that has become grotesquely real.

Pynchon further embellishes his macabre tale by including in it details from Puritanism. The narrator divides twentieth-century society into the "elect" and "preterite" (the damned), thus making explicit connections to the traditional, highly ordered Puritan society. Pynchon alludes to the ordered past of the Puritan elect and connects this to the power elite of the twentieth century: those who mysteriously and malevolently control the system that results in World War II and the Holocaust. A connection also is found between Tyrone Slothrop, an officer in the modern military, and the Puritan past. He is the "last of his line, and how far fallen," an absurd hero who "hangs at the bottom of his blood's avalanche, 300 years of western swamp-Yankees" (569, 25).

Pynchon contrasts Puritan morality with the randomness of contemporary society, but he also is critical of a tradition that presupposes the elect and preterition. He sardonically observes that Tyrone Slothrop's ancestor William wrote a heretical tract, *On Preterition*, which was "among the first books to've been not only banned but also ceremonially burned in Boston" (555). William had "argued holiness for these 'second Sheep,' without whom there'd be no elect." The narrator scornfully explains: "You can bet the Elect in Boston were pissed off about that" (555).[49]

In Thomas Pynchon's world, whether that of *Gravity's Rainbow, V.,* or *The Crying of Lot 49,* the perspective is not of the elect, but of the preterite. Epiphanies, ironically, are not of salvation but are of damnation, like that of the Baby Igor's daddy, who, close to death, seems to have figured out "You are for salvation; I am for the Pit" (*Lot 49* 27). In *Gravity's Rainbow* Pynchon ridicules the disturbing system of separation (between the elect and the preterite or "They" and the "Counterforce") through the use of slapstick, fantasy, comic songs, and paradox.

Like *V.*, *Gravity's Rainbow* is encyclopedic in scope, detailing activities by characters from the United States, South America, Africa, Central Asia, Russia, and Europe. There are over three hundred characters in the novel, connected to all aspects of society, including the military (the Allies and the Axis), scientists, politicians, secret agents, and "nonprofessionals [. . . and] just ordinary folks, little fellows" (105). References are made to chemistry, mathematics, film, song, art, and literature. And various languages are used: French, German, Latin, Italian, Herero, to name a few. Pynchon also, as Edward Mendelson points out, "asserts the inclusiveness of his vision" by developing " 'national' styles": the "dignified elegiac manner" for the British; the American dialect for Slothrop; and "a heightened solemn manner" employed in the German scenes.[50]

Gravity's Rainbow and the Jeremiad

Gravity's Rainbow gets much of its humor by parodying Puritan treatises and inverting Puritan themes. It parodies the jeremiad sermon, which consisted of "a recital of afflictions," such as diseases and droughts, followed by the "prescription," which delineated the causal path to a solution: "the sins exist, the disease breaks out; the sins are reformed, the disease is cured."[51] The colonial jeremiad encouraged people to repent their evil ways, prophesied eternal salvation, and celebrated God's promises. Cotton Mather used this form in *Magnalia* to encourage his contemporaries to change their ways and to follow the example of the first-generation Puritans. For Cotton Mather, the path to salvation was clear-cut. The third-generation Puritans were to follow the example of their forefathers and work toward Christian heroism.

The Puritan jeremiad sermon as presented by Samuel Danforth's *Brief Recognition of New England's Errand into the Wilderness* (1670) can serve as a model for this form. This address takes into account how far the Puritans were from achieving the Promised Land sought by the Pilgrims on the *Arbella* forty years earlier, but it praises the pilgrimage of the New Englanders, and encourages their meeting the spiritual challenge: "When men abate and cool in their affection to the pure worship of God which they went into the wilderness to enjoy, the Lord calls upon them seriously and thoroughly to examine

98

themselves."[52] Danforth condemns the colonists for their misdeeds and then refers to the prophet Jeremiah, who to stop the "backslidings" of the people of Jerusalem, reminded them of God's goodness to them and their following of him in the wilderness. He speaks of Jeremiah's criticism of the people for their rejection of God and their "following after their idols." The sermon indicates how the people repent and are thus converted from sin toward a condition of grace: "It is high time for us to 'remember whence we are fallen, and repent, and do our first works' " (Rev. 2:5).[53] On an anagogical level, the sermon points to how the sanctified soul will advance to the "house of the Lord." "The Lord Jesus, the great Physician of Israel, hath undertaken the cure."[54]

Gravity's Rainbow humorously focuses on man's lamentation in the twentieth-century world without countering it with any ability to atone and be forgiven by a just God. The novel exhibits the apocalyptic vision of the jeremiad but without the promise of salvation. Mom Slothrop has such a vision after drinking three martinis:

> It isn't starting to break down, is it, Joe? Sometimes, you know these fine Boston Sundays, when the sky over the Hill is *broken* into clouds [. . .] You know, don't you? Golden clouds? Sometimes I think—ah, Joe, I think they're pieces of the Heavenly City falling down. [. . .] but it *isn't* beginning to fall apart, is it. [. . .] it's very hard at such times really to believe in a Plan with a shape bigger than I can see. (682)[55]

Mom Slothrop's vision of apocalypse intensifies the irony implicit in an earlier jeremiad, *On Preterition,* by Tyrone Slothrop's ancestor William, for whom pigs instead of sheep form the basis for a parable. He pleads for his people, the nonelect "second Sheep," hell bound despite his prayer for their salvation. William Slothrop's lamentation, like traditional ones, expresses sorrow for the plight of a people. These are the preterite, in his argument, and for them there is "the squealing bloody horror at the end of the pike" rather than salvation (555).

Gravity's Rainbow contains fragments of the traditional plot of the jeremiad, with its dream of order and meaning, but emphasizes the opposite with the novel's theme of entropy. The protagonist Lieutenant Tyrone Slothrop longs for meaning and appeals to a higher power.[56] He prays, "at first, conventionally to God [. . .] for life to win out. But too many were dying, and [. . .] seeing no point, he stopped" (24).

Gravity's Rainbow and the Epic Quest

Pynchon uses not only the jeremiad but also the epic as a means for ironic reversals in his black humor comedy. For Pynchon, however, the fabulous aspects of the traditional epic are interchanged with the fantastic details of the modern tall tale, as in *V*. Like Benny Profane, the American Lieutenant Tyrone Slothrop, working in London, in 1944, for the ACHTUNG (Allied Clearing House Technical Units, Northern Germany), is a schlemihl. He has no goal or directing force, and—when he finally starts on a quest for the rocket—his search for information parodies rather than parallels the quest of the hero of traditional literature.

Slothrop's Puritan ancestors believed in the workings of God "in darkness above" and reflected this on tombstones as "the hand of God emerges from a cloud" (27, 26). Slothrop also shows an ironic and "peculiar sensitivity to what is revealed in the sky" (26). His connection, however, is with the V-2 rocket. His penis erects just before a V-2 rocket falls on the location. In fact, Slothrop has charted his sexual activities on a map in London. "They," the Firm, puzzle over the fact that these points are exactly the same as the "rocket strikes" (85) on their military map. Gradually, Slothrop realizes that his life and "The Penis He Thought Was His Own" (216) have been controlled since infancy like "a fixed roulette wheel" (209).

The fantastic nature of Slothrop's quest for meaning (that is, for information from the rocket station about his strange sensitivity) is compared by Pynchon (in a prefatory note to "In the Zone") to the adventures of Dorothy in *The Wizard of Oz*: "Toto, I have a feeling we're not in Kansas any more" (*Gravity's Rainbow* 279). Slothrop, too, has left the known and starts a series of adventures as part of a mock heroic quest.

The comic incongruities between Slothrop's serious quest for answers, as he infiltrates the Mittelwerke, where the Germans had manufactured V-1 and V-2 rockets (at this time taken over by the Allies), and the gamesome attitude of the rollicking, carousing Americans and Russians who now inhabit the station accentuate Slothrop's parody quest. That the people in the rocket station are singing songs, including one about a man named Hector who has intercourse with a rocket (306), and that Slothrop—and also the men—are unaware of Slothrop's connection to the song, adds to the bizarre comedy. Slapstick comedy is developed as Major Marvy spots Slothrop and, yelling "Go *git him* boys [. . . .] don't let that 'sucker git away!" (308), starts the chase.

Slothrop's quest parodies that of the traditional hero not only in terms of the first stage—leaving the known—but also in terms of his attitude toward adversaries such as Major Marvy. While the epic hero such as Ulysses or Achilles courageously overpowers the adversary, Slothrop fearfully tries to escape the enemy. One of the more hilarious episodes of this type is his escape from Major Marvy by balloon.

Believing the pilot Schnorp's declaration, "Nobody bothers a balloon" (332), Slothrop agrees to go anywhere, even Berlin, just to get away from Marvy. "Real unobtrusive getaway," Slothrop states as they go out to the brightly colored balloon, amid children who follow them on the lawn (332). Once up in the sky, Slothrop notices that Schnorp has brought along a dozen custard pies to sell in Berlin. Suddenly they spot a reconnaissance plane and, hearing the refrain "ja, ja, ja, ja! / In Prussia they never eat pussy" (a mock epic epithet signaling the presence of Marvy's men), they realize that they are in danger. The scene becomes sheer slapstick as Slothrop hurls pies at the approaching plane:

> Without planning to, Slothrop has picked up a pie. "Fuck you." He flings it, perfect shot, the plane peeling slowly past and *blop* gets Marvy right in the face. [. . .] "Now!" Schnorp yells, heaving a pie at the exposed engine. Slothrop's misses and splatters all over the windscreen in front of the pilot. By which time Schnorp has commenced flinging ballast bags at the engine, leaving one stuck between two of the cylinders.

The plane withdraws and the balloon is safe: "Schnorp is lying on his back, slurping pie, laughing bitterly. Half of his inventory's been thrown away, and Slothrop feels a little guilty" (334–36). The scene is followed by an epic digression, and it is not until twenty-three pages later that we return to the activities of Slothrop.

Echoes of the epic are suggested so that the reader will recognize a traditional system of values and will "enjoy" the way this postmodern novel will "ironically play on intertextuality."[57] The use of comic exaggeration, the fantastic, and bizarre incongruities in this incident are directly opposed to the elevated, spiritually significant, and unified sense customary in the epic. The scene and its comic ramifications develop laughter that is much freer than that in most of the novel, a novel that usually shocks its readers to laughter or presents serious questions that have no answers but "futile laughter,"[58] or reveals incongruities that blend fantasy and the grotesque to proportions that cause the reader to squirm rather than laugh at the black humor.

Slothrop's quest is diametrically opposed to quests of his Puritan ancestors, who always were certain of God's direction; different from those of the heroes of America's Puritan heritage, who had a mission and who were described as carrying out God's acts;[59] different from the quest in the great Puritan epic *Paradise Lost*, which influenced American epic writers like Cotton Mather.

Such reversals of motifs in earlier literature, as Umberto Eco points out, are a means of developing a new kind of postmodern comedy.[60] Pynchon's new type of comedy contrasts past literature with references from a twentieth-century context. The later context reveals how scientific mechanization and the Second Law of Thermodynamics have replaced the Holy Bible, a world in which people such as Pointsman affirm and depend on the "stone determinacy of everything, of every soul" (86).

Gravity's Rainbow and Milton's Puritan Epic

Gravity's Rainbow abounds in clear-cut theological allusions that have comic-apocalyptic and absurd ramifications in the modern world. Pynchon's rendering of a contemporary vision of hell invites comparison with famous traditional descriptions, such as that in *Paradise Lost*, which continually presents hell in relation to heaven. By caricaturing the traditional epic and by creating and then collapsing literary allusions to the rationally ordered universe that forms its context, Pynchon calls attention to the deflation of values that has occurred. He uses ironic and comic reversals of traditional values to satirize the shortcomings of a war-hungry, materialistic, "grab-all-you-can" world in which mechanical energy seems directed toward destruction.

The military weapons and the force of the rocket itself is an example of energy out of control, the "unchecked energy"[61] that is so different from the expansive power revealed in early American epics such as "Song of Myself." Ironically, the rocket's parabolic course resembles the arc of a rainbow. In the Bible and other religious works, the rainbow symbolizes God's covenant with man for peace; in *Gravity's Rainbow* it is a cynical allusion to the notion of God's justice, one that is absent in the irrational World War II society that seems to be a hell on earth.[62]

The opening scene in *Gravity's Rainbow* is set in a dusky atmosphere, an evacuation nightmare that probably is part of Pirate Prentice's dream.[63] The dream is similar to a vision of hell. Ironically, the images in Prentice's vision (in a chaotic world without salvation) echo the depiction in Milton's *Paradise Lost*, which shows hell in contrast to heaven. In Pirate's vision, the world is "a Universe of death . . . / . . . Where all life dies, death lives, and Nature breeds, / Perverse."[64] Ravaged by war, London is a darkened habitat, fit "to accommodate the rush of souls, . . . where all the rats have died, only their ghosts, still as cave-painting, fixed stubborn and luminous in the walls" (4). Because there is "no light anywhere," the horror seems "fixed", "luminous": what Milton has termed a "darkness visible."[65]

The streets of London are filled with stench and smoke from recent bombing; fumes rise from charred wood. There is a "smell [. . .] of old wood, of remote wings empty all this time just reopened to accommodate the rush of souls" (4). Smoke constantly emits from the rockets screaming across the sky. And never fully developed but always looming large in the background of all the other fire imagery is the incineration in the death camp, seen by the prison children as a huge fire "that always smoldered, day and night" (408).

In *Gravity's Rainbow,* the evacuees of darkened, bombed-out London streets move along "blind curves," down streets that get narrower and more broken, eventually finding that "there is no way out." The movement "is not a disentanglement from, but a progressive *knotting into*" (3–4). Pynchon ironically underlines the loss of meaning and salvation in his twentieth-century world: "You didn't really believe you'd be saved. Come, we all know who we are by now. No one was ever going to take the trouble to save *you,* old fellow" (4). Pynchon's hell is controlled by a mysterious Them, not by God. It is an absurd hell, not a deserved one as in *Paradise Lost*. And for Prentice the most tangible correlative of heaven is a "Banana Breakfast" (5–6).

The condition of the fallen in Milton and Pynchon is physical as well as spiritual. Satan's original brightness dims as he deteriorates from the angel Lucifer to the Archfiend. This changed state is acutely felt in *Gravity's Rainbow*, where people from all levels of society seem to be metamorphosed from animate to inanimate because of the war. Such deterioration is burlesqued early in the novel when Slothrop—still in Boston, before his army experience—makes his epic descent down the toilet bowl to retrieve his "mouth harp," which had dropped: "Either he lets the harp go, his silver chances of song, or he has to follow," reports the narrator. Slothrop, the last of his Puritan line, journeys down the plumbing to capture a bit of heaven's song. He becomes "shit-sensitized" as he tumbles, "if that indeed is what he's doing" (63, 65–66).

Later, however, in the actual hell of the Zone, Slothrop seems unable to counteract the "shit" around him. He gradually disintegrates before our eyes (740), his own way of being freed from the structure that has controlled him all along. Similarly, Franz Pökler, a technician for the group known as the *Verein fur Raumschiffart,* which provided a source of civilian volunteers for the rocket program, also gradually falls apart as the military gains more and more control over his life: "Pieces spilled into the Hinterhof, down the drains, away in the wind." He becomes "an extension of the Rocket" (*Gravity's Rainbow* 402), more inanimate than human.[66]

There are militaristic, satanic figures in *Gravity's Rainbow* who thrive on controlling others and developing a hellish world. These are the characters in power, such as Blicero/Weissmann, a psychologically frightening Nazi captain who, like Satan, seems inexorably bent on destroying.

Milton's Satan destroys because he wants revenge on God; Blicero's motivation and his desire for death are unknown. He has a death wish that makes perverse the Puritan dream of eternal life. His evil makes him appear to be a devil or a witch who feeds on the innocent—such as Katje and Gottfried (or Hansel and Gretel). No matter how much he engages in varied activities, Blicero, like Satan, finds no relief for his despair.[67] Whether Blicero is making Gottfried dress in women's clothes and Katje in men's before engaging in brutal sexual activities with both of them, or whether this commander of a V-2 base is cavorting before the men with his big African lover, Enzian—all of these machinations for Blicero are merely sexual "foreplay": "He only wants now to be out of the winter, inside the Oven's warmth, darkness, steel shelter [. . .] gonging shut, forever" (99). For Blicero, ironically, the rocket is the fetishistic means to ultimate sexual fulfillment.

Pynchon's world is a hell that offers the reader comic relief but no sense of divine promise of harmony, peace, or joy. Pynchon seems to take delight in undermining heavenly joy. In the "White Visitation" there is a religious painting on the wall depicting the lion and the lamb together. This is mocked by the narrator, who explains: "No one's expression is quite right. The wee creatures leer, the fiercer beasts have a drugged or sedated look" (82).

The conception of bliss in Pynchon's world reflects ironically on the nature of the beholder. For his characters, bliss is deflated to the level of the German *Rücksichtslos,* the "Toiletship." This vessel offers respite from the outside world, indicating that at least one can go to the bathroom and get away from it all: "The officers' latrines [. . .] are done in red velvet. [. . .] The toilet paper! The toilet paper is covered square after square with caricatures of Churchill, Eisenhower, Roosevelt, Chiang Kai-shek, there was even a Staff Caricaturist always on duty to custom-illustrate blank paper for those connoisseurs who are ever in search of the unusual." Yet, even here, Pynchon plays off images of "bliss" with those that would bother the navy personnel: "all over the walls, photograffiti, are pictures of Horrible Disasters in German Naval History. Collisions, magazine explosions, U-boat sinkings, just the thing if you're an officer trying to take a shit" (450).

The Absurd Quest

Pynchon's protagonist, Tyrone Slothrop, vainly tries to create an order from the clues that he finds in his epic journey through the Zone. In the process of seeking "signs of mystery" he develops a paranoid vision, opening into an "alternative world"[68] that is an ironic counter-part to the concept of salvation of Slothrop's Puritan ancestors. Para-noia becomes the focus in this world, where Slothrop ruminates over the comic-grotesque fact that he was sold in infancy to "spring" money for a scholarship for his Harvard education (286).

As Slothrop (and, in turn, the reader) searches for answers about the V-2 rocket, about Imipolex G, about the Forbidden Wing in his past, he travels through London, Nice, Zurich, Berlin, and other parts of the Zone. At the end of his epic journey this hero of the absurd not only fails to achieve fulfillment, but he also disintegrates, becoming "broken down [. . .] and scattered" (738). Seaman Bodine observes him just before the collapse is complete: "He's looking straight at Slothrop (being one of the few who can still see Slothrop as any sort of integral creature any more. Most of the others gave up long ago trying to hold him together, even as a concept—'It's just got too remote' 's what they usually say)" (740). One is left to ponder this transformation and also the following: " 'There never was a Dr. Jamf,' opines world-renowned analyst Mickey Wuxtry-Wuxtry—'Jamf was only a fiction, to help him explain what he felt so terribly, so immediately in his genitals for those rockets each time exploding in the sky . . . to help him deny what he could not possibly admit: that he might be in love, in sexual love, with his, and his race's, death' " (738). Slothrop's quest, his strange conditioning (if one can call it that) by Dr. Jamf, and his deterioration cause readers to search for a rationale by which to understand the unreasonable.

In an absurd World War II situation, frustrating searches abound. Slothrop continually quests for answers about "Them," an obsession that only leads him in circles; the mathematician Franz Pökler desperately seeks for his daughter, Ilse, who, he is told, is at a Nazi "re-education" camp (410); Tchitcherine searches for his soul brother Enzian and observes that "what might have been a village apocalypse has gone on now into comic cooperation, as between a pair of vaudeville comedians" (357). These characters are ceaselessly wandering, like the fallen angels in Milton's hell.

As the characters in *Gravity's Rainbow* quest for answers, go on geographical and psychological journeys, attempt to discover secrets or develop relationships or reveal motives, readers—because of their desire for correspondences—hope for a movement that will culminate in successful action. That they do not achieve this sense of an ending disappoints readers, but the imaginative process gives them a kind of pleasure in appreciating how they have been tricked.

In *Gravity's Rainbow,* the pain never totally blots out the humor. Slothrop's futile quest, his endless journey, is burlesqued by the tall tale of the meanderings, chance experiences, anger, and frustration of Byron, the immortal and rebellious light bulb. The reader laughs at the *reductio ad absurdum* of Byron the Bulb's journey from Osram, in Berlin, to an opium den in Charlottenburgh, to Hamburg, to Nuremberg, to various homes and factories and streets (647–55). The picaresque journey amuses the reader and eases anxiety over the bizarre quality of Pynchon's world. Then one learns that Byron, who once was an idealistic revolutionary—believing that "20 million Bulbs, all over Europe, at a given synchronizing pulse" (649) could dazzle mankind—eventually ends up controlled by the powerful light bulb organization.

On a more pessimistic level, one learns that the light bulb organization may be controlled by I. G. Farben—the company, one realizes, that supplied the death camps with lethal gas, the company that worked prisoners to death, the company that contributed to the genocide at

Auschwitz. The associations to I. G. Farben develop while readers are laughing and off guard. Pynchon then eases them back to the picaresque description of Byron the Bulb, who—the narrator explains—"is condemned to go on forever, [. . .] powerless to change anything." Eventually, he, like the human beings who people *Gravity's Rainbow* and also its readers, "will find himself, poor perverse bulb, enjoying it" (655).

In this world of black humor, traditionally advocated avenues of transcendence seem blocked. Roger Mexico attends an Advent service in a country church with his girl friend Jessica, even though he senses an irony in holding a service that celebrates redemption through Christ amid all the waste and loss of war. The evensong becomes a call to "leave your war awhile" for the refuge, the safer place, of the church service. Those who sing the evensong are a "pickup group" of people, not a harmonious choir that suggests representative angels singing their praise of God. For these people there is nothing in the church that can serve even as a physical focus for religious inspiration: "no counterfeit baby, no announcement of the Kingdom, not even a try at warming or lighting this terrible night." The communal event barely offers a glimmer of solace that could possibly illumine for these outcasts "alone in the dark" (134–36) the way home.[69]

At the close of *Gravity's Rainbow,* the ironically named Gottfried (God's peace) ascends to the heavens in a rocket. He holds the mystical belief that by this "transcendent" experience he carries out the will of his lover, Blicero/Weissmann. His ascent is suicide. From Gottfried's point of view there is a sense of ease and affection, a sense that death is a purification, "a whitening, a carrying of whiteness to ultrawhite" (759). The reader is uplifted by the mystical sense of "whitening," only to be abruptly disappointed: "what is it but bleaches, detergents, oxidizers, abrasives" (759). In *Gravity's Rainbow* "the real movement is not from death to any rebirth. It is from death to death-transfigured" (166), that is, to a death-in-life. This movement stresses the conflict between theological implications and a world in which such references are meaningless. As the rocket descends, there is a sense of anesthetized time, different by far from the religious promise of glorious eternity.

Here, as in the novel as a whole, Pynchon employs a succession of scenes to develop a comic counterpoint to the bleak picture of a twentieth-century world where rocket power is out of control: Steven Edelman explains the significance of the Kabbala while taking more and more Thorazine pills, which do not help anymore because his children, "mischievous little devils, have lately taken to slipping wafer capacitors from junked transistor radios into Pop's Thorazine jar" (753). The manager of the Orpheus Theatre (where the rocket is soon to fall), Richard M. Zhlubb (a thinly disguised Richard Nixon), complains about the "irresponsible use of the harmonica" (754), anarchistic behavior that upsets his theater. And the narrator, in the "Pre-Launch" section, makes sarcastic observations on the sexual implications of Gottfried's desire to be placed with the rocket where "deathlace" is the "bridal costume" for the boy who "fits well" and will "writhe among the fuel, oxidizer, live-steam lines, thrust frame, compressed air battery, exhaust elbow, decomposer, tanks, vents, valves [. . .] the true clitoris, routed directly into the nervous system of the 00000" (750–51). The scene has been called "a demonic inversion of the divine covenant,"[70] a jeremiad without hope for the future.[71] It has a frenzied black humor tone that is darkly ironic and strangely comic.[72]

Christian epics like the *Divine Comedy* and *Paradise Lost* have mystical levels vertically linked to a paradigm of divine providence. Such works assume correspondences between the mundane, temporal world and the transcendent, eternal new Jerusalem that is to be instituted on earth. They depend on a hierarchical mode of thought based firmly on absolute faith.

Dante's analysis of the four levels of meaning can be seen as a paradigm of a traditional allusive mode progressing vertically from the literal or referential meaning to the anagogical or mystical meaning that points to the eternal truth of God's glory. For Dante, the opening verses from Psalm 114, depicting the Exodus, conveyed the following: the literal departure of the sons of Israel; the allegorical significance of man's redemption through Christ; the moral emphasis on the conversion of the soul from sin to grace; and, finally, an ultimate spiritual sense that the sanctified soul, free from corruption and servitude, ascends to eternal glory and freedom.[73]

Black humorists like Pynchon depend on the readers' desire for traditional correspondences and all that they promise. George Levine and David Leverenz comment on Thomas Pynchon's success in trapping readers who look for correspondences: "The temptation, clearly, has been irresistible to take his allusions, his dropped clues, his metaphors, and run, right into the ordering patterns that welcome us into the Firm."[74] Black humorist Pynchon laughs at man's helplessness in an alien universe and in a social network that has grown way beyond his control, and he wants the readers also to laugh. He speaks of entropy with nonchalance. He encourages readers to attempt endless quests for order, causing them ultimately to respond with bitter laughter as their only release.

The experiences of Pynchon's characters, quite unlike those of traditional heroes, dramatize the deflation of the sacred to the profane, even though some of these characters, like Gottfried, experience something spiritual in rising to death in a rocket and, like Slothrop, have a sense of "feeling natural" when faced with symbolically charged phenomena. Deflation is the rule in the buildup and collapse of spiritual possibilities. Slothrop, in what seems to be a transcendent moment, observes a rainbow: "After a heavy rain he doesn't recall, Slothrop sees a very thick rainbow here, a stout rainbow cock driven down out of pubic clouds into Earth, green wet valleyed Earth, and his chest fills and he stands crying, not a thing in his head, just feeling natural" (626). The blatant depiction of the rainbow as a phallic symbol in "pubic clouds" deflates the scene's sacred possibilities. The chance for Slothrop to have a hallowing experience turns to mellowness, his "just feeling natural."[75] Such scenes become caricatures, allied, in many respects, to the burlesque evident in comic strips. The scene depicts the movement from the sacred to the earthy, and from the richly mythic to the cartoon.

The Comic Strip and Black Humor

Throughout *Gravity's Rainbow,* Pynchon parodies a multitude of genres, ranging from epic and jeremiad to pornography and the comic book. Slothrop connects himself to comic strip characters, ranging from super heroes like Plasticman to Porky Pig. As he reads the strips, he seems to foreshadow his own "destiny" as schlemihl, hero of the absurd—like Benny Profane. For example, he reads that Plasticman oozes out of a keyhole, then goes "up through piping that leads to a sink in the mad Nazi scientist's lab, out of whose faucet Plas's head [. . .] is just emerging" (207). This precedes Slothrop's incursion into the lab of Nazi guidance expert Zwitter. When Slothrop arrives on the scene, the narrator asks: "Plasticman, where are you?" (314), as though summoning an epic hero of old.

The novel gains much humor from Slothrop's attempt to emulate another comic hero, Rocketman, as he puts on a helmet, a cape of green velvet, and buckskin trousers (366). He is told, "No job is too tough for Rocketman," and is encouraged to set off for Potsdam to search for "2.2 pounds of hashish" (371), a peculiarly illicit mission for Rocketman. In the Rocketman sequence, Slothrop, because of his heroic garb, thinks that he will succeed—up until the moment he is *caught* digging up the cache of hashish![76]

Slothrop's deterioration accelerates as he changes from Rocketman to Porky Pig. He starts out in this role at a folk festival where the villagers ask him to play the part of Plechazunga, the Pig-Hero, who appeared in a thunderbolt, in the tenth century, to drive out Viking invaders (567). Though a success at the festival, where he ritualistically saves the town for another year, Slothrop has to flee pursuers and, like Porky Pig, is helped by a female pig who "smiles amiably, blinking long eyelashes" (573). Slothrop is chased by Russians who think he is a deserter, by the anti-black market police, and by others who pursue him because of his relationship with the V-2. Slothrop's last acts as pig take place at an old manor house that is used for all types of merriment: "bar, opium den, cabaret" (602). There, because of a chance exchange of costume, Slothrop escapes the men of Pointsman, the scientist who wants him for a guinea pig. The bizarre activities and their connections to comic strip events momentarily lessen the tension in a novel in which scientists think little of castrating someone for experimental purposes, soldiers take glee in brutalizing innocent members of a crowd, and the war wipes out multitudes with rockets.

At the conclusion of the novel, when Blicero/Weissmann launches Gottfried in a V-2 rocket, the narrator alludes to the collapse of myths that have traditionally sustained man and uses the comic strip mode to convey his point. He ruminates on the deterioration of super heroes, not traditional epic ones: the fading of Superman's cape and the "threads of gray" in his hair; Plasticman's losing his way among the Imipolex plastic chains, invented by the Germans; and the Lone Ranger's stormy arrival, only to find his friend Tonto hanged. For such heroes, "too late" had never been a problem, observes the narrator. But now things are different. In *Gravity's Rainbow* heroes are deflated, dreams are shattered, religion becomes meaningless, and decline increases. "The heroes will go on, kicked upstairs to oversee the development of bright new middle-line personnel, and they will watch their system falling apart [. . . and will not know] the meaning of it all" (751–52).

CHAPTER SIX

Ironic Allusiveness and Satire in William Gaddis's *The Recognitions*

William Gaddis's satire may be considered even more passionate than Pynchon's, his sense of mission more obvious. In "The Rush for Second Place," Gaddis satirizes the materialism of twentieth-century American society, which has exchanged "the remnants of the things worth being for those presumably worth having."[1] Gaddis uses farce and incongruity to criticize a society in which a good appearance, being liked, and influencing people enable a man to get ahead. He lampoons a society whose members are constantly on the move without meaningful direction, aimlessly drifting along what Nikolai Gogol has termed "tortuous, blind, impassable, devious paths," never able to find "eternal truth."[2]

In public lectures, Gaddis often praises Gogol's *Dead Souls*.[3] In fact, Gaddis in many respects is a twentieth-century Gogol. Certainly, they have expressed similar intentions. Referring to *The Recognitions*, Gaddis relates: "I thought that I was the first one to discover that the world was filled with false values and I was going to tell them. So I elaborated the 900 and some pages. It was a sense of mission." Making reference to *JR* (1975), he explains: "Twenty years later I did the same thing. I had to tell them that the stock market and this whole myth about free enterprise was just high comedy."[4] Gaddis's most recent novel, *Carpenter's Gothic* (1985), satirizes the power residing in society's religious, political, and business institutions. Gaddis's intent recalls Gogol's: "Who's going to tell the truth if not the writer?" Gogol points out that because of his humor, the reader may praise him for being "a cheerful sort of fellow," but this is not enough. Gogol desires that readers see and criticize themselves in his characters.[5]

Gaddis's distress over the materialism in twentieth-century America echoes Gogol's concern, a century ago, over the greed and corruption of Russia, its loss of spiritual goals. Both desire to expose counterfeits in their society. In *Dead Souls,* Gogol depicts counterfeits through his character Chichikov and those with whom the man comes in contact. The epic novel focuses on the development of a comic incongruity: dead serfs are treated as though they are alive for the purpose of the census. Through irony, the author emphasizes that the landowners not only exploit their living serfs but they also wish to profit from selling the dead. Gogol accentuates the comic aspect of this exploitation by having the protagonist, Chichikov, offer landowners the opportunity to sell him dead serfs, or dead souls, whose names are on the old census and for whom the landlords still have to pay a tax. The price of the dead serfs is subject to haggling, as is evident in the conversation between Chichikov and the landowner Sobakevich:

> "God damn it," Chichikov thought, "this one's talking of selling before I've even mentioned the idea!" And he said aloud: "And what price would you have in mind? Although it's really rather strange to use the word price in speaking of such merchandise." "Well, since I don't wish to charge you a kopek above the proper price, it'll be one hundred rubles apiece," Sobakevich said. "A hundred!"Chichikov cried. . . . I, for my part, would suggest . . . eighty kopeks per soul." . . . "But it's not bast sandals I'm selling," [responded Sobakevich].[6]

The similarity between Gaddis and Gogol goes beyond mission. Both authors use black humor and the comic-grotesque as a means to develop their satiric epics. To criticize the materialistic orientation of society, Gaddis, instead of naming his characters, often represents them in terms of their possessions. A large diamond ring tells us Recktall Brown is present; a Mickey Mouse watch points to Agnes Deigh. This develops a "gloomy but also grotesquely comic"[7] vision reminiscent of that of Gogol, who ridicules Russia's businessmen and petty officials by reducing them to objects they sell and garments they wear: in looking at a store window, people appear unable to differentiate between the red-faced vendor and the samovar that he markets except for the fact that "one of them had a pitch-black beard";[8] in a government office Chichikov observes "an ordinary light gray jacket . . . *its* head twisted to one side . . . as, with zest and flourish, *it* wrote out some court decision" (italics added).[9]

In "The Rush for Second Place," Gaddis criticizes twentieth-century society for making appearances and material success all important, for carrying out the advice of Willy Loman in *Death of a Salesman*, to aim to be liked,[10] advice similar to that which Gogol mocks when he relates Chichikov's father's parting counsel to his son: "Always try to please your teachers and your superiors." This, he explains, is the way to "get ahead." If Chichikov is to have friends, he is instructed to "pick the richer ones. . . . Money will do everything for you."[11]

Ironic Allusiveness

Gaddis's major means of ridiculing the shallow, materialistic bent of society is through ironic allusiveness. Like Pynchon and other post-modern epic writers, he uses this method extensively to develop satiric comedy. While traditional writers like John Milton and Cotton Mather use allusions to strengthen the connection between the themes and values in their works and similar ones in earlier epics, Gaddis alludes to earlier literature in order to show an ironic contrast with the precepts of his era. He returns to literary depictions of traditional beliefs and behavior from earlier centuries to show—by contrast—the superficialities of twentieth-century America.

By allowing the reader to enjoy the disparity between twentieth-century concerns and traditional values evident in the original sources, Gaddis laughingly exposes the counterfeits.[12] He depends on what Umberto Eco calls the " 'encyclopedia' of the spectator,"[13] the literary knowledge of the reader, which can be called upon to develop ironic contrasts between an earlier work and the present one. In *JR* Gaddis alludes to his own *The Recognitions* and calls attention to the comic incongruity between the book itself and the banal and arrogant comments of some twentieth-century book reviewers. He cites reviews of seven novels, all anagrams for *The Recognitions.*[14] Comments include: "a narrow and jaundiced view, a projection of private discontent"; "so ostentatiously aimed at writing a masterpiece"; "nowhere in this whole disgusting book is there a trace of kindness or sincerity or simple decency" (*JR* 515).[15]

In order to mock the false assertions masquerading as the truth in twentieth-century American society, Gaddis tries to strip the contemporary scene of its apparent normality. By defamiliarizing the present reality for readers, he calls attention to the need for an inner reality that has traditional meaning and basic truths. Gaddis's method is spelled out in *The Recognitions* by Wyatt Gwyon as he speaks of seeing Picasso's *Night Fishing in Antibes:* "When I saw it all of a sudden everything was freed into one recognition. [. . .][16] You don't see it in paintings because [. . . .] the instant you see them they become familiar, and then it's too late" (92).

Recognizing includes "the action or fact of perceiving . . . a thing as having a certain character or belonging to a certain class" (that is, in terms of others of its type). It also includes the experience of being able "to know again," of being capable of viewing an object as being "identical with something previously known."[17] When the present perception is contrary to expectations (that have been set by what had been known), readers laugh at the contemporary scene and appreciate its inadequacies.

In order to ridicule the present, Gaddis encourages readers to draw upon an encyclopedic range of earlier writings: transcendental works, alchemical tracts, Flemish paintings, the third-century *Clementine Recognitions,* Goethe's *Faust,* and T. S. Eliot's *The Wasteland* and *Four Quartets.* He focuses on these lofty works of the past, steeped in religious and philosophical significance, to satirize the "materialistic, grab-all-you-can" twentieth-century American society.[18]

Transcendental References

Gaddis often develops ironic references to transcendental themes and to great transcendentalist thinkers like Ralph Waldo Emerson. He begins one of his party scenes in *The Recognitions* with an epigraph from Emerson's essay "Old Age": "America is a country of young men" (169) who, Emerson writes, are "too full of work hitherto for leisure and tranquillity."[19] Emerson's notion of the energetic and productive work of young men and the wise balancing of solitude and sociability in old age makes ironic and comic the futile activity in the novel's contemporary American gatherings "full of people who spen[d] their lives in rooms" (176): the young people, alienated from each other and from the natural environment; the poet, myopic and unable to see beyond the printed page instead of having an eye that "can see far," an eye that "seems to demand a horizon";[20] the poet capable only of viewing "simply a series of vague images [. . . to be] faced with lowered eyes as though seeking a book at hand to explain it all" (*Recognitions* 179). With sharp humor, the narrator ridicules different types of shallow behavior of contemporary party-goers. Some engage in incommunicative dialogue: "—*Him* Byronic? Miss Stein demanded.—I said *moronic*, said Mr. Schmuck's assistant" (656). Others mask their identities: Ed Feasley meets a girl whom he finds attractive. After the party, he exclaims to a friend: "Chrahst, I found her, the girl in the purple dress. Standing right beside me at the next urinal" (315). Others appear to be arguing philosophically over such inane points as whether a death should be classified as a suicide or an accident because the man, who had attempted to hang himself, fell to his death when the rope broke (180).

To see clearly the lack of meaning in twentieth-century society's social gatherings, Gaddis suggests that one think about where America had been and where it is. His description of contemporary parties directly contrasts with those more meaningful gatherings in American history of the "Transcendental Club" in which Emerson, Alcott, Frothingham, Fuller, and others exchanged ideas on such subjects as "American genius—the causes which hinder its growth," "the actuality of intuition," and "the immanence of God."[21] Such significant issues are never topics of conversation at the parties Gaddis describes.

The author sounds like a comic prophet, a modern Jeremiah, listing the transgressions of his contemporaries, whose thoughts center on trivialities. Such people deflate religion by telling banal jokes about how it is "all right to kiss a nun [. . . .] as long as you don't get into the habit" (103); others treat lightly an author's endeavors, as does the critic who, when asked "You reading that [book]?" responds: "No. I'm just reviewing it. [. . .] All I need is the jacket blurb to write the review." That the omniscient author describes the book as *The Recognitions* compounds the cynicism: "It was in fact quite a thick book," whose dust jacket has bold lettering that stands forth "in stark configurations of red and black" (936). In such a society, the author cynically prophesies that nothing is holy.[22] In such a society, materialism has supplanted transcendentalism and science has replaced religion. The narrator, with wry humor, explains:

> Science assures us that it is getting nearer to the solution of life, what life *is*, . . . ("the ultimate mystery"), and offers anonymously promulgated submicroscopic chemistry in eager substantiation. But no one has even begun to explain what happened at the dirt track in Langhorne, Pennsylvania about twenty-five years ago, when Jimmy Concannon's car threw a wheel, and in a crowd of eleven thousand it killed his mother. (566)

Flemish Art

Gaddis creates much of his ironic dialogue with the past by developing allusions to fifteenth-century Flemish art. He evokes a desire for a lost age that produced painters whose art "would bring tears to the eyes of the devout."[23] In *The Recognitions* the protagonist yearns for the piety and devotion he believes were part of the context of fifteenth-century Netherlandish painters—Roger van der Weyden, Hubert and Jan van Eyck, Dirc Bouts, and Hans Memling. Wyatt wishes to be part of an age when painters displayed an exquisite sense of piety, such as van der Weyden and Bouts conveyed in their Madonnas and their Descents from the Cross. Copying these fifteenth-century Flemish masters, Wyatt mixes tempera to approximate their paint and attempts a psychic affinity with their philosophical and emotional states of mind. He paints masterpieces that connoisseurs judge to be the work of the original Netherlandish painters. He seems to transport himself to their golden age and virtually presents his gift to the guild as an artist in Flanders. He thinks of the guild oath, "to use pure materials, to work in the sight of God" (*Recognitions* 250).

Gaddis develops the ironic allusive mode by caustically contrasting Wyatt Gwyon's nostalgia for painterly beauty with the present world, where randomness and disconnections abound. For a time, the transforming power of Wyatt's imagination creates a sense of meaning and beauty for readers. But the shift of focus from the sacred and serious to the profane and the ludicrous jars readers. The black humor tone that emerges from the depiction of these incongruities mixes components of pain with humor, horror with farce.

The title of Gaddis's postmodern comic epic novel indeed derives from the third-century *Clementine Recognitions,* in which Clement, seeking salvation, journeys to Palestine and becomes a follower of Saint Peter. Basil Valentine, a central character in Gaddis's *Recognitions,* holds the same name as the Renaissance author of the alchemical treatise *The Triumphant Chariot of Antimony.*[24] The novel also can be considered a "bop version" (661) of Goethe's *Faust,* which centers on the issue of redemption. Such references call to mind a physical journey in Palestine and the quest for a new Jerusalem, the redemption of matter and the redemption of the soul, man's desires and the justification of God's ways. These are the major sources that are called upon and contradicted in the novel. As the expectations created by these are frustrated, the reader appreciates the "ironic ploy" and, with a combination of pleasure and pain, enjoys the grim joke that comes from the incongruity.[25]

Allusions to the *Clementine Recognitions*

From early childhood, Gaddis's twentieth-century protagonist, Wyatt Gwyon, is fascinated by the story of Saint Clement, who was martyred by being tied to an anchor and thrown into the Black Sea (44). According to theological tracts, Clement had argued for apostolic succession against Gnosticism and other heretical beliefs. Legend relates that when Clement was thrown overboard, the waters parted and a tomb appeared at the bottom of the sea, signifying the beatification of Clement.

Wyatt connects the story of Saint Clement and a legend his father had told him about a celestial being who came down a rope into the atmosphere of this world and drowned (44). Wyatt continually ponders the possibility that human beings are fished for by celestial beings who watch their actions: "Can't you imagine that we're fished for? Walking on the bottom of a great celestial sea, do you remember the man who came down the rope to undo the anchor caught on the tombstone?" (115) he asks his wife years later. Wyatt wants to be fished for; he yearns for salvation, for signs of God's grace in a fallen world.

References to the legend of Saint Clement point out ironic connections between the hero of the *Clementine Recognitions* and Wyatt Gwyon, hero of the absurd. The *Clementine Recognitions,* a long, episodic work, describes the young adulthood of Saint Clement of Rome (first century A.D.). The treatise affirms orthodox Christian doctrine by emphasizing the traditional connection between this world and a new Jerusalem, between the protagonist Clement and every man seeking eternal salvation.

In the twentieth-century *Recognitions,* however, the character Basil Valentine explains to an acquaintance:

> Tell your [writer] friend *Willie* that salvation is hardly the practical study it was then. What? . . . Why, simply because in the Middle Ages they were convinced that they had souls to save. Yes. The what? The *Recognitions?* No, it's Clement of *Rome.* Mostly talk, talk, talk. The young man's deepest concern is for the immortality of his soul, he goes to Egypt to find the magicians and learn their secrets. It's been referred to as the first Christian novel. (372–73; first italics added)

Basil Valentine's comment on the *Clementine Recognitions* reveals the comic-ironic contrast between the sacred and the profane, between religion and Mammonism. In addition, his comment has a significant error. He says that Clement goes to Egypt to find the magicians and learn their secrets. In the original, though Clement wishes to consult with magicians about immortality, he quickly turns from such actions because "transactions of this sort are hateful to the Divinity" (*Clem. R.* 78). Instead of traveling to Egypt, land of magic and the occult, Clement sails to Palestine, where he meets Saint Peter, who teaches him how to progress toward salvation. Accompanying Peter on his missionary journeys to various cities, Clement sees Peter heal the sick and give peace to those in turmoil (*Clem. R.* 136). As he hears Peter discourse on the consistency of Christ's teaching and listens to him debate with Simon Magus, he appreciates how goodness and logical argumentation can convince people to believe the teacher of truth and abhor Satan and his followers. United with his lost father, mother, and brothers, Clement watches his father repent for having been seduced by Simon Magus, and he hears Peter explain: "As God has restored your sons to you, their father, so also your sons restore their father to God" (*Clem. R.* 210). The journey with Peter through Palestine enables Clement to appreciate the ultimate significance of things, the "Alpha and Omega, the beginning and the end, the first and the last" (Rev. 22:13).

The progression of the hero in the *Clementine Recognitions* provides a framework by which to compare Wyatt Gwyon's ironic quest for salvation in Gaddis's twentieth-century novel. Wyatt is estranged from his father, Reverend Gwyon; he has no guide like Saint Peter to reconcile him with father or God. When he finds a souvenir from the basilica of Saint Clement in Rome, Wyatt appeals to his father for information about the martyred saint. Reverend Gwyon gives the boy no Christian counsel; instead, he is engrossed in the fact that under the basilica geologists found a pagan temple for worshipers of the Persian god, Mithras. The "subterranean sanctuary [. . .] afloat with vapors from two thousand years before" (44) is more vital to him than Wyatt's concern about salvation. Reverend Gwyon's comments suggest that his pilgrimages to Rome and Spain are an ironic reversal of the voyages of early Christian pilgrims. Instead of pilgrimages heightening his connection to the Church, they alienate him from Christianity, his congregation, and his son.

The pattern of father-son estrangement is evident throughout Gaddis's *Recognitions*. As a young boy, Wyatt accidentally kills a wren and goes to his father's study to confess. Instead of atoning and receiving guidance, Wyatt stands waiting outside his father's forbidding study door, while the minister remains silently facing him from inside the room. As an adult, Wyatt again wants to repent his actions. He travels home to the New England parsonage but again is unable to communicate with his father.

In the carriage barn of the New England parsonage, amid peals of thunder and lightning, Wyatt finally blurts out: "Father . . . *Am I the man for whom Christ died?*" "Louder than laughter," the narrator relates, "the crash raised and sundered them in a blinding agony of light in which nothing existed until it was done." The narrator continues, "Then it seemed full minutes before the cry, pursuing them with its lashing end, flailed through darkness and stung them to earth. Water fell between them, from a hole in the roof. The smell of smoke reached them in the dark" (440). In the traditional allusive mode, lightning and thunder would signify a prophetic moment full of God's presence; water would imply Baptism and regeneration. This scene, however, comically frustrates all expectation for Baptism, reducing to nothing the reader's vision of the grand image of John the Baptist and Christ. Contrary to expectation, the scene deflates all prophetic symbolism to the gross details of a metal washtub whose water is wasted. The lightning drives a hole in the washtub and the water gushes out. Unlike the Baptism of Christ, which brings the Father and the Son together, this gush of water physically enforces the separation of the father and son. There is no sign of God's presence or of salvation in this black humor scene. There is no link that will connect Wyatt to his God or to his father. There is only the ironic "denseness and that strangeness of the world [which] is the absurd."[26]

Wyatt's eventual communication with the Reverend Gwyon takes on a sharper tone of black humor. At the age of thirty-three (Christ's age at the Crucifixion),[27] Wyatt's Puritan guilt leads him to a penitential act. He goes to the town of San Zwingli, near Madrid, and visits the grave of his mother, Camilla, who died when he was three.[28] Then he travels south to the Spanish monastery in Estremadura, where his father had stayed after Camilla's death. In these surroundings, Wyatt, now known as Stephen (name of the first Christian martyr), unwittingly eats his father's ashes baked in the bread that the monks have served. The monks have mistaken the ashes (mailed to them in an oatmeal box) for wheat germ.

The monks use the ingredients in the cereal box to bake bread, which is served to Wyatt: "The bread crumbled because of its fine gray texture. He [Wyatt] crammed half of it into his mouth [. . .] As he chewed, a thoughtful expression came to his face for the first time." "His eyes," we are told, were fixed upon a painting but were "focused far beyond it. He chewed on" (870–71). By eating the ashes, Wyatt inadvertently carries out the form as well as the spirit of his penitential act. Wyatt's eating this bread made from the ashes parodies the ceremonial action of the Eucharist: the Sacrament that conveys to the believer the Body as well as the Blood of Christ; the Sacrament that signifies Christ's gift of eternal life to mankind through His death and resurrection. That Wyatt eats the bread made from his father's ashes is Gaddis's satiric response to the ultimate question of faith. In this bizarre way Wyatt becomes one with the Father/father.[29]

Adding to the distress and comedy of the situation is the outrageous punning on the protagonist's newly acquired name, Stephan Asche: the name on the forged passport that Mr. Yák has prepared for him (795). Black humor intensifies as apparently random happenings begin to coalesce. We recall that Stephen was Reverend Gwyon and his wife Camilla's original choice of the name for their son (27). Now, thirty-three years later, the counterfeiter Mr. Sinisterra (known as Mr. Yák) restores Stephen's name by giving him a forged passport.[30] Mr. Sinisterra was responsible for Camilla Gwyon's death thirty years before, when he posed as a ship's surgeon and accidentally killed her during an operation for appendicitis. Recollection of these happenings increases the dual tone of seriousness and humor that accompanies the bizarre communion of father and son.

The absurdities surrounding Wyatt's quest for communion with his father and its parodic connections with the Eucharist help develop the broader ironic contrast between Wyatt and the hero of the third-century *Recognitions* who affirms his belief in God and is united with his father as well. The ironic contrast also is developed by means of Wyatt's futile quest for Camilla, as opposed to Clement's successful meeting with his mother after years of separation. Wyatt's longing for his mother also connects to his implicit desire for help from Mary, the Blessed Virgin.

The Virgin Mary's divine motherhood, the belief that Mary intercedes on behalf of man and dispenses God's grace with a mother's love, provides a range of associations that connect to Wyatt's sense of the mystical presence of his mother, who died when he was three. As a child, he believes he has a vision of his dead mother. As an adult, he notices that his paintings of the Madonna resemble Camilla. Wyatt seems to pursue intimations of Camilla as he would suggestions of divine motherhood. He seems to be appealing to Mary's intercessory power, higher than all other saints. The mystique around Camilla, envisioned by Wyatt, is ironically fulfilled when the Church mistakes her body for that of the eleven-year-old Spanish girl whom it has declared a saint and accidentally canonizes Camilla in her place (791–92).

An absurdist vision and a black humor tone emerge as we recall the description of the violent killing of the little Spanish girl and the odd reaction that greets the announcement of her canonization years later. The girl is assaulted on her way home from her first Communion by a man who believes intercourse with a virgin will cure his disease (16), a rationale evidently used by others in history. The narrator explains that New Yorkers, like Mr. Pivner, avidly read newspaper accounts of the Spanish girl's beatification, not because she will be a saint but because they are anxious to gather information about her rape and murder (291).

Incongruities between the sacred and the profane reach farcical proportions in the cemetery near Camilla's grave, as Wyatt, seeker of salvation, accidentally meets and befriends Mr. Yák, who becomes virtually a guide and a father surrogate for him. Mr. Yák's actions as guide are in direct contrast to those of Clement's guide, Saint Peter; Mr. Yák does not explicate the Law but evades the law. In San Zwingli, Spain, as in New York City, he is in disguise. In false mustache and toupee, he gestures rigidly and automatically like a mechanical slapstick actor: he keeps "tugging at his mustache [. . .] and then pressing it anxiously back in place" and, we are told, he "might have worn a hat, but for fear his hair [might] come off with it when it was removed" (777–78). The counterfeiter, Mr. Yák, is a Bergsonian caricature of "something mechanical encrusted on the living,"[31] a comic buffoon, the object of laughter.

Laughter, essentially, is·a reaction to perceived contradictions or incongruities, and these reach an extreme in the interchanges between Wyatt and Mr. Yák. Wyatt, the idealist, feels burdened by the sinful accumulation in the fallen world, while Mr. Yák, the materialist, has always easily accommodated himself to sin, as when, after accidentally killing Camilla, he crosses himself and murmurs, *"The first turn of the screw pays all debts"* (5), or when, sought for counterfeiting charges, he leaves New York for Spain, thinking of himself as a pilgrim on a voyage to the "Eternal City, in a Holy Year, [. . .] like those early pilgrims to the Holy Land" (496), or when, thirty years after killing Camilla, he justifies his counterfeiting activities to Wyatt: "I'm not a bum. [. . .] I'm a craftsman, an artist like, see? . . . and they got jealous of my work" (785). Mr. Yák is a caricature of the twentieth-century decadent, in contrast to the devout young artist who yearns for salvation. Brought together, these dissimilar figures generate laughter, but the laughter wavers when we comprehend that Wyatt, who searches for communion with father and mother, is virtually adopted by the degenerate Mr. Yák.

Mr. Yák shows paternal interest in Wyatt, who, in contrast to Yák's own son, Chaby Sinisterra, is intelligent and industrious. A comic-ironic tone develops as this degenerate surrogate father keeps telling the sensitive aesthetician, the deeply religious Wyatt: "I knew you weren't a bum" (786). It is equally strange that the surrogate father, essentially a father of lies, continually insists, "I'm an artist," when in reality he is a counterfeiter. Wyatt's accidental meeting with his surrogate father, Mr. Yák, and the incongruities that ensue contribute to a frenzied tone of black humor, as memories of death and distress mingle with details of farce. Irony seems to be implied by the surroundings themselves, particularly the fact that villagers of San Zwingli seem unaware that their Catholic town is named after Huldreich Zwingli, the

Swiss Protestant reformer whose treatises argued against the major tenets of Catholicism.

An ironic allusiveness emerges as events in Wyatt's twentieth-century world are recognized as being in stark opposition to those in the third-century *Clementine Recognitions*. This emphasizes the difference between people in early Church history, who looked to Scripture for guidance, and those in the twentieth century, like Mr. Pivner, who lack spiritual inclination and turn to newspapers as a guide for a meaningful life. Intertextuality emphasizes the comic incongruity between the early Christians who affirmed their faith when told of miracles, like the appearance of a tomb at the beatification of Saint Clement, and those twentieth-century readers who are feverishly drawn to the story of the little Spanish girl's canonization for its sensational details.

The intertextual focus also emphasizes the contradiction between the early Christian treatises, which handle the story of Saint Clement with reverence, and Gaddis's black humor novel, which uses the subject of saints as material for comedy. The little Spanish girl, whose body is left behind in the graveyard, is a comic counterpart to Saint Clement. Her body remains in the graveyard while Camilla's is mistakenly taken in her place to be canonized in Rome: "When they took her out of the graveyard here to put her somewhere else when she was beatified they thought she looks [*sic*] kind of big for an eleven-year-old girl, but the way the body was preserved after forty years almost, so that made them sure it's a saint" (791).

The incident is extended to ludicrous proportions as Mr. Yák/Sinisterra carries out his intention of using the "left behind" corpse as a basis for a mummy that he wishes to sell. Mr. Yák exclaims, with glittering eyes and trembling hands, "This is just what we want" (793). Once in his room, in a nearby pensión, Mr. Yák sets up his materials for mummy making. He pours colorless liquid from one test tube to another, changing it to red and then back to colorless. Parodying religious ritual, he chants: "Water into wine, wine into water. [. . .] Water into blood, blood into a solid. Remember the miracle at Bolsena? Watch." He then quickly drops from the sacred to the material details of science: "A little aluminum sulphate dissolved, a few drops of phenolphthalein" (794).

Yák is a cartoon figure: he grabs for his hairpiece, putting it on backward; he uses clichés repeatedly, such as "You're safe as a nut";

and he sounds like a poor imitation of a middle-class businessman as he promotes the fraudulent enterprise of making a mummy: "There's work to do. [. . .] You don't want to do nothing? That's the way you get into mischief. You get into mischief, doing nothing" (795–96).

This farce ends with Yák and Wyatt walking the mummy to the railway station: "Be careful. We pretend it's an old woman, see? Only when we get on the train she's real stiff in the joints, see?" In the train's compartment, Yák, a caricature of a counterfeit man, "patted down the shock of black hair, pressed the mustache, and cleared his throat with satisfaction." The narrator comments on all three of them "looking in what light there was through the smoke like a weary and not quite respectable family. The conductor, at any rate, showed no rude curiosity when he tapped at the glass panel, slid the door open, and took three tickets from Mr. Yák, who had bounded to his feet to meet him" (811–12). When the shawl partially falls off the mummy, a woman gasps, grabs her husband, and they politely leave the compartment: "—And my God! . . . did you see her face?—Syphilis, her husband said" (815).

In Gaddis's black humor novel, chance occurrences seem to coalesce in a bizarre design that is an ironic reversal of the meaning found in literature depicting traditional heroes, such as Saint Clement, in the *Clementine Recognitions*. With Peter as guide, Clement learns about God's goodness, affirms his faith, and is reunited with his parents. In direct opposition, Wyatt Gwyon seems to fulfill the ludicrous role of absurdist hero that Basil Valentine had, by chance, predicted for him: "I suppose you . . . well, let's say you eat your father, canonize your mother, and . . . what happens to people in novels? I don't read them" (262).

Allusions to Alchemy

Gaddis's second major inversion of the allusive mode to develop absurdist comedy is based on medieval alchemy: the traditional pursuit of the redemption of matter and the redemption of the soul.[32] The narrator in *The Recognitions* refers to famous masters such as Raymond Lully—"a poet, a missionary, a mystic" (77)—figures who spoke in religious terms and believed they could bring mankind back to the golden age before the Fall. Such men "had seen in gold the image of the sun, spun in the earth by its countless revolutions, then, when the sun might yet be taken for the image of God" (131–32). The incongruity between the spiritual nature of the traditional alchemical pursuit of gold, on the one hand, and on the other, the material focus in the world of the twentieth-century novel is a source of comic irony. The narrator's crude language underlines the reduction: "once chemistry had established itself as true and legitimate son and heir, alchemy was turned out like a drunken parent." The child, continues the narrator, "had found what the old fool and his cronies were after all the time"; they had found gold in all its varieties. The narrator deflates the present status of gold by ironically juxtaposing it with that of the past: "a cube capable, at the flick of a thumb, of producing a flame, not, perhaps, the *ignis noster* of the alchemists, but a flame quite competent to light a cigarette" (132–33). Contemporary man is satirically portrayed as placing material possessions over spiritual concerns. For the alchemist, on the other hand, "being and having the stone were the same thing."[33]

One of the central figures in *The Recognitions,* Basil Valentine, is obviously linked to the medieval alchemist Basilius Valentinus, who called himself a Benedictine monk. The early alchemist's ostensible concern was with the soul; Basilius admonishes, "You must truly repent you of all your sins, confessing the same, and firmly resolve to lead a good and holy life . . . by opening your hand and your heart to the needy."[34] In contrast, Gaddis's Valentine is purely concerned with matter, with accumulating gold artifacts: a signet ring, cuff links, a cigarette case, a bull figurine.

Gaddis, however, like Pynchon, develops a comic-ironic perspective that relates not only to the present but also to the past. The alchemist Basilius Valentinus, as was mentioned earlier, was a shadowy figure whose background was suspect. He signed his treatises as a Benedictine monk, yet his name never appeared in records of the order.[35] He prefaced his works, including *The Triumphal Chariot of Antimony,* with the admonition that people repent of their sins and lead a virtuous life, yet, according to legend, he may have poisoned monks by giving them an alchemical elixir derived from antimony.

Gaddis's Valentine is a comic variation on Valentinus. He is a Jesuit-educated art critic, a mysterious man who gives the acquisition of wealth top priority in all his dealings. He has a contractual agreement with the dealer Recktall Brown and, for a fee, praises as originals the forgeries (including Wyatt's) that Brown places for sale.

The scheme Valentine and Brown work out goes something like this: Valentine arrives at the showing, engages in discussion with other art critics, who have access to the latest scientific methods of detecting art forgery (for example, X-ray pictures, infrared and ultraviolet rays, different types of microscopes; 250). Valentine states that he is satisfied that the paintings are original; his comments convince others; the forgeries command high prices from patrons of the arts looking for originals. And Valentine shares in the profit with Recktall Brown, whose descriptive name denotes his coarse behavior.

In this satiric novel, Wyatt also enters into an agreement with Recktall Brown, creating paintings that the latter sells as originals. The comic ploy that Gaddis uses is that, despite his desire for salvation through art, Wyatt still agrees to a sinful contract for money with the Devil. When Valentine inquires of Wyatt, "Tell me, does Brown pay you well?" Wyatt responds, "Pay me? I suppose. The money piles up there." When Valentine asks about the money, Wyatt answers: "The money? you . . . can't spend love" (261–62).

Painting, for Wyatt, is a religious act of devotion, an act of purification. By preparing his artist's medium and his study as an alchemist would prepare his complex materials and laboratory, Wyatt sets up an alchemical paradigm that acts as a touchstone for the redemption of his soul.[36] In Wyatt's study, pots of paint are always boiling and changing color; eggs are used to make tempera; and the oil of lavender, used in the base for Wyatt's paints, emits a mysterious "odor of sanc-tity" (270), akin to the fragrance of the holy water used by Egyptian alchemists in processing their color theory of alchemy (248).[37] Black humor develops, however, because despite his intelligence and expertise, Wyatt naïvely agrees to a contract with Brown without appreciating its deleterious effect.

Wyatt is engaged in a refining process. He employs an alchemical paradigm to pursue spiritual purification, a means of virtually leaving behind the sinful accumulations of a fallen world as he uses his imagination to create the world anew in art.[38] His practice of preparing tempera by hand and of creating colors that approximate those of the fifteenth-century artists parallels the experimentation of alchemists, whose series of changes and renewals of matter were aimed at deriving a universal solvent, an "elixir" that would refine matter and cause it and the alchemist to regain a prelapsarian state: achieving heaven's gold and the perfection of Adam and Eve.[39] Like the traditional alchemists, Wyatt is driven by a vision of perfection. However, though Wyatt works feverishly and sleeps little, he increasingly becomes dismayed by the barren existence of an absurd world.

126

At the end of the book, Wyatt seems psychologically shattered by personal disasters: the loss of his paintings, his separation from Esme (the model who shares his yearnings), and his inability to be reconciled with his father or with God. He lives in the Spanish monastery in Estremadura. There he occupies himself by scraping off paint from original masterpieces (for example, a Valdes Leal and an El Greco) in an attempt to free the paintings of the accumulations of time that damage color and obscure beauty. Ironically, Wyatt goes so far in his restoration as to razor blade the paintings themselves and return the canvases to their original emptiness (870–75). Accentuating the grotesquely comic nature of the act, so incongruous with what one believes to be Wyatt's sensitive, artistic nature, is the exclamation of the fat man in a brown suit: "Boy, that big picture was some mess wasn't it, the Rubins" [*sic*] (879).

Now, it would be comforting to believe that Wyatt (Stephen) "is pushing on to a more comprehensive idea of restoration—namely, the restoring of reality to itself," that he is "making a gesture of 'recalling' the 'falsifications' of even the greatest artists."[40] However, the absurdist novel, like Camus's *The Myth of Sisyphus,* withdraws such soothing answers. The recognition here is that when one divests the world of all accumulations, one reaches only an empty purification, signifying nothing. To illuminate the comic absurdity of the endeavor, Gaddis has the character Ludy caution: "But you can't [. . .] take that painting and . . . and do what you're doing" (872).

It is ironic that Wyatt, who forever yearns to "soar in atonement," never meets the devout Stanley, the musician who appears to be his soul mate in the novel. Like Wyatt, Stanley dwells on the past, and, like him, he wishes to reach God through his artistic creation—a Requiem Mass to be played on an organ in the ancient Italian cathedral Fenestrula. Stanley finally completes the work and plays the concerto in the church, without paying attention to the warning of the Italian priest: *"Per favore non bassi . . . e non strane combinazioni di note, capisce"* [Please, no bass . . . and no strange combination of notes, understand] (956). The resounding music causes the structure to collapse: "Everything moved, and even falling, soared in atonement" (956).[41] That the "gigantic" organ in the small church was the "gift" of a well-meaning American adds to the tragicomic character of the scene.

The grotesque, cartoon quality of the cathedral scene is underscored by our recollection of an earlier episode (in France) in which the reader—with a Hobbesian sense of eminency—observes another edifice destroyed by an American's inability to understand a foreign language: Arny, in trying to eliminate smoke from his hotel room, rushes to open the window without reading the sign on it: *"On est prié de n'ouvrir pas ce fenêtre parce que le façade de l'hôtel lui compter pour se supporter"* [It is requested that the window not be opened because the front of the hotel counts on it for support] (942). The narrator explains that "with some effort he opened the window, smoke billowed out, and the facade of Henry's Hotel collapsed" (942). Gaddis further deflates the significance of Stanley's act of atonement by informing the reader that the concerto was recovered and "is still spoken of, when it is noted, with high regard, though *seldom played"* (956; italics added).

We react to Stanley's death as we do to that of his mother, who believes in meeting God for the Last Judgment in as whole a body as possible. Doctors have removed her leg, her appendix, and her tonsils. Finally, after watching her dentures dissolve in a solution a nurse has administered incorrectly, she leaps to her death from the hospital window: "It was too much. She must get where she was going while there was still time" (561).[42]

The quest of Stanley's mother for salvation is a parody of all absurd quests in the novel, ranging from Wyatt's desire to achieve salvation through art and the author Willie's desire to write about salvation in a novel that looks back to the *Clementine Recognitions* and Goethe's *Faust*. Calling attention to his own artifice, the postmodernist Gaddis has Basil Valentine warn that the writer Willie would be ill advised to use the *Clementine Recognitions* and Goethe's *Faust* as sources for his novel because their subject, salvation, is no longer a "practical study." *The Recognitions,* like Stanley's Requiem Mass, will be written for "a rather small audience" (373), one, the novel satirically implies, that will not be influenced by its position in the marketplace.

Goethe's *Faust* and *The Recognitions*

Gaddis's third major inversion of the allusive mode, for satiric purposes, is to Goethe's *Faust,* an epic that celebrates the growth of its hero in this world and his eventual redemption in heaven. Gaddis calls attention to his ironic-comic stratagem by having a character say: "We're shooting *Faust* now, a sort of bop version, we've changed him to this refugee artist" (661). The importance of this farcical intertextual dialogue with *Faust* is stressed at the opening of the novel by means of an epigraph from the "Laboratory" scene where Wagner is making Homunculus.[43]

> MEPHISTOPHELES *(leiser)*: Was gibt es denn? [(whispering) What is it, then?]
> WAGNER *(leiser)*: Es wird ein Mensch gemacht. [(whispering) A man is being made.] *(Recognitions* 3)

Other details that echo Goethe's work include the black poodle Wyatt encounters on the street (135), the intimation that Brown, like Mephistopheles, has "cloven feet" (676), Brown's "contract" with Wyatt, and the allusion, in the first line of Gaddis's novel, to the "Carnival Masque" scene in *Faust* (227–58 [II.i.5065–5986]).

"Even Camilla [Wyatt's mother] had enjoyed masquerades" (3), explains the narrator in the opening line of *The Recognitions*. Camilla liked masquerades "of the safe sort where the mask may be dropped at that critical moment it presumes itself as reality" (3). She would shun, the reader infers, the sort of satire evident in the "Carnival Masque" scene in *Faust,* which discloses the crowd's avarice as they push and scramble for the gold and jewels thrown to them by characters in the parade. She would be grieved by the satirist in Goethe's procession who wishes "to sing, and utter, / That which no one wants to hear" (235 [II.i.5297–98]). This reference cautions us that Gaddis, like Goethe's satirist, will mock the characters as they parade before us.

Many details in Camilla's procession in the Spanish town of San Zwingli echo those in Goethe's "Carnival Masque" scene. The maidens in Goethe's great Roman Masquerade are away from home, in the German court, inhabited by Catholics. The American Camilla is in a *Catholic* ritual march in Spain. The maidens from Florence, however, are beautifully dressed and sell their wares to prospective suitors (232 [II.5198ff.]); Gaddis's grand *"Spanish affair"* in San Zwingli contradicts such promise, for it carries Camilla not to a prenuptial masquerade but to her grave, to be buried (as Protestant Aunt May exclaims) "with a lot of dead Catholics" (3). The contradiction of such meaning develops derisive humor in *The Recognitions*.

Gaddis plays off his piece against *Faust* in order to exhibit the comic futility of Wyatt's yearning for salvation in a world in which vanity and hypocrisy are the norm, and in which God no longer seems to exist. This method develops an intertextual dialogue with the earlier text.[44] Such a conversation is fraught with comic irony.

The early scenes in *Faust* clearly establish that God is watching man's activities, that He will reward good and punish evil. The "Prologue in Heaven" contrasts the following: God's goodness and the Devil's evil; God's creativity and Mephistopheles's urge toward destruction; God's assertion of man's sufficiency to stand firm against dark inclinations, his ability to advance toward the "true way" (14 [I.329]), and the Devil's wish to tempt Faust to damnation. These early passages in the drama emphasize the importance of man's activity in this world as preparation for eternity. The Lord explains to Mephistopheles: "While Man's desires and aspirations stir, / He cannot choose but err" (13 [I.317]). A "good man" (14 [I.328]) has the ability to advance toward the light of salvation. This idea is reiterated by the angelic choral as it tells Faust: "Thus is the Master near,— / Thus is He here! (34 [I.806–7]). The affirmation culminates in the final angelic celebration of Faust: "Whoe'er aspires unweariedly / Is not beyond redeeming" (500 [II.v.11936–37]). These lines stress celestial love and grace as angels bear Faust's immortal essence to heaven.

Faust, in Part I, vacillates between romantic hopes of heavenly ascent and pessimism and despair over the straitened circumstances of life (62 [I.1545]). Dissatisfied with the natural world while at the same time mocking man's delusion about higher things, he spurns man's belief in God: "Cursed, also, Hope!—cursed Faith, the spectre! / And cursed be Patience most of all!" (64 [I.1605–6]). The chorus cries out that Faust has destroyed "the beautiful world" (64 [I.1609]). As the epic progresses, however, the hero learns patience and turns from self-absorption to concern for his fellowmen and for God.

Before signing the contract with Mephistopheles, Faust makes the following stipulation: "When on an idler's bed I stretch myself in quiet, / There let, at once, my record end! / . . . Canst thou with rich enjoyment fool me, / Let that day be the last for me!" (66–67 [I.1692–97]). It is to this that Faust signs his name in blood. As a result of his pact with Mephistopheles, Faust travels and partakes of a range of pleasures: carousing in taverns, participating in festivals at the imperial court, wooing the innocent Gretchen, and meeting and wedding the beautiful Helen of Troy. Yet, throughout, whether with Gretchen or later with Helen, Faust is never satisfied with this world. He continually aspires and thus never loses to the Devil. This need to be ever aspiring brings him close to God and, eventually, wins him salvation.

Goethe, in a conversation with Eckermann, explains the religious significance of Faust's actions. He indicates that the continual striving, the refusal to be satisfied with the offerings of a fallen world, shows a divine spark in Faust and makes him worthy of redemption: the striving "becomes constantly higher and purer . . . and from above there is eternal love coming to his aid."[45] For Goethe, this conforms to the religious belief that divine grace is needed to assist man to heavenly bliss. Goethe acclaims the heroic potential in man and God's "eternal love."[46]

Wyatt also makes a pact with the Devil. Recktall Brown finds Wyatt in his apartment, despondent and despairing. He offers him a "contract" in the form of a business agreement. He proposes that Wyatt shall create his own art works. Recktall Brown, the art dealer, will sell these as newly discovered originals, and Wyatt will share in the profits.

The incongruity between Recktall Brown's materialistic perspective and Wyatt's spiritual orientation gives a comic-grotesque edge to the contractual episode. This is evident in the incommunicative dialogue in which Brown and Wyatt engage as they use the term "significance." Brown informs Wyatt: "We're talking business. [. . .] Money gives significance to anything." Wyatt, missing the point, tries to explain: "A work of art redeems time." Brown responds, "And buying it redeems money" (144).

Wyatt's involvement with the art dealer is as serious for him as is Faust's with Mephistopheles. Gaddis parallels the important actions of Wyatt with the farcical behavior of the minor character Otto, just as Goethe burlesques Faust's actions with those of his comic counterpart Wagner.[47] Otto is a caricature of Wyatt in almost all respects. Wyatt is a sincere artist; Otto, a pretentious plagiarist whose work sounds unusually familiar to all who hear it. Wyatt travels to Spain because he wishes to become spiritually close to the journey of his father and mother; Otto goes off to a banana plantation in South America so that he can look glamorous when he returns to New York. Wyatt is loved by the model Esme; Otto, after what he believes was a night of memorable lovemaking, finds that Esme does not even remember who he is (207). Otto also makes a travesty of the search for the father motif, so important for Wyatt. Otto and his father, Mr. Pivner, hope to recognize each other by their green scarves. However, when Otto, in the lavatory, sees Pivner looking intently at him (actually "staring [. . .] down at the bit of wool protruding from the coat's pocket") he fears the man intends to accost him sexually and thus looks at him with contempt. This frightens the father: "After a shrugged fluster and buttoning beside him, he [Otto] was alone" (566–67).

Comic parallels to Wyatt's conduct also are created by the contract between Recktall Brown and his servant, Fuller. Brown, who first meets Fuller while on a Caribbean cruise, buys the ignorant Fuller with a "set of gold teeth, and a promise of magic" (223). Their contract is that Fuller will work for him, submit to his punishments, and Brown, in turn, will turn his servant's skin white. Fuller's belief in the magical ability of Brown and of his black poodle provides comic relief for the evil power of Brown over Wyatt like that of Goethe's Mephistopheles over Faust (Mephistopheles, of course, transforms himself into a poodle before the "Pact Scene" in *Faust*). Fuller believes that the "poodle and their master communicated" (223). He asks the poodle: "You goin to write it down in your report. [. . .] Some day I goin to discover where you keep it and destroy every page" (345).

In Wyatt's first and last meetings with Recktall Brown, the scenes overflow with Faustian echoes that relate Brown to Mephistopheles and Wyatt to Faust. A brittle humor develops, in spite of the danger to Wyatt, because of the exaggerated details that make the characters appear to be cartoon figures of the Faustian originals. When Brown first knocks at Wyatt's study door, something ominous causes Wyatt to draw "back as though threatened" (140). Then, as a parody of the Devil, Brown complains that people say bad things about him: "You'd think I was wicked as hell, even if what I do for them turns out good" (141). In addition, a strange thing happens to Brown's face as he confirms the contract with Wyatt: "His eyes, which had all this time seemed to swim without focus behind the heavy lenses, shrank to sharp points of black, and like weapons suddenly unsheathed they penetrated instantly wherever he turned them" (146). This calls attention to Mephistopheles and his spirit dog, which had "fiery eyes" and was "terrible to see" (51 [I.1255]).

In Goethe's drama, Faust, alone in his study, picks up the Bible and labors to translate the opening verse in the Gospel of Saint John (50 [I.1224]). Wyatt contradicts this religious tone, when, in a parallel situation, he chants: "*Dog! Dog! Dog!*" The narrator observes that "no sound contested his challenge [. . .] for spelling the Name of God backwards, no response to God, if not the Name, reversed three times" (139).[48] The black poodle in the study scene and the "contract" with Brown foreshadow the later allusions to Mephistopheles during the

Christmas party, the locale where expectation of Wyatt's possible atonement is—in a comic-grotesque manner—reduced to nothing.

The deflation of the sacred at the Christmas party sets the tone
for Wyatt's mock heroism and his ironic quest for redemption. At the
party Brown (seeming to have the fearful concern of the Devil) swerves
as he passes the low Bosch tabletop of the Seven Deadly Sins near the
fireplace (663). Valentine, as though reacting to the allusion, asks:
"What the devil's the matter with you." The dark humor increases as
Brown replies: "Not a God damn thing the matter with me." Brown's
laughter, calling to mind hell fires, rises "in an eructation of smoke"
(663–64). When he pulls on his prized suit of armor over his legs,
one guest states that he might be "wearing false calves" like Mephistopheles in "that ponderous thing by Goethe [. . .] to cover his cloven
feet" (676).

In this context, surrounded by party-goers whose banality is
transparent, such as Mr. and Mrs. Schmuck, Wyatt tries to redeem
himself by revealing that the valued paintings Brown is selling are
forgeries, and that he, Wyatt, is the forger. The scene develops more
cartoon qualities as the distressed Wyatt, eyes aglitter, wearing one suit
on top of another, tries to inform the people that the paintings are
frauds. The incongruity between the seeker of salvation and the crass,
moneyed people causes bitter laughter. For these people, the sensitive
artist is a "lunatic come back again," a person ready to "go up in
flames." Wyatt's attempted atonement is the object of ridicule: "Won't
do, won't do at all . . . can't hev this sort of thing, invading a private
gathering, eh? A man's home is his mphht what d'you-call- it, don't you
know," observes one man, unable to complete the literary allusion. The
man then turns to a fellow guest: "I say, my dear fellow do be a bit
more careful, you're spilling your drink all over me" (676–77). The
seeking of atonement at this sacrilegious Christmas party is ludicrous.
Some people "turn their attention, and some their backs, on this di-
verting visitor who stood looking feverishly round, holding up a hand-
ful of charred wood, whispering—Where is he? [. . . .] Brown!" (677).

Wyatt and Brown—Faust and Mephistopheles—face each other.
The scene evokes echoes of Goethe's *Faust*, when Mephistopheles tries
to prevent the saved Faust from being carried off to heaven. In *The
Recognitions*, however, all becomes slapstick. Mephistopheles is de-
terred from evil action not because angels carry the hero away but
because the devil himself, who has just managed to put on a suit of

armor, crashes from his perch on the balcony to the room below and lands not far from the Bosch tabletop of the Seven Deadly Sins, near the rising flames of the fireplace (677).

There is an important difference between the ridicule in *Faust* and that in *The Recognitions*. Goethe balances indignation at man's greedy activities with a vision of man's possible goodness and creativity in this world, and his eventual redemption in heaven. *The Recognitions,* on the other hand, emphasizes man's futile efforts in a meaningless world. The major difference between Faust and Wyatt is that Faust achieves redemption while Wyatt does not.

Some critics believe that Wyatt, at the close, does progress toward hope and renewal. They point to his remarks to the popular religious novelist Ludy—"Love, and do what you want. [. . .] Now at last, to live deliberately. [. . .] Yes, we'll simplify" (899–900).[49] They point to the time Wyatt spends with the Spanish woman Pastora, finally living for the moment, instead of always thinking of the past. However, an intertextual reading of *The Recognitions* and Goethe's *Faust* clarifies that Wyatt's situation is a comic deflation of Faust's.

Faust's pact with Mephistopheles to remain ever aspiring speaks obliquely to Wyatt's activities after he leaves New York City for Spain. Wyatt's new philosophy to "love, and do what you want" (899), to luxuriate with Pastora, emphasizes taking joy in the "moment" and abandoning his former aspirations. In response to Mr. Yák's warning— "You don't want to let yourself go to hell like this, do you hear me?"— Wyatt says, "No, [. . .] It's just the other way" (803). He believes that he and Pastora are in love.

At first glance, this change in Wyatt seems to be healthy. He has shifted from being a withdrawn recluse, engaged solely in his art, to being an active lover. He even insists that giving love to Pastora can atone for withholding it from another woman in the past, thus expiating his guilt for the mistreatment of Esme (guilt similar to Faust's because of his neglect of Gretchen). On the other hand, however, Wyatt, in thinking only of being with Pastora, shows the contentment with the moment that Faust withstands.

Wyatt's aim to live deliberately burlesques his former yearning for the ideal past. In addition, according to the Faustian pact, to be caught up entirely in life is damning. It shows no yearning for eternal love or divine grace. The allusions to *Faust* thus ironically comment on Wyatt's final "affirmation." The reader recalls Faust's caution to Euphorion— "touch but with thy toe the surface, / Like the son of Earth, Antaeus"

(406 [II.9610–11])—which locates Faust in relation to both the physical and spiritual, this world and the next. Faust grows to appreciate the importance of the two. Wyatt, on the other hand, never does.

The tragicomic absurdity of Wyatt's situation is also underlined by the comparison he makes between himself and the great epic hero Odysseus. When with Pastora, he thinks of himself as Odysseus, but with a significant twist. In contrast to Odysseus's slaying the suitors whom Penelope has kept in abeyance, Wyatt connects himself to the suitors and wishes "to supersede where they [lovers of the prostitute Pastora] failed, lie down where they left." He intends to live the moments through "where they happened," insisting, "It's only the living it [sin] through that redeems it" (898).[50]

Wyatt's activities in the last stages of his quest parody the meaningful close of Faust's life on earth when he is welcomed to heaven by the angelic choir. There is a sharp irony in Gaddis's novel through contrast with the last vision of Faust amid the melodious strains of the angelic chorus:[51]

> All things transitory
> But as symbols are sent:
> Earth's insufficiency
> Here grows to Event:
> The Indescribable,
> Here it is done:
> The Woman-Soul leadeth us
> Upward and on! (506 [II.v.12104–11])

The last glimpse we have of Wyatt is at the Spanish monastery where he, intent on "restoring" paintings, razor blades them into fragments. His reach for the spiritual through the restoration of art, like his earlier quest for connection with the Reverend Gwyon, culminates in bizarre action. In the earlier scene at the monastery, he becomes one with the father/Father in a parody of the Eucharist. In this later effort at spiritual satisfaction, he cuts away at the creative work of great artists, literally denuding the canvas of Rubens's nudes. He destroys rather than restores. The fact that Wyatt meticulously razors the paintings, despite the warnings of Ludy and the exclamations of the man in the brown suit, shows how rigid and mechanical this Bergsonian figure has become. Wyatt's actions confuse the reader, causing him not to know whether to laugh or cry at the humor emerging in the artist's absurd quest for meaning.

Wyatt, throughout his life, looked at the Bosch tabletop of the Seven Deadly Sins (owned first by Reverend Gwyon and later by Recktall Brown). He always trembled while observing the eye of Christ in the center of the tabletop, and reading the inscription: *"Cave, Cave, D^s videt"* [Take care, take care, God is watching] (25). Now, at the end of the book, Wyatt no longer believes in God's presence. Not only does he feel that God is not watching him, but he also concludes that the masters of the golden age of Flemish art created paintings that seemed to show a vain effort in handling the "fear there was no God" (875).

For Wyatt, the world seems analogous to a hellish sea in which celestial people would be doomed to drown, just as Saint Clement drowned in the Black Sea with an anchor around his neck. But in Wyatt's twentieth-century world there is no miraculous sepulcher, no salvation. Instead, there are only continual parties and chance meetings; people often seem to be all afloat in the dusky ambiance of a Stygian flood. The narrator relates: "Like undersea flora, figures stood weaving, rooted to the floor, here and there one drifting as though caught in a cold current, sensing [. . .] what one expressed as— Something submarine, as he paddled the air before him, and went on" (656–57). People glide past one another like variously colored fish, blinded by self-preoccupation.

In this setting, the hero's journey has been reduced to the movement from one party to the next. His company includes crass members of society: Cremer, the art critic who requires a percentage of a painter's sale price for a good review; Radcliffe graduates who misspell words and perversely place a *t* in *genial;* and a husband and wife who separate when each publishes a novel with the other as protagonist.

The Recognitions presents a world in which the artist Wyatt continually searches for meaning, a glimpse of a lost paradise, a sign that God is watching. Instead he finds only randomness. People are recognized by surface details of trivia (a green scarf, a fedora hat, a gold signet ring, a large diamond ring) and by their cartoon behavior (repeating an unusual pronunciation such as "Chr-ah-st" or showing a propensity to make counterfeit twenty-dollar bills). Such a flattening of human beings deflates the dignity of man.

The Recognitions is a book about false resurrections, such as the mistaken canonization of Camilla Gwyon in place of the young girl chosen by the Church. It is a book about counterfeiters who parody God's creation. It is a book about the ironic desire to soar in atonement in a world in which God is not watching, a world in which God may never have been watching.

The Recognitions is a comic epic about a world in which people are guided by a Bible of commercialism whose readers range from the monks in the Spanish monastery in Estremadura to the inhabitants of crowded tenements in New York City. In Estremadura, a monk enthusiastically peruses the books of a visiting religious novelist with the hope of finding a copy of *Como Ganar Amigos y Vencer Todos los Otros* [How To Win Friends and Influence People] (859). In Manhattan, Mr. Pivner avidly reads Dale Carnegie's explanation about "a new way of life," an alchemical "elixir" (the narrator sarcastically interjects) that exchanges "the things worth being for the things worth having." Continuing the ironic reversal of the sacred to the material, Carnegie emphasizes: "You owe it to yourself, to your happiness, to your future, and *TO YOUR INCOME!*" (498–500).

In this upside-down world, a minor and rather negative character—Benny—proclaims: "We're comic. We're all comics. We live in a comic time. And the worse it gets the more comic we are" (640).[52] Thus does Gaddis use jest to spend his rage, as he recognizes the absurdist vision that emerges from the contrast between the ideal and its loss.

CHAPTER SEVEN

The Absurd Quest and Black Humor in Ken Kesey's *Sometimes a Great Notion*

Sometimes a Great Notion—more so than the novels of John Barth, Thomas Pynchon, and William Gaddis—focuses on traditional heroic subjects: the conflict between two brothers, the Oedipal bind, and the reaction to the death of a loved one. Its tone however, like that of the other postmodern novels, is one of black humor. It also shares with these novels an encyclopedic, epic scope and an absurdist vision.

Sometimes a Great Notion (1964), which has received less critical attention than *One Flew Over the Cuckoo's Nest* (1962),[1] stresses an encyclopedic spectrum of expectations and hopes that fail. Examples include Indian Jenny's reliance on magic, Jonas Stamper's appeal to Old Testament affirmations, Joe Ben's belief in New Testament fundamentalism, and the union's message of mutual support. Kesey portrays the courage, energy, and aspirations of Henry and Hank Stamper but then ironically makes the reader aware of the frailty of these characters in an alien universe. Frustrated hopes are a constant reminder of what has been defined as the nature of the absurd: "The senselessness of the human condition and the inadequacy of the rational approach."[2] Kesey conveys the phantasmagorical aspects of this phenomenon with a mixture of pain and humor, virtually combining Kafka and Mark Twain.[3] This black humor tone gives compelling power to the epic novel, *Sometimes a Great Notion*, just as it did for Kesey's shorter and more popular novel, *One Flew Over the Cuckoo's Nest*.

A comic-absurdist vision is evident in the opening passages of *Sometimes a Great Notion*. The narrator invites the reader to *"come look"* at the tributaries of the Wakonda Auga, *"a river smooth and seeming calm, hiding the cruel file-edge of its current"* (1). The reader gradually notices an arm placed dangling from a pole, outside an upper window of the Stamper house. All the fingers of the hand but the middle one are tied down, giving the world "the finger," making a "gesture of grim and humorous defiance" (9). The finger defies not only an absurd universe but also the hostile Wakonda townspeople, who support the lumber union and oppose the independent Stampers. The severed arm of old Henry Stamper, tied in place by his son Hank, succeeds in conveying the double-edged aspect of horror and the comic. This *"macabre prank"*[4] pictorially reflects the black humor tone in *Sometimes a Great Notion*.[5]

Kesey, like the other American black humor novelists, alludes to our post–World War II era, in which the memory of the bombing of Hiroshima looms: *"that mighty first boom was only the first faintest murmur of an explosion that is still roaring down on us, and always will be"* (505). These concerns about modern technological destruction contrast with the heroic, pioneering spirit and the courageous desire to return to nature. With cynical humor, the narrator observes, *"Who played at Dan'l Boone in a forest full of fallout?"* (116).[6]

Two scenes in *Sometimes a Great Notion* show the ephemerality of life and man's ludicrous and ineffectual attempts to cope with a senseless universe. The episodes—one from Hank Stamper's youth, the other from his adulthood—act as touchstones for the comic-absurd. The first describes pet bobcats that Hank has retrieved by tunneling through blackberry vines. Hank and his uncle construct a cage for them that sits "majestically" on four high legs near the river's edge. Hank is worried that the kittens might drown; to reassure himself as he returns home, he reasons: "The river would have to rise a good fifteen feet to reach even the legs, and by that time the house, the barn, probably the whole town of Wakonda would be washed away." The narrator satirically points out that the boy, following this logical reasoning, says: "I guess I'll go on in an' hit the sack" (101). The next day "the boats

[are] fine and the river [isn't] much higher than usual." Hank runs out to the bobcats. However, *"the whole bank where the cage stood is gone; the new bank shines bright and clean . . .* [as if cut by] *a huge moon-stropped razor"* (102). The kittens have drowned.

In the second scene—the woodcutting incident—Hank, his aged father, Henry, and cousin Joe Ben work against the union to fulfill their logging contract with Wakonda Pacific. Working together in the forest, the three Stampers feel in perfect harmony. "The three of them meshed, dovetailed . . . into one of the rare and beautiful units of effort . . . [like] a jazz group . . . swinging together completely" (476). Suddenly the tone changes. The splintered bark from a fallen tree causes the buzz saw to jump out of Hank's hand and bound onward to sever Henry's arm. The accident is described in surreal details: "a bright yellow-white row of teeth appear splintering over the mossy lips to gnash the saw from his hands fling it furiously to the ground it claws screaming machine frenzy and terror trying to dig escape from the vengeful wood" (478). The "runaway log" springs downhill, slams into Joe Ben, and pins him under water.

Joe Ben is a member of Brother Walker's "Pentecostal Church of God and Metaphysical Science"; he is a fundamentalist believer who sees signs of God's goodness in all, including "the number of Rice Krispies that might have snapped, crackled, and popped over the top of his bowl onto the breakfast table ('Four of 'em! See? See? It's the fourth month and this is my fourth bowl of cereal and Jesus said to Lazarus, Come forth')" (276). When, as a youngster, Joe finds horse manure in his Christmas stocking, his eyes glitter with happiness and he runs out to find the pony that got away (282). The author sardonically exploits these cross-references to increase the irony of Joe Ben's actions as he, pinned under the log, finds that his thoughts move from the sacred to the profane: *"He leadeth me through the valley of the shadow!* Come on now, sonny, don't make me laugh; you know better than that bullshit. *It ain't funny! Or bullshit"* (488).

In spite of Hank's efforts to save him, Joe Ben drowns: "A bubbling of hysterical mirth erupted in Hank's face just as he was bending to deliver another breath to Joe. . . . [whose mouth was] open and round with laughing" (488). Joe's laughter, Kesey indicates, shows his gradual perception of the absurd and his attempt to face it, but, iron-ically, the open-mouthed laughter also causes his death.[7]

Multiple levels of absurdity appear in the story: the *metaphysical* conveys the *"treacherous impermanence"* (95)[8] of nature, whose rivers overflow all apparent boundaries on the water-soaked Oregon coast; the *historical* reveals the memory of Hiroshima, which contradicts the productive aspirations of the mid-twentieth-century world; the *psychological* shows the bizarre ramifications of an Oedipal relationship involving Hank, Lee, Myra, and Viv; the *social* demonstrates that absurd men "secrete the inhuman"[9] as the townspeople use the organization of a large labor union to fight the independent activity of the Stamper Lumber Company. Beneath all other ramifications of the absurd is the painful awareness of man's mortality, the realization that tomorrow brings each person closer to death.

One of the ways of dramatizing the tragicomic awareness of man's absurd mortality is the employment of the quest motif: "our recent writers portray the universe as a 'vast practical joke'—and the joke is on everybody, novelist, characters, and readers alike." In such fiction, "any quest at all is the quest absurd."[10] The black humor tone accompanying the absurd quest, so powerful throughout *Sometimes a Great Notion* as a whole, is particularly pronounced in three episodes: Hank's defiant struggle following his attempt to save Joe Ben's life; the experience of Hank and his half-brother, Lee, in their final pilgrimage to the Stamper house; and the awkward family boat trip that precedes Myra's and Lee's eastern journey, their quest for a new life (early in the novel).

Kesey uses Wakonda, a logging town in the Pacific Northwest, to provide a setting for the "heroic quest." In traditional quest literature, the hero leaves the known, undergoes a series of adventures, and returns to his people, where heroism is rewarded. In Kesey's contemporary version there is no reward. In *Sometimes a Great Notion* the protagonists confront an alien universe that renders all heroic aspirations absurd.

Hank's efforts to rescue Joe Ben from the river fail, and he drowns. The narrative commentary that prefaces Hank's ruminations over the death, in Chapter 10,[11] focuses on man's alienation in a universe where heroic potential is constantly shattered by death. By alluding to the *"survivors of Hiroshima"* and that *"mighty first boom"* (505), the bomb that has changed man's world view, Kesey shows how Hank's alienation mirrors the aloneness of contemporary man who experiences the "confrontation between [his] human need and the unreasonable silence of the world."[12] Hank feels isolated from the universe and from mankind as well. The grotesque nature of Hank's aloneness is revealed in his confrontation with the townspeople, who are depicted as caricatures of optimism. This exaggeration accentuates the incongruity between the depressed Hank and these cartoon figures, creating a comic-ironic theme that has Kafkaesque overtones.

There is a tragicomic incongruity between Hank's ruminations (revealed in interior monologue) and the townspeople's optimistic fantasies about an early spring. On the day of Joe Ben's funeral the sun is unusually bright. Now that the Stamper company has submitted to union wishes and called off its deal with Wakonda Pacific, the townspeople look at the November sun and think of the rebirth that comes with an early spring. Their clichéd observations are used by the author to mock their hyperbolic optimism and religious fervor. The real estate man, "tingling with joy and ease," exclaims, "We're out of the woods; around that old corner." Brother Walker cheerfully adds, "The Lord is merciful . . . and eternally *just*." Both men seem to be cartoon figures "beaming their brightest and dreaming of great transactions of earth and air . . . masters of the bright outlook" (507–8). Brother Walker is filled with desire for rebirth, for an affirmation of his religion. He callously states that "the Lord needed the use of Joe to make Hank Stamper see the Light, so to speak" (515). In contrast to these ludicrous banalities is the serious interior monologue of Hank, for whom the bright sun's glare, like that of the atom bomb, shines on a world denuded of life and meaning. For Hank "the sun comes out bright as hell, like it was lit with more than light" (520). Dazzling "like somehow it scrubs both [his] eyeballs," the light pierces Hank; it is an "open-eyed dream," a white light that seems, like "steel wool," to "rub *everything* away" (520–21). For Hank, the world is denuded of meaning, of joy— the sun gives no warmth, only a glare as though all of nature has been washed away. There is no sense of God's love or a Promised Land, only a darkness visible, a hell on earth. Calling upon the reader's knowledge of the culmination of the heroic quest, Kesey ironically frustrates all expectations and presents a bizarre counterpart of hopelessness in a world where randomness prevails—where the chance meeting of a splintered bark and a buzz saw causes devastation.

Camus emphasizes the impossibility "of suppressing the absurd." He insists: "It is essential to know whether one can live with it or whether, on the other hand, logic commands one to die of it,"[13] and states: "There is a direct connection between this feeling [absurdity] and the longing for death."[14] The will to live is achieved through defiance, but simultaneously evident is man's sense of isolation and death.

This underlying pessimism is apparent in the following lines by Lead-belly, with which Kesey prefaces *Sometimes a Great Notion*:

> Sometimes I live in the country,
> Sometimes I live in the town;
> Sometimes I get a great notion
> To jump into the river . . . an' drown.[15]

The second scene to be examined in terms of the absurd shows Hank and his half-brother, Lee, as they make their way to the Stamper household in the last stage of their quests. Hank's quest has been to get the logs to the Wakonda Pacific Company (and, following the accident, to save his cousin Joe Ben from drowning). Lee's quest has been to leave his sheltered eastern academic life, return to Stamper Hall, and assert himself as a man. Hank is for Lee a father image: the one who rescued him from the dune's stovepipe hole when he was a child (303) and from the teenage Dayglo Gang on the beach years later (299). Hank is a courageous individualist who braves the unknown. Ironically, he also is the object of Lee's hatred and vengeance, the half-brother/father figure whom Lee has observed having sexual intercourse with his mother Myra,[16] the man Lee blames for his loss of Myra's love: "I needed it *more* than he did, Viv. But I found . . . that he was too much for me. . . . Because I couldn't . . . ever take his place" (251).

In psychoanalytic theory, a boy's Oedipal fantasies evoke a sexual desire for the mother, followed by a fear of the father. Kesey gives Freudian theory a comic twist by having Lee, in his homeward journey, fantasize about supplanting brother Hank as a sexual partner with Hank's wife, Viv. The incongruity between the seriousness of Lee's past suffering and the trite language he uses to express present fantasies causes laughter. "I'm sprinting hell-bent backwards," Lee observes. "*I'm taking a running jump at the womb*" (293), he continues, as he thinks about Viv. Analyzing his strange situation, Lee exclaims: "All that obscure Oedipal pap . . . might be approaching some kind of truth" (69). To put himself in the place of Hank with Viv seems to offer Lee what Oedipal fantasies often promise: the mother's love and the power of the father.[17] Sharpening the ludicrous quest is Lee's hope that the completion of the fantasy will transform him into a contemporary superhero, "a Captain Marvel" (503).

The ridiculous incongruity of Hank's and Lee's actions underlines the absurdity of the situation. One observes Hank's courage versus Lee's timidity; Hank's fortitude versus Lee's clandestine plan of revenge; Hank's physical and psychological exhaustion versus Lee's puny self-pity; Hank's appreciation of the absurd versus Lee's sorely limited wish fulfillment dream of supplanting his half-brother/father in bed with Viv in order to be transfigured into a superhero.

Kesey contrasts Hank's and Lee's interior monologues and their experiences prior to their journey homeward, the last stage of the quest. Juxtaposed with Hank's heroic endeavors in the woods are Lee's cartoon actions in his pilgrimage from town to Stamper Hall, with his plan to seduce Viv. While Hank valiantly attempts to save Joe Ben and then his maimed father, Lee—limited by his comically exaggerated self-engrossment and feelings of rivalry—ruminates "over dreary cups of drugstore coffee" in town (468). He variously indulges in self-pity and in wish fulfillment fantasies, vacillating between being Billy Batson and being Captain Marvel. Lee's self-indulgent comic book references and juvenile clichés make his endeavors laughable. Then farce and pathos seem to collide, and readers find themselves disoriented and strangely disconcerted by the phantasmagorical quality of black humor that becomes prominent in the homeward journeys of Hank and Lee.

In town, Lee hurries out into the rain, exclaiming: "Viv, here I come, ready or not" (477). Then he trudges home, grimly telling himself he can make it, "by gosh." At the same time, Hank, in the forest, is attempting to explain to Joe Ben that he cannot succeed in freeing him: "I can't! The log here! . . . I mean look at the goddam waterline where I have to" (481). Lee makes his pilgrimage along the wet highway, "stoically" refusing a ride to punish himself "with rain and cold for the sin" he plans to commit with Viv (489). At the time, Hank is trying valiantly to cope with the reality of Joe Ben's death and also with his awareness of the treacherous ease with which nature covers her tracks in the smooth surface of water that covers Joe: "He stared, frowning, at the now placid spot where the strange laughter had exploded" (488).

The conflicting scenes take on surreal proportions as Hank swims across the Wakonda River and enters the house. Then, with bizarre swiftness, everything collapses to a cartoon scene. Kesey depicts Lee as a Billy Batson whose metamorphosis to a superhero fails to materialize: "I don't know what I expected—perhaps to actually find myself swollen to Captain Marvel magnitude, flying away replete with cape, spit-curl, and neon-orange leotard." Lee thinks to himself: "It was the end of my incantations . . . finishing the last half of a broken 'Shazam!' that all-powerful word that would transform Billy" (503). The use of comic book language and simplistic wish fulfillment thinking contributes to the farcical quality of the situation.

The bedroom scene moves swiftly to the painful aspects of the absurd. Hank peers at Lee through the same hole in the wall that Lee had formerly used to spy on his mother and Hank (500). On a psychological level, this touches on what Freud analyzes as being central to the uncanny: the "inner repetition-compulsion" that brings one back to the same situation whether it is being lost and returning to the same street or coming across a number or a name several times. This "involuntary return" causes a "feeling of helplessness and of something uncanny."[18] It adds a strange dimension to the ludicrous position of Lee, who, after seducing Viv (the mother surrogate), admits that rather than feeling akin to Captain Marvel, he has "merely created another Billy Batson" (503), "a scrawny and ineffectual punk" (135).[19] The "involuntary return" to the same helplessness in the bedroom scene (even though the brothers' positions are reversed) develops the comic-grotesque ramifications of the situation.

In this bedroom scene, Hank, who has struggled against nature and society, realizes that *"strength ain't real"* in an alien world. Cuckolded and defeated, he perceives his helplessness in relation to the treacherous impermanence of life. As he realizes that all that he cherishes, suddenly and without warning or reason, can vanish—his bobcats, his cousin Joe Ben, and even the love of his wife, Viv—he is overcome by retching (502–3).[20] Hank's experiences border on the tragic, but, unlike tragedy, Kesey's absurdist work makes no final affirmation of meaning, order, or divine intervention.[21] There is only the uncanny unpredictability of nature and the impermanence of life, forces that undo the heroic quests in *Sometimes a Great Notion*.

The trip toward Stamper Hall, at the end of Hank's and Lee's trials, is in ironic contrast to the early family boat ride away from the Stamper house, at the first stage of Lee's quest (the third scene to be examined). To describe the retreat of twelve-year-old Lee and his mother, Myra, across the Wakonda Auga River (37–40), Kesey moves back and forth in time, creating a quality of "anesthetized time" (35), in which past, present, and future events merge. Kesey describes Lee as wanting to separate his mother, Myra, from her twenty-four-year-old stepson, Hank, with whom she has engaged in an incestuous relationship. The young Lee meditates on fantasies of revenge: "Shazam . . . *my* magic phrase that would turn me instantly enormous and invulnerable" (135).

To burlesque Lee's situation, the author exploits its ironic connections to that of classical heroes. Lee thinks: "My one great hero, Captain Marvel, still head and shoulders above such late starters as Hamlet or Homer. . . . Shazam: S for Solomon and wisdom; H for Hercules and strength; and so on with Atlas, Zeus, Achilles, and Mercury" (135).

The early boat trip scene shows that each member of the Stamper family is involved in a futile quest and, also, that each member's sense of alienation causes him to engage continually in the incommunicative dialogue of the absurd. The departure of wife and son brings to full circle old Henry Stamper's quest East (fourteen years earlier, at age fifty-one) for a wife to care for his ten-year-old son Hank. The narrator explains, ironically leveling (and thus reducing) all Myra's acquisitions in the East, that Henry had convinced the attractive twenty-one-year-old coed to leave her three horses, two lovers, and a parrot to depart for the exciting wilds of Wakonda, from which, fourteen years later, she flees.

At sixty-five, Henry still thinks of himself as a robust hero, one of those western loggers with the independence of a frontiersman.[22] He, therefore, never doubts Myra's ostensibly sensible reason for leaving Wakonda: to find an eastern school for their twelve-year-old son, Lee. No question of "his young wife's fidelity ever penetrated the old man's cock-certainty," explains the narrator with bawdy humor, "for the fourteen years she lived in his wooden world." When his friend Boney Stokes insists, "You can't be the stud you once was—ain't you concerned for her . . . alone over yonder?" old Henry replies that some men are "so special, they can keep a woman pantin' with the *pure mem'ry* an' the *wild hope* that what has happened once is liable to happen again!" (35).

Hank also is unaware of the full dynamics of the flight. It is doubtful that he surmises that Lee hates him because of the clandestine affair with Myra, for he thinks of himself as Lee's big brother protector.[23] That each of the Stampers is enveloped in his own "notion" makes it difficult for the family members to harmoniously communicate on an emotional level. Myra apologizes to Henry for having so much baggage and quickly adds: "But I'll be back as soon as possible. I'll be back just as soon as possible." Henry winks at Hank and says,

"Can't go too long on san'wiches an' salad when she's used to steak an' potatoes" (37).

To expand the boat scene, Kesey presents the interior monologue of Lee, projected into the future, as he thinks back on his father's superficial comments about the eastern schooling the boy supposedly wanted: " 'Well now'—old Henry spaces his words between oar strokes. 'Well now, Leland'—in a detached, remote, inviolable voice— 'I'm sorry you think you need'—cords snapping in his neck as he leans backward with the pull—'need a back East schooling . . . but that's the long and short of it, I reckon.' . . . *A litany spoken over me, Lee thinks later, listened to only for the rhythm . . . anesthetized time"*(38–39).

> (Now it's done, Hank thought. . . . Now it's finished, and I won't ever see no more of her again.) . . . They row through the glittering water. And reflections swirling gently among the flower petals. Jonas rows alongside, muffled from the neck down in green fog: *You have to know.* Lee meets himself coming back across twelve years after with twelve years of decay penciled on his pale face. . . . *You have to know there is no profit and all our labor avoideth naught.* Jonas pulls, straining at the fog. Joe Ben goes into a state park with a brush knife and an angel's face, seeking freedom. Hank crawls through a tunnel of blackberry vines. . . . "I'm hollowed out with loneliness," the woman cries. The water moves. The boat moves with measured heaves. (39)

The passage alludes to many examples of the comic-absurd quest. There is the cross-reference to Lee's grandfather Jonas, who leaves Kansas because he believes the pamphlet messages promising a new life in the frontier westward in Oregon where "There is Elbow Room For a Man To Be As Big And Important As He Feels It Is In Him To Be!" (20). Once there, he ironically realizes that all "had sounded good on paper" (19). This waterlogged land of Wakonda frightens him and he flees. Parodying the last stage of a hero's quest, Jonas undergoes an ironic "return" to his people when his body is shipped back and buried in the very river that was his means of escape (24–26). The reference in the passage to Joe Ben reveals his hopes that his knife-marred face will enable him to start life anew and break the pattern set by his handsome, debauched father, who died in a cabin strewn with girlie magazines (Joe, of course, dies as a result of the buzz saw accident). The reference to Hank's quest recalls his laborious tunneling through blackberry vines to secure the bobcat kittens that later drown.

During the pauses in Old Henry's conversation, Kesey inserts the interior thoughts of Lee and his half-brother, Hank. The brothers' contrary fantasies, or notions, estrange them and cause their conversations to be incommunicative dialogue of the comic-absurd. For Lee, his rival brother, Hank (lover of his mother), seems to lack humanity and threatens his own male identity. Hank, on the other hand, sees himself as a helping father/protector of Lee. Their lack of communication is analogous to that in the absurdist dialogue between Yossarian and Milo Minderbinder in Heller's *Catch-22*, where the characters speak at cross-purposes during the funeral of Snowden (one mentioning the loss of life while the other keeps lamenting the possible loss of profit in chocolate-covered cotton).[24] Hank jovially observes: "What ya say, bub? You going to like New York for a home? . . . All them cute little college mice after you, you being such a big stud logger from the north woods?" Henry adds, "That's right, Leland . . . that's how I got your mama." The irony in Henry's words and the arrogance in Hank's cause Lee to glare at his brother and exclaim: "You . . . just . . . wait." Hank indignantly cries, "Me? *Me*? . . . You're lucky I don't bust your scrawny little *neck!*" Henry, missing all cues, comments: "*What!* . . . In God's *creation!* Are you two *talking* about!" When no more is said, he "takes up the oars again, apparently satisfied, and rows on" (39–40).

To intensify the absurdity in Lee's quest for freedom, the narrator refers to his later attempt at suicide with "twelve years of decay penciled on his pale face." Twelve years after leaving for his eastern quest, Lee tries to asphyxiate himself. First, he turns on the burners of the stove; then, with mock religious fervor, he goes to the water heater and "kneel[s] piously at the little door" to blow out the pilot light as "the flame spew[s] symbolically from three jets, describing a fiery cross." Parodying Hamlet, he relates: "I draw a breath . . . 'There's a divinity that shapes our'—*pfft*—'ends' " (63). The stove explodes; its blast tosses the mailman to the middle of the lawn, and Lee steps forward with "comically blackened face . . . more a caricature of contempt than an affectation—like a mime's expression" (55). Incongruities and exaggeration give a grotesque-comic edge to the episode. Lee explains to the irate mailman: "I *think*—I'm attempting to kill myself, thank you; but I'm not quite sure I've found exactly the right method" (55). The scene flashes on the inept Lee and, then, on the postman, who, sneezing blood over mail bags, tries to figure it out but finally concludes: "I think it was too *perfect* to be coincidental. . . . I think the blast was *planned*" (81). The reader, with Hobbesian eminency, laughs at the infirmities of these foolish figures; however, the merriment is dissipated by the emotional reaction to the pain Lee experiences. One realizes how futile is his quest for a transformation by way of a change of residence (by journeying East with Myra). One realizes that Lee cannot wipe out the image of Hank and Myra together: "That tangle of arms and legs, sighs and sweat-wet hair telescoped through my bedroom peephole . . . *that* was what burned out my innocent eyes!" (217).

The Grotesque

The range of humor in Kesey's novel of comic absurdity progresses from the comedy of farce to the edge of black humor. At the farcical tip of the continuum is the union president Jonathan Bailey Draeger, who believes that all men behave in predictable patterns. He continually jots down anecdotal answers to life's experiences and refers to this material on subsequent occasions. Draeger is an archetype of Bergsonian humor, a personification of "something mechanical encrusted on the living." The reader, with superiority, laughs at Draeger in much the same way that one takes glee in observing Bergson's clowns as they jump up and down till they seem like inanimate "bundles of all sorts, falling and knocking against each other." "Gradually," Bergson explains, "one lost sight of the fact that they [the clowns] were men of flesh and blood like ourselves." The phrase "like ourselves" shows that when laughing at "the transformation of a person into a thing," one affirms the belief in a clear separation between what is human and what is inanimate. One experiences something close to Hobbes's feeling of "sudden glory" or "eminency" at the "infirmities" of the clown, the object of laughter.[25]

The "sudden glory" perspective then resides at one end of the humor continuum. At the opposite end, images of the grotesque disorient us. From the dark-edged vantage point, bouncing clowns would exhibit the uncanny merger of animate and inanimate, mirrored in nature and human nature. We would have no feeling of "eminency" when observing them because we would be unable to separate clearly "men of flesh and blood" from the inanimate. Laughter from such a vantage point would be a helpless, hostile response to the world that reduces man to the inanimate through death.

At this dark tip of the humor continuum, common sense fails and, as Ruskin points out, the "ludicrous" and the "fearful" seem to merge. Wolfgang Kayser observes that laughter at this point reaches "the comic and caricatural fringe of the grotesque." There is "a play with the absurd," an awareness of the "demonic aspects of the world," and rationalism ceases to be of use. On a psychological level, laughter at the dark end of the humor continuum can be explained as a "grotesque-comic sublimation," when "the function of the comic is to overcome anxiety while at the same time it is based on already mastered anxiety," giving the comic a "double-edged character,"[26] and bringing about the nervous laughter of black humor.

The merging of animate and inanimate, so central to the grotesque aspects of black humor, also is evident in Joe Ben's recollection of "the dark portent he had seen stamped into his father's face—like an expiration date stamped into a borrowed book" (255–56). In another episode, plant and animal merge. The reader peers with Lee at the Darlingtonia plant's "round hole resembling a mouth" and sees at the bottom of the tube a "clogging liquid containing the carcasses of two flies and a honey bee" (292). In another passage, the moon seems to take on animation as the young Lee looks at it after falling into a deep dune stovepipe hole on Halloween. The moon seems to be grinning like a Cheshire cat: "everything gone but the black reminder and the jeering grin" (301). The grin is reminiscent of the man-made jack-o'-lantern that appears to laugh at goblins at Halloween (277). The grotesque progression from inanimate to animate and vice versa adds a sharp-edged tone to the depiction of the alienated, absurd world.

Kesey's continual movement from the ludicrous to the calamitous is disorienting. As a result, one becomes aware that people live in a bizarre cartoon world, where abortive suicides show up in blackface, "a caricature of contempt" (55); where ruined, handsome old men (like Joe Ben's father) die in a "lonely mountain cabin full of girlie books" (112); and where depressive young academicians, like Lee, are told by psychiatrists: "So . . . you may be neurotic as hell for the rest of your life, and miserable . . . but I'm afraid never completely out. . . . Sorry to disappoint you" (68). There is a frenzied tone to this brittle humor that accompanies the absurd. It is the comic-grotesque tone of black humor, the same as that which emerges as the reader observes old Henry's grim gesture of the finger of defiance against a senseless universe in which heroic energy is annihilated by a chance incident.

One recalls Bromden's observation in *One Flew Over the Cuckoo's Nest:* "It's the truth even if it didn't happen" (25). This perspective encourages the reader to appreciate the connection between dream and reality. In *Sometimes a Great Notion,* Kesey guides the reader by explaining: "Besides, there are some things that can't be the truth even if they *did* happen" (70). This point of view indicates the possible fictionality of our nightmare world, a fitting subject for a modern tall tale: Lee's mother, Myra, could not have plummeted forty-one floors to her death (72), nor can we be *"trapped* by our existence" (72); heroes such as Hank cannot be destroyed; he and Lee must fulfill their logging contract with Wakonda Pacific. One refuses to think that they are on the same river that Jonas tried to use as a vehicle for escape but was buried in, the river that Lee and his mother, Myra, traveled across in an effort to escape their past. Hank and Lee cannot be "the two tiny figures leaping *foolishly* from log to log" (598; italics added).[27]

Such grim absurdity in *Sometimes a Great Notion* is reminiscent of that in *Catch-22*, when Yossarian uses a raft to row to Sweden, and in Bruce Jay Friedman's *Stern*, when the protagonist imagines that the prejudiced Kike man will eventually treat him as a human being: "Stern saw himself writing and producing a show about fair play, getting it shown one night on every channel, and forcing the man to watch it since the networks would be bare of Westerns."[28] This grim humor also is similar to that in *One Flew Over the Cuckoo's Nest,* when McMurphy jocularly asks for a "crown of thorns" before getting shock treatment (237), little knowing that he will eventually act out the role of savior. It also is similar to the closing scene in *Cuckoo's Nest* when Bromden yearns to follow the path he had seen the frolicking dog take, without recalling that the dog had galloped to the same spot as an oncoming car (272). *Sometimes a Great Notion,* like *One Flew Over the Cuckoo's Nest,* has an absurdist thrust and black humor tone that make us "shiver as we laugh."[29]

The Comic Strip and the Absurd in *Sometimes a Great Notion* and *One Flew Over the Cuckoo's Nest*

For Kesey, comic strip heroes—Captain Marvel, Superman, Plasticman, the Flash—replace the mythic heroes Hercules, Ulysses, and Aeneas,[30] thus flattening reverential, complex figures to one-dimensional ones. In his days as a cult hero, Kesey enjoyed appearing at psychedelic happenings dressed in a white cape and leotards: "Captain America! The Flash! Captain Marvel! the Superhero, in a word."[31]

In *Sometimes a Great Notion* and *One Flew Over the Cuckoo's Nest,* Kesey uses a comic book style, reducing exalted, multifaceted figures and their opponents to cartoon representations of good and evil. Primarily, Kesey is a caricaturist, simplifying patterns of good and evil—the individualistic Stamper clan, who "NEVER GIVE A INCH" (*Notion* 30), versus the labor union, which wishes to institute a pattern of conformity for all. In *Cuckoo's Nest,* in a manner similar to that in *Sometimes a Great Notion,* the action involves the mythic conflict between good and evil: a liberating hero versus the stultifying combine and the hospital, "an exemplary he-man versus a machine-tooled, castrating matriarch."[32]

In *Cuckoo's Nest,* McMurphy's opponent, Nurse Ratched, is variously described as a Circean creature, carrying a bag filled with magical devices to transform patients as she pleases (10); a huge machine, "crooking . . . sectioned arms" around patients (11); a sinister creature sitting in the center of wires, controlling everything "with mechanical insect skill" (30); a Medusan figure with petrifying power to freeze all who disobey her, like Billy Bibbit, who looks "only straight ahead at her face, like there was a spiraling light there . . . hypnotizing swirl" (264–65).

In *Sometimes a Great Notion* cartoon figures lack the phantasmagorical magical dimension of evil of a Nurse Ratched, so prominent in comic books. They are lower-keyed, but still caricatures of opponents of the hero. Hank's major opponent is his half-brother, Lee, who aspires to be the hero Captain Marvel when, in fact, Lee is a foolish cartoon figure of the physically weak, neurotic intellectual, one who is ultra self-conscious about "that obscure Oedipal pap" (69). Lee also is an exaggeration of the arty intellectual, self-consciously interrupting his own narration of his problems with the comic explanation: "Looking back (I mean now, here, from this particular juncture in time, able to be objective and courageous thanks to the *miracle of modern narrative technique*)" (67–68; italics added). Hank's other opponents are union members. Among them is the president, Jonathan Bailey Draeger, an uneducated bully who has supreme faith in the foolish aphorisms he constructs and who, with a group behind him, threatens the Stamper clan: "You heartless sonofabitches better be prepared to suffer the conch-aquences!" (307). Another is Les Gibbons, a sneaky, manipulating character who brags when it is safe to do so. Even though Hank ferries him back and forth across the river, he tells others in the union: "I'll foller him right to his hole and kick the hound outa him there!" (542).

Sometimes a Great Notion can be seen as expanding upon the formal structural qualities that invigorate Kesey's earlier novel. *One Flew Over the Cuckoo's Nest* has been called an "archetypal Western."[33] Its hero is a cowboy who "walked with long steps . . . and he had his thumbs hooked in his pockets." The iron in his boot heels "cracked lightning out of the tile" (*Cuckoo's Nest* 172). McMurphy is the "ultimate Westerner, the New American Man."[34] He is the Lone Ranger: "a giant come out of the sky to save us from the Combine," says Bromden (*Cuckoo's Nest* 224). Harding underlines this point at the end of the big party when he expects McMurphy to escape: "I'd like to stand there at the window with a silver bullet in my hand and ask 'Who *wawz* that'er masked man?' as you ride" (258). McMurphy, as Sherwood explains, is "like the comic strip savior, whose silver bullet annihilates Evil."[35]

McMurphy is the logger, "the swaggering gambler, the big red-headed brawling Irishman, the cowboy out of the TV set walking down the middle of the street to meet a dare" (*Cuckoo's Nest* 172). He also is inflated to a Christ figure. Shock treatment is given to him on a table shaped like a cross, emitting a "crown of electric sparks in place of thorns" (*Cuckoo's Nest* 65); he is surrounded by twelve followers on a fishing expedition (*Cuckoo's Nest* 211–12); and he dies to save the men.

Similarly, in *Sometimes a Great Notion*, Hank is a superhero: a strong individualist exhibiting "berry-vine toughness" (23); a man who is "always surprised just how much he can do by himself" (589); a cowboy type who knows he has to fight "on account of that's his place, no matter how he don't like it" (309). He is the energetic, rugged, nature-loving hero of the American frontier, evoking in the reader a longing for the heroism of America's early settlers: a Captain John Smith developing new territory; a Daniel Boone making his way in the wilderness. The descriptions of Hank cause the reader to make connections to the nation's early settlers and their westward movement. However, the narrator quickly mocks this by pointing out that Hank comes from a clan of "west walkers" who moved "*not* as pioneers . . . blazing trail for a growing nation" but as restless men with "itchy feet" (16; italics added).

In both works, Kesey adds to his comic presentation an underlying pessimism. Beneath the comic book antics of the hero is the sense of death and decay present in black humor literature. At the conclusion of *Cuckoo's Nest,* Bromden finally lifts the control panel and smashes it through the screen and window: "The glass splashed out in the moon, like a bright cold water *baptizing* the sleeping earth" (271–72; italics added). Bromden, with joy, anticipates happiness similar to that which he experienced in childhood before the white men took over his father's land. In his exhilaration, he recalls the dog he had seen loping in the breeze under a moonlit sky. The dog was intoxicated with freedom: "The night, the breeze full of smells so wild makes a young dog drunk" (142). Above the loping dog Canada honkers were flying. The dog ran in the direction of the Canada honkers, toward the highway. Bromden, at the close of the novel, recalls the loping dog but forgets the fact that the dog was headed for death. In his optimism, he remembers only the movement toward freedom. He forgets that "the dog and the car [were] making for the same spot of pavement" (143).

The reference to the dog presents the underlying pessimism that Bromden had once appreciated as he watched McMurphy, under strain, play out his role as hero for the men: "The thing he [McMurphy] was fighting, you couldn't whip it for good. All you could do was keep on whipping it, till you couldn't come out any more and somebody else had to take your place" (265). This cynical outlook stresses the connection between the oppressiveness of the mental hospital and that of society as a whole, the fact that "the ward is a factory for the Combine . . . for fixing up mistakes made in the neighborhoods and in the schools and in the churches" (40); the fact that the regimentation of the hospital is reflected in society, where people live in "five thousand houses punched out identical by a machine" (203).

Such grim absurdity in *Cuckoo's Nest* is similar to that in the last scene in *Sometimes a Great Notion* when Hank and Lee, in a grand gesture, attempt to move the logs on the river in order to carry out their contract with Wakonda Pacific. Lee, finally, heroically acknowledges that he has to win "back the pride [he] had exchanged for pity" (594). Looking at the severed arm of Henry Stamper, he grins and says, "The devil . . . But if he thinks I've had enough . . . !" (595). Hank, surprised and happy to see that Lee has joined him, asks, "Can you swim, bub? You may have to do a little swimming, you know" (597). Here the reader appreciates the near impossibility of two men—alone on the river—being able to deliver the logs to Wakonda Pacific. The reader is reminded of man's frailty, of the absurd impermanence of man's achievements when he contemplates the difficult quest of the brothers as they jump from log to log (598). He is reminded that man may live in a "cartoon world, where the figures are flat and outlined in black, jerking through some kind of goofy story that might be real funny if it weren't for the cartoon figures being real guys" (*Cuckoo's Nest* 34).

The flattening of themes and characters to the comic strip accentuates irony: whether it is caused by being unable to return to a land of promise and meaning, like Bromden; or trying to be Captain Marvel but remaining a Billy Batson, like Lee; or being unable to act out the role of grand explorer in a land full of fallout, like Hank. The black humor tone of *Sometimes a Great Notion* and *Cuckoo's Nest,* however, prevents these statements from sounding contrived or trite. This, perhaps, is Kesey's strongest achievement. He, like Barth, Pynchon, and Gaddis, may use heavy-handed devices—banal jokes, clichés, exaggerated contrasts—and yet these are sustained by the texture of the comic epic. The combination of pain and humor allows the reader to laugh at the absurdity of the human predicament and go back to the "struggle itself toward the heights."[36]

CHAPTER EIGHT

Conclusion

To compare the epic novels of Barth, Pynchon, Gaddis, and Kesey to the grand epics *Paradise Lost* and *Magnalia* and *Leaves of Grass* is not only to attempt to define the form of these contemporary labyrinthine works but also to praise them in the highest terms. The epic, traditionally, has been the most prestigious literary genre, one that authors have chosen for weighty purposes.

The novels of Barth, Pynchon, Gaddis, and Kesey adapt the epic to their comic objective. *Giles Goat-Boy* parodies the epic by beginning with lengthy prefatory materials ostensibly meant to determine the work's authorship; this is followed by the narrative, with its swelling rhythms and archaic syntax (for example, "I am he that was called in those days" [41]), which gradually collapse to the banal and comic.[1] Similarly, *Gravity's Rainbow* burlesques the traditional epic in passages such as Slothrop's descent into the toilet (63–67), Byron the Bulb's odyssey (647–55), and Slothrop's airborne pie fight with Major Marvy (332–36). Similarly, there also are the details of George Goat-Boy's "heroic" assignment and the depiction of the twentieth-century god, the computer WESCAC, as being no more than a compilation of the ideas people have fed into it.

These postmodern works have their roots in the traditional epic and also are linked to the comic tradition of Rabelais's *Gargantua and Pantagruel*, Cervantes's *Don Quixote*, and Fielding's *Joseph Andrews*. They, like *Joseph Andrews*, are comic epics in prose. They, too, expose the pervading attitudes of vanity, hypocrisy, and concern with worldly pursuits.[2] However, while *Joseph Andrews* attacks follies and vices by contrasting them with the ideal values of charity and good-heartedness, the twentieth-century comic epics mock *all* ideals, emphasizing man's foolishness in seeking them. All these postmodern epic novels are encyclopedic in scope, focus on the ironic quest of the hero of the absurd, and use exaggeration to satirize all institutions. Highly allusive and full of farce, satire, and the grotesque-comic aspects of black humor, these contemporary comic works are philosophically grounded in existentialism and the absurd.

Encyclopedic Epic Qualities

The postmodern comic epic novels are encyclopedic in scope, consisting of many subjects, styles, and forms. In this respect, they are like earlier epics: the *Iliad* and the *Odyssey*, which incorporate history, philosophy, religion, and various forms of literature; *Paradise Lost*, which refers to political events, religion, astronomy, mythology, and earlier literature, and which uses different forms of literature—drama, pastoral, dialogue, ode, domestic farce, and masque;[3] and Joyce's twentieth-century epic novel *Ulysses*, whose breadth ranges from the development of the English language to the growth of an embryo, whose references range from the varied people of Dublin to figures in classical literature,[4] and whose style combines many literary genres, such as narrative, drama, and comedy.

Encyclopedic qualities of the postmodern comic epic novels include their voluminous size and their multiple cross-references to a variety of ways of life and systems of knowledge: science, art, philosophy, and music. The epic form enables contemporary novels to display a panoramic view of members of society including college graduates and artists, those who shoot alligators in the sewers of Manhattan, those who travel in the Zone, and those who are loggers in Wakonda, Oregon. The form also affords many opportunities for farce because the novels contrast these members and their quests with the epic heroes of a literary past.

A significant aspect of this encyclopedic epic is its similarity in nature to the encyclopedia itself, with its wealth of data—names, places, and facts. Like Joyce's *Ulysses,* the American comic epics exploit "the physical bulk, the numbered pages, the facilities for endless cross-reference"[5] that are used in an encyclopedia. As in *Ulysses,* to make sense of the narrative, readers must understand the cross-references from section to section, the constant interrelation of parts. After several readings, they are increasingly able to see how the book's sections build on one another. The readers, understanding the continuities in the new epic, then wish to connect them to the "world" as a whole and also to customary ideals as they would in the traditional epic.

Ulysses rejects formal, classical connections to patterns of human perfection but instead implicitly upholds new ideals. It develops a re-interpretation of the world in the light of modern experience of heroic quests, yoking together irreverent and reverent details as it moves toward an ambiguous sense of meaning and order. The American post-modern epics differ from *Ulysses* in that they set up complex allusions to different systems of knowledge—as evident in religious treatises, alchemical tracts, literary masterpieces—but they do not uphold new ideals. They encourage the reader to unite the systems in a spiritual or holistic way but then reject any connection between the novel's allusions and ultimate answers about the world, allowing the clues to fade through encyclopedic disjunction. In *Ulysses* ironic and parodic action culminate in a coming together of Bloom and Stephen, virtually father and son, and an emphasis of "love . . . Word known to all men."[6] In the contemporary American novels, however, the "sense of an ending" is frustrated repeatedly.[7] The ironic quests parody all meaningful endings, as in *The Recognitions,* where the only connection between Wyatt and the Reverend Gwyon is the bizarre Eucharist.

The new epic novels depend on what Umberto Eco refers to as the " 'encyclopedia' of the spectator," the reader's vision that is called upon as the reader reacts to repetition of traditional themes and types.[8] The novels allude to a variety of social systems such as religion, alchemy, psychology, business, and art. They also ironically refer to basic concepts in Western literary works: information about the early Christian catechumens in *Goat-Boy;* the dream of developing a nation in *V.;* early Christian and pagan legends in *The Recognitions;* and mystical rites of the American Indian in *Sometimes a Great Notion.* Postmodern encyclopedic novels also reveal firsthand knowledge of national archives (Barth), films (Pynchon), painting (Gaddis), and folk songs and legends (Kesey). These authors mock man's reliance on all systems of knowledge at the same time that they use these to structure their literary works.

The "epic territory" in these novels, instead of pointing to the creation and celebration of a nation, is an " 'inverse mapping' of what it once was and might be."[9] The contemporary epics indicate a disappointed desire for order in an irrational twentieth-century world. They emphasize a culture that seems to have lost confidence in norms and in heroic subjects, a culture of people whose quests are—in the end—absurd. These mock epics suggest a decline in revered values within a twentieth-century community devoid of heroic meaning.

The Ironic Allusive Mode

The complex assimilation of epic patterns and themes develops a highly allusive, poetic texture in the new comic novels. Cotton Mather, as was mentioned earlier, discusses the importance of an allusive texture in his prose epic *Magnalia*. Mather knows that the intricate, embellished style causes difficulty for readers. Mather, however, insists that the embellishments prepare the reader for connections between the Puritan heroes and classical and biblical ones. The process serves to develop and enrich the moral and aesthetic values of the past.[10]

Twentieth-century black humor writers also use an embellished, allusive texture, but the ironic interconnections cause their works to be satiric rather than celebrative like the traditional epic. Their ironic allusive mode turns customary epic themes and unifying patterns inside out. In this way, they develop a comic-ironic tone that underscores man's desire for unity and his disappointment in a fragmented world. This ironic comedy becomes the vehicle for their satire of man's false values and lack of spiritual concerns. They show passionate anger at a society whose heroes of the absurd compete for second place.

The Absurd and Black Humor

Rather than using a prophetic voice like that in *Paradise Lost, Magnalia,* or "Song of Myself," postmodern novelists create an epic voice that calls attention to itself as fabricator of a fictional reality. These writers self-consciously emphasize that they are formulating a fiction and so deflate man's pretensions to transcendence. They create illusory worlds, like that in Borges's *Encyclopedia of Tlon,* which gradually blur the real world, causing one to "know nothing with certainty—not even that it [the fiction] is false."[11] "We are deep, these days, in the counterfeit," explains Hugh Kenner, "and have long since had to forego easy criteria for what is 'real.' "[12]

A myth underlying and giving absurd meaning to the postmodern epic novel is that of Sisyphus: pushing his rock though aware that it will roll down again and again. Often, the excitement of the story causes the reader, like Sisyphus, to get caught up in the traditional hope for culmination. The reader, therefore, follows clues until they dissolve into nothingness. This evokes the brittle laughter of black humor as one realizes each situation's horror and farce. The reader responds in such a way to George/Giles in *Goat-Boy,* when he concludes that passage and failure are the same; to Stencil, in *V.,* as he wonders whether to conclude his quest, realizing that it, however apparently fruitless, is all that gives significant order to his life; to Slothrop, in *Gravity's Rainbow,* who looks for cause and effect, only to find the disturbing fact that his father had sold him in infancy for experimentation purposes; to Wyatt Gwyon, in *The Recognitions,* who becomes one with his father/ Father by eating the bread that the monks have made from Reverend Gwyon's ashes; and to Lee Stamper, in *Sometimes a Great Notion,* who wonders if things can be fiction even if they did happen.

These postmodern novels use traditional epic devices to structure their black humor comedies, works that have no answers but that involve the reader in life's quest for meaning. Such works keep one foot in the literary past and one in the present as they bombard the reader with an encyclopedic range of meanings that spell out no ultimate truths but are the stuff of twentieth-century thought. Consequently, the highly ordered comic epic novels show that man is capable of creating imagined worlds that transform despair over lost ideals into newfound comedy.

The thrust of the postmodern comic novel is well described by Malcolm Bradbury when he states:

> Satire and comedy are, at their best, among the greatest forms of human intellectual energy. They displace, distort, subvert and dispel the familiar structures of reality, truth and history, replacing these rule-making systems with the rule-breaking laws of humor, at once the most humane and subversive of our impulses. At the same time they can intervene in reality and history, and . . .

have forced us to reconsider and reconstruct our view of human nature and the political future. It is when the world we live in no longer seems pervious to the anarchy of human need that satire and comedy are most called for, and become necessary vision.[13]

NOTES

Chapter One

1. Sir William Davenant, "Preface to *Gondibert,*" in *Critical Essays of the Seventeeth Century,* ed. J. E. Spingarn (1908; reprint, Illinois: Interstate Printers, 1957), 2:2.

2. Aristotle, *The Poetics,* trans. William Hamilton Fyfe (Cambridge, Mass.: Harvard University Press, 1932), chaps. xxiv.9; xxv.13. See also E.M.W. Tillyard, *The Epic Strain in the English Novel* (London: Chatto & Windus, 1958), 16, 24.

3. John Milton, *Paradise Lost,* in *John Milton: Complete Poems and Major Prose,* ed. Merritt Y. Hughes (New York: Odyssey, 1957), I.26 (all references to *Paradise Lost* are to this edition, hereafter referred to as *PL*); *Reason of Church Government* (Hughes 669); Cotton Mather, *Magnalia Christi Americana,* ed. Kenneth B. Murdock (Cambridge, Mass.: Harvard University Press, 1977), 89.

4. Northrop Frye, *Anatomy of Criticism* (Princeton, N.J.: Princeton University Press, 1957), 303–14; see also Edward Mendelson's excellent discussion of the subject: "Gravity's Encyclopedia," in *Mindful Pleasures: Essays on Thomas Pynchon,* ed. George Levine and David Leverenz (Boston: Little, Brown, 1976), esp. 161–64.

5. François Rabelais, *The Histories of Gargantua and Pantagruel,* trans. J. M. Cohen (Middlesex, England: Penguin, 1983), 52–53.

6. Rabelais 597.

7. Rabelais 93.

8. Rabelais 83.

9. Rabelais 83–85.

10. Rabelais 74.

11. Rabelais 74; see the excellent discussion by M. M. Bakhtin, *Rabelais and His World,* trans. Helene Iswolsky (Bloomington: Indiana University Press, 1984), 188–89, who points out that the openness of the Renaissance marketplace emphasizes, by contrast, the dangers of the controlling closed world view of the medieval scholastics. Similarly, the zany activity of Pynchon's characters who try to disregard the war contrasts with and brings out the twentieth-century controlling group, ominously called "They," the new "elect."

12. Miguel de Cervantes, *Don Quixote,* ed. Kenneth Douglas and Joseph R. Jones (New York: Norton, 1981), 386.

13. Henry Fielding, *Joseph Andrews,* ed. Martin C. Battestin (Middletown, Conn.: Wesleyan University Press, 1967), 4. Fielding, in the "Introduction" to his sister's [Sarah Fielding] *The Adventures of David Simple* (1744; reprint, New York: Oxford

162

Notes

University Press, 1969), 6, defines the work as *"a comic Epic Poem"* that focuses on *"a Series of Actions"* in the manner of Cervantes.

14. Henry Fielding 4.
15. Henry Fielding 5, 4.
16. Henry Fielding 4; Sarah Fielding 7.
17. See Martin C. Battestin, *The Moral Basis of Fielding's Art* (Middletown, Conn.: Wesleyan University Press, 1959), 30–43.
18. Herman Melville, *Moby-Dick*, ed. Harrison Hayford and Hershel Parker (New York: Norton, 1967), 355. See Edward H. Rosenberry's excellent discussion on the comic, *Melville and the Comic Spirit* (Cambridge, Mass.: Harvard University Press, 1955), 116–27.
19. Melville 360.
20. Melville 31–32, 147.
21. Nathaniel Hawthorne, *The English Note-Books*, ed. Randall Stewart (New York: MLA of America, 1941), 433.
22. James Joyce, *Ulysses: The Corrected Text*, ed. Hans Walter Gabler (New York: Vintage Books, 1986), 250.
23. Joyce 644. In the Preface to *The Corrected Text* of *Ulysses*, Richard Ellmann points out that Hans Walter Gabler has provided the manuscript lines, "Do you know what you are talking about? Love, yes. Word known to all men," in the National Library scene (161). This gives a positive answer to Stephen's later question to his mother's ghost: "Tell me the word, mother, if you know now. The word known to all men" (474). Joyce xii.
24. Joyce 3.
25. Joyce 270.
26. See David Hayman, "Cyclops," in *James Joyce's Ulysses*, ed. Clive Hart and David Hayman (Berkeley: University of California Press, 1974), 267. Hayman observes that the chapter's "incoherence and irreverence are in complex ways yoked to reverence and a respect for forms and even for human values. This is also true of the obvious satirical content, since satire *always* implies respect for some sort of reason and a positive if implicit order" (Hayman 267; italics added). This calls attention to a major difference between Joyce's satire (and also traditional satire) and that of the postmodernists. Postmodern comic-satiric epics expose the false, the affected, and the hypocritical, but they do not do this by clarifying intrinsic values. The postmodern absurdist novels obviously do not have a clear synthesis, an establishment of an ideal, and have been reproached for this lack. See, for example, Earl Rovit's criticism of Barth's parody for being based on a system that indicates that "nothing is of intrinsic value." Such "parody becomes employed without the rigorous passion that can make effective satire." "The Novel as Parody: John Barth," in *Critical Essays on John Barth*, ed. Joseph J. Waldmeir (Boston: G. K. Hall, 1980), 118–19.
27. Joyce 278.
28. See Rudolf Arnheim, *Entropy and Art* (Berkeley: University of California Press, 1971), 8–12. See also Stephen G. Brush, "Thermodynamics and History," *Graduate Journal* 7, no. 2 (1967): 481.
29. Albert Camus, *The Myth of Sisyphus and Other Essays*, trans. Justin O'Brien (New York: Vintage, 1955), 21. For discussions on the absurd, see Martin Esslin, *The Theatre of the Absurd* (New York: Doubleday Anchor, 1969); Eugène Ionesco, who defines the absurd condition as one "devoid of purpose." It afflicts man when he is "cut off from his religious, metaphysical, and transcendental roots" (quoted in Esslin 5). See also Jean-Paul Sartre, *Nausea*, trans. Lloyd Alexander (New York: New Directions, 1964), 129–31, who recounts Antoine Roquentin's experience of the absurd. He notes that "the world of explanations and reasons is not the world of existence," that no one can explain existence. For Roquentin, a feeling of physical nausea spreads like a "black,

amorphous . . . presence." This "nausea" grows out of man's desire for meaning and its inevitable disappointment in an absurd universe (Camus 11).

30. Vladimir Nabokov, *Lolita* (1955; reprint, New York: Berkley Medallion, 1970), 255; Mathew Winston, "Humor Noir and Black Humor," in *Veins of Humor*, ed. Harry Levin, Harvard English Studies 3 (Cambridge, Mass.: Harvard University Press, 1972), 275–77, includes the above three points in his discussion of how a black humor work disorients the reader. Max F. Schulz, in his Introduction to *Black Humor Fiction of the Sixties* (Athens, Ohio: Ohio University Press, 1973), 5, defines black humor as "a phenomenon of the 1960s, comprising a group of writers who share a viewpoint and an aesthetics for pacing off the boundaries of a nuclear-technological world intrinsically without confinement." The dramatist Friedrich Dürrenmatt, *Problems of the Theatre* and *The Marriage of Mr. Mississippi,* trans. Gerhard Nellhaus (New York: Grove Press, 1965), 31, states that black humor comedy seems to be the only thing "suitable" for conveying man's absurd predicament in our contemporary world, "a world like that of Hieronymus Bosch whose apocalyptic paintings are also grotesque." See also Bruce Jay Friedman's Foreword to *Black Humor* (New York: Bantam, 1965), vii–xi; Brom Weber, "The Mode of 'Black Humor,' " in *The Comic Imagination in American Literature,* ed. Louis D. Rubin (New Brunswick, N.J.: Rutgers University Press, 1973); Douglas M. Davis, Introduction to *The World of Black Humor* (New York: Dutton, 1967), 13–26; Conrad Knickerbocker, "Humor with a Mortal Sting," in Davis 299–305; Richard Kostelanetz, "The American Absurd Novel," also in Davis 306–13; Burton Feldman, "Anatomy of Black Humor," in *The American Novel Since World War II,* ed. Marcus Klein (New York: Fawcett, 1969), 224–28; Hamlin Hill, "Black Humor: Its Cause and Cure," *Colorado Quarterly* 17 (1968): 57–64; Sarah Blacher Cohen, Introduction to *Comic Relief: Humor in Contemporary American Literature* (Urbana: University of Illinois Press, 1978), 2–5; Walter Blair and Hamlin Hill, *America's Humor: From Poor Richard to Doonesbury* (New York: Oxford Univesity Press, 1978), 498–506; Elaine B. Safer, "The Allusive Mode and Black Humor in Barth's *Sot-Weed Factor,"* *Studies in the Novel* 13 (Winter, 1981): 424–25. Blair and Hill point out that no one "has managed to define the exact qualities of black humor to the satisfaction of anyone else" (498). An eighteenth-century example of black humor appears in *The Idler,* no. 22 (September 9, 1758). Samuel Johnson relates the words of an old vulture to her children: " 'We have not the strength of man,' returned the mother, 'and I am sometimes in doubt whether we have the subtlety; and the vultures would seldom feast upon his flesh, had not Nature, *that devoted him to our uses,* infused into him a strange ferocity, which I have never observed in any other being that feeds upon the earth. Two herds of men will often meet and shake his earth with noise, and fill the air with fire. . . . you will then find the ground smoking with blood and covered with carcasses, of which many are dismembered and mangled *for the convenience of the vulture.'* " *Samuel Johnson,* ed. Donald Greene (New York: Oxford University Press, 1984), 283; italics added.

31. Umberto Eco, "Innovation and Repetition: Between Modern and Post-Modern Aesthetics," *Daedalus* 114, no. 4 (1985): 171.

32. *PL* I.14–15.

33. *PL* VII.1–5.

34. Alan Prince, "An Interview with John Barth," *Prism* (Spring 1968): 48.

35. For example, *Sot-Weed* parodies the actions of the Whitmanesque "cosmic lover" as Burlingame strokes the pig Portia. Direct allusions to Whitman's hero and his love for everything in the world create a contrast with the rigid concerns of Ebenezer Cooke. However, the comparison not only mocks Eben, it also acts as an absurdist corrective to the excessive exuberance of Whitmanesque idealism. Similarly, in *Gravity's Rainbow,* Pynchon uses "elect" and "preterition" as central ordering metaphors, even though his narrative emphasizes profound disadvantages in separating people into haves and have-nots. In *The Recognitions,* Gaddis refers to alchemical treatises by Raymond

Lully to contrast historic spiritualism with twentieth-century materialism. Yet, he also stresses a negative view of alchemists by choosing as a major referent Basilius Valentinus, a psuedo–Benedictine monk whose motives are questionable. (See John Read, *Prelude to Chemistry: An Outline of Alchemy* [1936; reprint, Cambridge, Mass.: MIT Press, 1966], 183, 187.) And Kesey connects the hero Hank to early American pioneers, but simultaneously deflates Hank's own ancestors by characterizing their westward journeys as "foolish roaming" (*Notion* 16).

36. Cotton Mather, *Magnalia Christi Americana*, ed. Thomas Robbins (Hartford: Silas Andrus and Son, 1853; photo-litho reprint, Pennsylvania: Banner of Trust, 1979), II.339–486, in an enlargement of Increase Mather's book of tales, devotes Book VI to detailing many examples of God's intervention. These range from stories of how children are saved—e.g., a carpenter does "let fall accidentally, from an upper story, a bulky piece of timber just over these little children. . . . 'O Lord, direct it!' [cries the man] and the Lord did so direct it, that it . . . canted along on the floor between two of the children, without ever touching one of them all" (356)—to how evildoers are destroyed with lightning "whereby the *inward* parts are burnt, while the *outward* are not hurt" (362).

37. Perry Miller, *The New England Mind: From Colony to Province* (Cambridge, Mass.: Harvard University Press, 1953), 33.

38. Frye 167.

39. Robert S. Haller, trans. and ed., "The *Letter to Can Grande*," *Literary Criticism of Dante Alighieri* (Lincoln: University of Nebraska Press, 1973), 100.

40. Wylie Sypher, "The Meanings of Comedy," in *Comedy*, ed. Wylie Sypher (New York: Doubleday, 1956), 222.

41. Frye 167–70.

42. See Leonard J. Potts, *Comedy* (London: Cheltenham Press, 1948), 45; Roger Cox, "The Structure of Comedy," *Thought* 50 (1975): 82.

43. Jerry C. Beasley, *Novels of the 1740s* (Athens: University of Georgia Press, 1982), 192.

44. *PL* XII.549–51.

45. I use Pynchon's spelling of *schlemihl* throughout.

46. See John O. Stark, *Pynchon's Fictions: Thomas Pynchon and the Literature of Information* (Athens: Ohio University Press, 1980), 51–52; Harold Farwell, "John Barth's Tenuous Affirmation: 'The Absurd, Unending Possibility of Love,' " *Critical Essays on John Barth*, ed. Joseph J. Waldmeir (Boston: G. K. Hall, 1980), 67; Barry H. Leeds, *Ken Kesey* (New York: Frederick Ungar, 1981), 88.

47. Camus points out that the universe "without a master seems to [Sisyphus] neither sterile nor futile. . . . The struggle itself toward the heights is enough to fill a man's heart. One must imagine Sisyphus happy" (91).

Chapter Two

1. Cotton Mather, *Magnalia Christi Americana*. Books I and II of *Magnalia* are taken from Cotton Mather, *Magnalia Christi Americana*, ed. Kenneth B. Murdock (Cambridge, Mass.: Harvard University Press, 1977), and are referred to parenthetically in the text as Harvard. Books III–VII are from *Magnalia Christi Americana*, ed. Thomas Robbins (reprint, London: Hartford: Silas Andrus and Son, 1853; photo-litho reprint, Pennsylvania: Banner of Trust, 1979), 2 vols. References to this edition will cite volume and page. *Magnalia* has been variously called "the most stupendous American historical work undertaken in the seventeenth century" (Howard Mumford Jones, *Ideas in America* [Cambridge, Mass.: Harvard University Press, 1944], 97); the "greatest effort in the century to organize the experience of this [American] people" (Perry Miller, *The New*

England Mind: From Colony to Province [Cambridge, Mass.: Harvard University Press, 1953], 33); an epic from which emerges a picture of the "representative American" (Sacvan Bercovitch, " 'Nehemias Americanus': Cotton Mather and the Concept of the Representative American," *Early American Literature* 8 [1974]: 231); the *"magnum opus* of the Massachusetts theocracy" (Vernon Parrington, *Main Currents in American Thought* [New York: Harcourt, Brace, 1930], 1: 116); and a "colossal jeremiad" (Perry Miller, *From Colony,* 33). Of Mather, Kenneth Silverman, *The Life and Times of Cotton Mather* (New York: Harper and Row, 1984), has observed: "No other person born in America between the time of Columbus and of Franklin strove to make himself so conspicuous . . . as an American." Continues Silverman, "The titles of some of his major works—'Biblia Americana,' *Magnalia Christi Americana,* 'Curiosa Americana,' *Psalterium Americanum*—announce his affection for the place and his hope of putting America on the cultural map" (425–26). Carmela Perri, "On Alluding," *Poetics* 7 (1978): 306, explains that because "the structural elements, styles, modes, meters, genres . . . have accrued rather specific associations throughout the ages, a poet's choices among them might be deliberate evocations of (allusions to) past uses of them." Referring to eighteenth-century literature, James Swearingen, "Philosophical Hermeneutics and the Renewal of Tradition," *The Eighteenth Century: Theory and Interpretation* 22 (1981): 207, observes that "understanding the past consisted in a transformation that constituted renewal." Stephen Behrendt, "The Best Criticism: Imitation as Criticism in the Eighteenth Century," *The Eighteenth Century* 24 (1983): 7, points out that "the imitative work . . . not only perpetuates but expands . . . tradition in itself while generating still further expression . . . within the consciousness of the reader/viewer." See also Reuben Brower, *Alexander Pope: The Poetry of Allusion* (Oxford: Clarendon, 1959), 14; Harold Bloom, *A Map of Misreading* (New York: Oxford University Press, 1975), esp. 125–206; Christopher Ricks, "Allusion: The Poet as Heir," *Studies in the Eighteenth Century,* ed. R. F. Brissenden and J. C. Eade (Toronto: University of Toronto Press, 1976), 209–40; Donald Mell, "Dryden and the Transformation of the Classical," *Papers on Language and Literature* 17, no. 2 (1981): 146–63, esp. 150–52.

2. This is an alteration of *Aeneid* I.8–11; trans. in Harvard 90.

3. Cotton is extending the definition of "types" and "antitypes" as traditionally used. For example, Cotton's uncle Samuel Mather defines a type as "some outward or sensible thing ordained of God under the Old Testament, to represent and hold forth something of Christ [the Antitype] *in the New.*" Samuel Mather, *The Figures or Types of the Old Testament* (New York: Johnson Reprint Corporation, 1969), 52; see also Kenneth Murdock, who points out that Cotton Mather read his uncle's book "avidly" when it was published in 1683 and "found many typological interpretations of Biblical words, phrases, and allusions with which he loaded the pages of the *Magnalia*" (Harvard 45); see also George Miller, "Archetype and History," *Modern Language Studies* 10, no. 3 (Fall 1980): 15–18.

4. Ursula Brumm, *American Thought and Religious Typology,* trans. John Hooglund (New Brunswick, N.J.: Rutgers University Press, 1970), 46, points out that "the history of the American Puritans . . . [develops] toward the fulfillment of prophecies and the repetition of exemplary models." William Manierre, "Cotton Mather and the Biographical Parallel," *American Quarterly* 13 (1961): 156, observes that, through parallels with biblical figures, the author is able "to magnify the subject of his biography, to remind his readers of New England's mission [and] to suggest the purposefulness of history."

5. Biblical citations are to the King James Version.

6. See Sacvan Bercovitch's excellent discussion of this subject in "New England Epic: Cotton Mather's *Magnalia Christi Americana,*" *ELH* 33 (1966): 337–50.

7. Bercovitch, "New England Epic," 350; see also Roy Harvey Pearce, *The Continuity of American Poetry* (Princeton, N.J.: Princeton University Press, 1961), 60.

Notes

For further discussion of the American epic tradition, see also James E. Miller, *The American Quest for a Supreme Fiction: Whitman's Legacy in the Personal Epic* (Chicago: University of Chicago Press, 1979), 13–29.

8. George Sensabaugh, *Milton in Early America* (Princeton, N.J.: Princeton University Press, 1964), 38, explains that Mather found Milton's scenes of battle had pictorial and transcendental value. He paraphrased them to "enlarge his own exposition in describing Indian warfare [in Book II] and twice to heighten particular [battle] scenes [in Book VII]." Thomas Goddard Wright, *Literary Culture in Early New England, 1620–1730* (New York: Russell & Russell, 1966), 143, points out that Mather "was familiar with 'Paradise Lost' " and "there must have been at least one copy of 'Paradise Lost' . . . lying open on Cotton Mather's table as he wrote his greatest book."

9. See G. K. Hunter, *Paradise Lost* (London: George Allen and Unwin, 1980) 56–59; James Holly Hanford and James G. Taaffe, *A Milton Handbook* (New York: Appleton-Century-Crofts, 1970) 161.

10. *PL* I.19–22.

11. See Bercovitch's comments on epic conventions in *Magnalia* ("New England Epic," esp. 338–45); see also C. S. Lewis, "The Style of Secondary Epic," *A Preface to 'Paradise Lost'* (1942; reprint, London: Oxford University Press, 1979), 40–51.

12. Mather alters the opening lines from Virgil's epic and draws connections between the heroic founding of America and that of Rome. He adapts the lines from the *Aeneid* to his own purposes, changing Virgil's focus on the one man, Aeneas, to the many Puritan pious heroes who "traverse so many perils" and "face so many trials" in the building of the nation. Virgil's lines are: "Tell me, O Muse, the cause; wherein thwarted in will or wherefore angered, did the Queen of heaven drive a man, of goodness so wondrous, to traverse so many perils, to face so many toils." Virgil, *Aeneid*, trans. H. Rushton Fairclough (Cambridge, Mass.: Harvard University Press, 1978), bk.I.8–10.

13. There are more than forty biographies, in addition to biographical sketches. See the discussions by R. E. Watters, "Biographical Technique in Cotton Mather's *Magnalia*," *WMQ*, 3rd series, Vol. 2 (1945): 154; and Gustaaf Van Cromphout, "Cotton Mather as Plutarchan Biographer," *American Literature* 46 (1975): 465.

14. John Winthrop, "A Model of Christian Charity," *Old South Leaflets* (Boston: Directors of the Old South Work, 1883), no. 207.

15. Both Barth and Gaddis, in their use of the genre saints' lives, are thinking in terms of Catholic, not Puritan, saints. Marjorie M. Malvern, "The Parody of Medieval Saints' Lives in John Barth's *Giles Goat-Boy or, The Revised New Syllabus*," *Studies in Medievalism* 2 (1982): 59–76, traces connections between four of the characters in *Goat-Boy* and saints in Jacobus's medieval *The Golden Legend*; see also John Tilton's comments on Giles's name deriving from Saint Giles in "*Giles Goat-Boy:* An Interpretation," *Bucknell Review* 18, no. 1 (1970): 96.

16. See Sacvan Bercovitch, *The American Jeremiad* (Madison: University of Wisconsin Press, 1978), 9–11; and Perry Miller, *From Colony*, 27. See Smith and Tololyan's discussion of Pynchon's "deep involvement with American Puritanism" and his "brilliant reworking" of the Puritan jeremiad in "The New Jeremiad: *Gravity's Rainbow*," *Critical Essays on Thomas Pynchon*, ed. Richard Pearce (Boston: G. K. Hall, 1981), 169.

17. *The Theological Dictionary of the New Testament*, ed. Gerhard Kittel, trans. and ed. Geoffrey W. Bromiley (Grand Rapids, Mich.: Eerdmans, 1965), 3:455, 459, explains that "there is no certainty as to the original meaning [of *kairos*]." The editors emphasize the "fateful and decisive point . . . the fact that it is ordained by God." Frank Kermode, *The Sense of an Ending* (1967; reprint, New York: Oxford University Press, 1968), 48, writes of "the coming of God's time (*kairos*) . . . as against passing time, *chronos*." Edward Tayler, *Milton's Poetry: Its Development in Time* (Pittsburgh: Duquesne University Press, 1979), 8, interprets *kairos* as "the way God's providence

works in and through time." See also Joseph Anthony Wittreich's discussion of the prophetic mode, which lays stress on inspiration, on unlocking visionary meanings, and on "teaching men to see not *with* but *through* the eye," in *Visionary Poetics* (San Marino, Calif.: Huntington Library, 1979), 26.

18. *PL* IV.684–721.

19. George Herbert, "The Church Militant," *The Works of George Herbert*, ed. F. E. Hutchinson (Oxford: Clarendon, 1970), 235–36. Mather's reverence for the theme is particularly noticeable in that he, like his fellow Americans, selectively uses Herbert's positive statement, while ignoring the lurking irony in the context of the lines, the point that as the Church moved, sin followed: "Yet as the Church shall thither westward flie / So Sinne shall trace and dog her instantly" (Herbert 197, lines 259–60). People in the later eighteenth century often cited Bishop [George] Berkeley's "Westward the course of empire takes its way," from "Verses on the Prospect of Planting Arts and Learning in America," in *A Collection of English Poems, 1660–1800*, ed. Ronald S. Crane (New York: Harper, 1932), 340 (published after *Magnalia*, in 1752). See J. A. Leo Lemay's summary of materials on the *translatio* theme: "The Frontiersman from Lout to Hero," *Proceedings of the American Antiquarian Society* 88 (1979): 198–99; see also Lemay, *Men of Letters in Colonial Maryland* (Knoxville: University of Tennessee Press, 1972), 131–32 and *passim;* Harold Jantz, "The Myths about America: Origins and Extensions," *Deutschlands literarisches Amerikabild*, ed. Alexander Ritter (New York: Georg Olms, 1977), 43–44; Rexmond C. Cochrane, "Bishop Berkeley and the Progress of Arts and Learning: Notes on a Literary Convention," *Huntington Library Quarterly* 17 (May 1954): 229–49; Karl H. Dannenfeldt, "The Renaissance and the Pre-Classical Civilizations," *JHI* 13 (1952): 435–49; William Brennan, "Milton's *Of Education* and the *Translatio Studii*," *Milton Q* 15 (1981): 55–59.

20. Barrett Wendell, *Cotton Mather: The Puritan Priest* (1891; reprint, New York: Harcourt, 1963), 162, explains that "Mather makes you by and by feel what the Puritan ideal was: if he does not tell just what men were, he does tell what they wanted to be, and what loyal posterity longed to believe them."

21. Alan Prince, "An Interview with John Barth," *Prism* (Spring 1968): 50–51. The *Archives of Maryland* has a wealth of historical material that was easily available to Barth. Compare, for example, Barth's references to William Claiborne's plots to get the Island of Kent in the years following 1634 (*Sot-Weed* 90–91) and the records of charges of "piracy and fellony" in the *Archives of Maryland 5, Proceedings of the Council of Maryland 1667–87*, ed. William Hand Browne (Baltimore: Maryland Historical Society, 1887), 172, 157–239.

22. Samuel Eliot Morison, "William Pynchon: The Founder of Springfield," *Proceedings of the Massachusetts Historical Society* 64 (1932): 69, calls attention to the fact that William Pynchon (1590–1662) was a staunch Puritan, that he helped establish the church in Springfield, Massachusetts, and that "it was on a small point of theology, not a fundamental of Puritan belief, that he fell out with his fellow-magistrates." Morison gives details on the condemnation of Pynchon's book, *The Meritorious Price of Our Redemption* in "William Pynchon, Frontier Magistrate and Fur Trader," *Builders of the Bay Colony* (Boston: Northeastern University Press, 1981), 371–75. He also recounts William's journey to America sailing on the ship *Ambrose*, " 'rear admirall' of the Winthrop fleet." During the journey Pynchon was asked to board the *Arbella* and dine with John Winthrop (Morison, "The Founder of Springfield," 72), an incident that is used for comic purposes in *Gravity's Rainbow*, with regard to Tyrone Slothrop's ancestor William, "vomiting a good part of 1630 away over the side of that *Arbella*" (364). See also Ruth McIntyre, *William Pynchon: Merchant and Colonizer* (Springfield, Mass.: Connecticut Valley Historical Museum, 1961), 34, who explains that William Pynchon's book was condemned as heretical and "burned publicly in the market place at Boston"— just like the work of Slothrop's ancestor William in *Gravity's Rainbow* (555). See also

Notes

Frank Foster, *A Genetic History of the New England Theology* (New York: Russell and Russell, 1963), 15–21; Carl Bridenbaugh, ed., *The Pynchon Papers*, I (Boston: Colonial Society of Massachusetts, 1982), xxx–xxxi; Mathew Winston, "The Quest for Pynchon," *Mindful Pleasures: Essays on Thomas Pynchon*, ed. George Levine and David Leverenz (Boston: Little, Brown, 1976), 254–55.

23. Irving Howe, ed. *Literary Modernism* (Greenwich, Conn.: Fawcett, 1967), 35.

24. Joseph Campbell, *The Hero with a Thousand Faces* (1949; New York: Meridian, 1956), 388, explains that one no longer knows "toward what one moves . . . [or] by what one is propelled"; see also David Galloway, *The Absurd Hero in American Fiction*, 2d ed. (Austin: University of Texas Press, 1981), 13.

25. Mather takes the description of these Pilgrims from the account in William Bradford's *Of Plymouth Plantation, 1620–1647*, ed. Samuel E. Morison (New York: Knopf, 1952), one of the best sources on colonial America.

26. See also William Bradford's *History of Plymouth Plantation*, ed. Worthington Chauncey Ford (Boston: Houghton, 1912), 1: 33; hereafter referred to parenthetically in the text as Ford.

27. Ursula Brumm, "Did the Pilgrims Fall Upon Their Knees When They Arrived in the New World? Art and History in the Ninth Chapter, Book One, of Bradford's *Of Plymouth Plantation*," *Early American Literature* 12 (Spring 1977): 29, points out that the description of the landing in America "is the very apex of the whole book," a scene in which Bradford "witnessed the birth of a new nation."

28. Mather's account is not as detailed as that in *Plymouth Plantation*, which it causes us to recall.

29. Albert Camus, *The Myth of Sisyphus and Other Essays*, trans. Justin O'Brien (New York: Vintage, 1955), 49. See Sartre's comment that without God we are not "provided with any values or commands that could legitimize our behavior"; without God "man is condemned to be free." "Existentialism Is a Humanism," in *Existentialism from Dostoevsky to Sartre*, ed. Walter Kaufmann (New York: New American Library, 1975), 353. See David Galloway's excellent discussion, *The Absurd Hero in American Fiction*, 2d ed. (Austin: University of Texas Press, 1981), 7–16. See also R.W.B. Lewis, *The Picaresque Saint* (Philadelphia: Lippincott, 1959), 60–65.

30. For further discussion of *Plymouth Plantation's* communal sense, see Walter Sutton, "Apocalyptic History and the American Epic: Cotton Mather and Joel Barlow," in *Toward a New American Literary History*, ed. Louis J. Budd et al. (Durham, N.C.: Duke University Press, 1980), 70; see also Walter P. Wenska, "Bradford's Two Histories: Pattern and Paradigm in *Of Plymouth Plantation*," *Early American Literature* 13 (Fall 1978): 159–60.

31. See the excellent discussion by John Griffith, "*Of Plymouth Plantation* as a Mercantile Epic," *Arizona Quarterly* 28 (1972): 231–42, emphasizing the "mercantile economics." "The enemy," explains Griffith, "is poverty, and Bradford's history is primarily the story of how the Pilgrims triumph by obtaining economic sufficiency—a story of material acquisition, albeit for 'good and honourable ends' " (232).

32. See Bradford, *Of Plymouth Plantation*, ed. Morison, xxix. Moses Coit Tyler, *A History of American Literature, 1607–1765* (Ithaca, N.Y.: Cornell University Press, 1949), 103, places Bradford's *History* "at the head of American historical literature."

Chapter Three

1. "Song of Myself" sec. 52.1333. In this chapter, references to Whitman's poetry and prose (unless otherwise stated) are to Walt Whitman, *Leaves of Grass*, ed. Sculley Bradley and Harold W. Blodgett (1965; reprint, New York: Norton, 1973). For prose references, title and page number will be given; for poetry, the title and line number

and, at times, the name and page number for the source poem. For "Song of Myself," the section and line number will be given.

2. The young Whitman's hope for his nation, conveyed in the image of shaking his "white locks at the runaway sun," is reminiscent of Milton's aspirations for his country "rousing herself like a strong man after sleep, and shaking her invincible locks . . . and kindling her undazzled eyes at the full midday beam" (*Areopagitica* 745). The exuberance here mainly exists in the earlier Whitman of the "1855 Preface," a poet full of vitality and life. The later Whitman of *Democratic Vistas, Prose Works 1892*, ed. Floyd Stovall (New York: New York University Press, 1964) was more critical of a society whose "democracy grows rankly up the thickest, noxious, deadliest plants and fruits of all" (2:422). Even in *Democratic Vistas*, however, Whitman shows faith that man's goodness will come to fruition, that "man at last arises . . . with wonder and love" (425).

3. Critics who stress this phenomenon are Tony Tanner, "Caries and Cabals," *Mindful Pleasures: Essays on Thomas Pynchon*, ed. George Levine and David Leverenz (Boston: Little, Brown, 1976), 49, who speaks of the "the urban wasteland, thick with the rubble and dead of our century of total wars"; and Raymond M. Olderman, *Beyond the Wasteland: A Study of the American Novel in the Nineteen-Sixties* (New Haven, Conn.: Yale University Press, 1972).

4. Malcolm Cowley, ed., *The Complete Poetry and Prose of Walt Whitman* (New York: Pellegrini & Cudahy, 1948), 38.

5. R.W.B. Lewis, *American Adam: Innocence, Tragedy and Tradition in the Nineteenth Century* (1955; reprint, Chicago: University of Chicago Press, 1971), 198; see also John F. Lynen, *The Design of the Present: Essays on Time and Form in American Literature* (New Haven: Yale University Press, 1969), 324; Justin Kaplan, *Walt Whitman: A Life* (New York: Simon and Schuster, 1980), 238.

6. Gay Wilson Allen, *Walt Whitman Handbook* (Chicago: Packard, 1946), 291–92, explains: "As a poet Whitman was not only trying to *express* the cosmic scheme, in which all creation was eternally evolving into something better, but . . . trying to contribute his own effort toward achieving the divine plan."

7. See Joseph W. Slade's discussion of other alienated characters riding on the subways—"beggars, nomads, migrant farmers, the ethnic poor . . . schlemihls of the city"—in *Thomas Pynchon* (New York: Warner, 1974), 111.

8. Brackets are used to distinguish editorial ellipses from those in the text of Pynchon.

9. Lewis, *American Adam*, 49; see also Roy Harvey Pearce, *The Continuity of American Poetry* (Princeton, N.J.: Princeton University Press, 1961), 168, who points out that Whitman's "subject, as he wrote in a preliminary note for the first section of *Leaves of Grass*, was 'Adam, as central figure and type.' "

10. See Lewis's analysis of Whitman as Adamic poet in "Crossing Brooklyn Ferry" (*American Adam* 52–53); see also James E. Miller, *A Critical Guide to "Leaves of Grass"* (Chicago: University of Chicago Press, 1957), 6, who calls "Song of Myself" a "dramatic representation of a mystical experience."

11. In a footnote, Sculley Bradley and Harold W. Blodgett, *Walt Whitman: Leaves of Grass* (New York: Norton, 1973), 52, cite the phrases of the first three editions: "Walt Whitman, an American, one of the roughs, a kosmos."

12. Pynchon calls Benny Profane a "schlimazzel" (*V.* 110); the word *schlimmazel* is from the German *schlim* (bad) and the Hebrew *mazel* (luck).

13. Vernon Parrington, *Main Currents in American Thought* (New York: Harcourt, Brace, 1930), 3:70; Whitman's celebration of country is a wonderful response to Emerson's request in "The Poet": "I look in vain for the poet whom I describe. . . . with tyrannous eye, which knew the value of our incomparable materials, and saw, in the barbarism and materialism of the times, another carnival of the same gods whose picture he so much admires in Homer." See Ralph Waldo Emerson, *Collected Works*, ed. Alfred

Notes

R. Ferguson et al. (Cambridge, Mass.: Harvard University Press, Belknap Press, 1971–83), 3:21–22; hereafter referred to as *CW*.

14. Gay Wilson Allen, *Walt Whitman Handbook*, 284. Whitman, as Cowley states, "recognized the value of our incomparable materials, the Northern trade, the Southern planting and the Western clearing" (8); see also Lynen, who speaks of Whitman's "spiritual brotherhood" with mankind (284).

15. "What is commonest, cheapest, nearest, easiest, is Me" (14.259).

16. Octavius B. Frothingham, *Transcendentalism in New England* (Boston: American Unitarian Association, [1876]), 182. Whitman explains: "Your facts are useful, and yet they are not my dwelling, / I but enter by them to an area of my dwelling" ("Song" 21.491–92). This comment on his "dwelling" calls to mind Evelyn Underhill's description of the other "order of reality," the "Transcendental Feeling," the mystic's response to "intimations received in [the] awakening," in *Mysticism: A Study in the Nature and Development of Man's Spiritual Consciousness* (New York: Dutton, 1930), 233. See also Marghanita Laski's discussion of "trigger" experiences that seem to give messages in *Ecstasy: A Study of Some Secular and Religious Experiences* (Bloomington, Ind.: Indiana University Press, 1961), 341–42. James Miller points to the mystical experience whereby there is a "fusion of the physical and spiritual . . . [enabling one] to know transcendent reality. The poet's mystical state of consciousness results in immediate 'knowledge' " (*Critical Guide* 10).

17. See also Emerson: "The philosophy of six thousand years has not searched the chambers and magazines of the soul. In its experiments there has always remained, in the last analysis, a residuum it could not resolve" ("The Over-Soul," *CW* 2:159).

18. Henry David Thoreau, *Walden and Civil Disobedience*, ed. Owen Thomas (New York: Norton, 1966), 66.

19. Emerson, "Compensation," *CW* 2:59. Parrington points out that Whitman "was a transcendentalist" (3:77); Hyatt H. Waggoner, *American Poets: From the Puritans to the Present* (1968; Baton Rouge: Louisiana State University Press, 1984), 160, observes that Whitman's poetry implies "the whole body of Emerson's Transcendental doctrine"; see also Lawrence Buell, "Transcendentalist Catalogue Rhetoric: Vision Versus Form," *American Literature* 40 (November 1968): 325–39; and Lynen 332–33.

20. Emerson, "Nature," *CW* 1:18.

21. Emerson, "Compensation," *CW* 2:60.

22. Emerson, "The Over-Soul," *CW* 2:160.

23. Emerson, "Nature," *CW* 1:22; italics added.

24. Thoreau 146.

25. "The Transcendentalist was satisfied with nothing so long as it did not correspond to the ideal in the enlightened soul; and in the soul recognized the power to make all things new" (Frothingham 182). Whitman's illuminations have caused him to be called "a romantic, a transcendentalist, a mystic" (Parrington 3:70); one who had "intuitive and almost mystical experience by which he achieved vision" (Leon Howard, *Literature and the American Tradition* [New York: Doubleday, 1960], 189); and one who "believed the poet was the agency of a transcendent power and created 'rapt verse' in an 'ecstasy of statement' " (Kaplan 189). Whitman's experiences incorporated aspects of thought ranging from transcendentalism and mysticism to pantheism. Gay Wilson Allen, *Walt Whitman Handbook*, 314, cites three "sources and parallels for Whitman's thought: (1) American Transcendentalism. . . . (2) European philosophy, especially German Idealism, and (3) Oriental mysticism, especially Hindu."

26. The novel has been called "Pynchon's Paranoid History," by Scott Sanders, "Pynchon's Paranoid History," *Twentieth Century Literature* 21 (1975): 177. Mark Siegel, *Pynchon: Creative Paranoia in 'Gravity's Rainbow'* (Port Washington, N.Y.: Kennikat Press, 1978), 107–8, sees this paranoia as a means of understanding the system in *Gravity's Rainbow*, a system that is "rooted in a theology from which God has been

withdrawn." It is a concept that "structures Pynchon's fiction" (Sanders 140). Jerome Klinkowitz, *Literary Disruptions: The Making of a Post-Contemporary American Fiction* (Urbana: University of Illinois Press, 1975), 12, who writes very little on Pynchon, observes that in *V.* "technique becomes theme; development is suspicion, plot becomes paranoia, and Pynchon is able to exploit the whole theory that 'the plots men see may be their own inventions.' " Klinkowitz quotes Richard Poirier, *The Performing Self: Compositions and Decompositions in the Languages of Contemporary Life* (New York: Oxford University Press, 1971), 9.

27. See Tony Tanner, *Thomas Pynchon* (New York: Methuen, 1982), 79.

28. Wernher von Braun, the "man whose allegiance / Is ruled by expedience," is ridiculed by Tom Lehrer in his recording *That Was the Year That Was.* Among the song's most cutting lines are: "Once the rockets are up, / Who cares where they come down. / That's not my department, / Says Wernher von Braun"; or "In German or English, / I know how to count down / And I'm learning Chinese, / Says Wernher von Braun." Reprise Records 6179.

29. See Richard Pearce's discussion of "Whitman's view of 'Nature without check' " as compared with Pynchon's emphasis on "nature that only knows transformation," in *The Novel in Motion* (Columbus: Ohio State University Press, 1983), 84.

30. See the excellent discussions of entropy by Stephen G. Brush, "Thermodynamics and History," *Graduate Journal* 7, no. 2 (1967): 477–565; and David Porush, *The Soft Machine: Cybernetic Fiction* (New York: Methuen, 1985).

31. Rudolf Arnheim, *Entropy and Art* (Berkeley: University of California Press, 1971), 9.

32. William Gaddis, "The Rush for Second Place," *Harper's* (April 1981): 36.

33. Gaddis makes this point in "The Rush for Second Place" 35.

34. Saul Bellow, "Some Notes on Recent American Fiction," in *The World of Black Humor,* ed. Douglas M. Davis (New York: Dutton, 1967), 336–37; Robert Alter, *After the Tradition* (New York: Dutton, 1971), 48–49; John Gardner, "The Sound and Fury over Fiction," as interviewed by Stephen Singular, *New York Times Magazine* (8 July 1979): 14; John Gardner, *On Moral Fiction* (New York: Basic Books, 1978), 94.

35. The tone that develops is black humor. See Chapter 1 and its n. 30.

Chapter Four

1. "The Literature of Replenishment," *Atlantic Monthly* 245 (January 1980): 71. Page references to "Replenishment" and to the following works will be identified parenthetically: "The Literature of Exhaustion," *Atlantic Monthly* 220 (August 1967): 29–34; Jorge Luis Borges, *Labyrinths,* ed. Donald A. Yates and James E. Irby (New York: New Directions, 1964). The emphasis on revitalization answers Barth's observation in "The Literature of Exhaustion" that since certain possibilities seemed to have been exhausted, some could believe: "the novel's time as a major art form is up" ("Exhaustion" 32). The statement on exhaustion also was expressed by José Ortega y Gasset, "Decline of the Novel," trans. Helene Weyl, in *The Dehumanization of Art and Other Essays on Art, Culture, and Literature* (1925; reprint, Princeton, N.J.: Princeton University Press, 1968), 58–59: "Whether a genre is altogether done for can, of course, never be decided with mathematical rigor; but . . . at least, that the material is getting scarce may appear frankly evident." Charles B. Harris, *Passionate Virtuosity: The Fiction of John Barth* (Urbana: University of Illinois Press, 1983), discusses "Exhaustion" and "Replenishment" as springboard for an analysis of Barth's method. Harris's focus is different from mine. He relates "Exhaustion" to *Lost in the Funhouse,* and he uses "Replenishment" as a means to discuss *Letters,* pointing to Barth's emphasis on combining "premodernist and modernist modes of writing." The material in this chapter is

Notes

taken in part from my article, "The Allusive Mode and Black Humor in Barth's *Sot-Weed Factor,*" *Studies in the Novel* 13, Winter, 1981. Copyright 1981 by North Texas State University. Used with permission.

2. Barth distinguishes his fictional poet by spelling his name "Cooke" rather than "Cook," the spelling most frequently used by the eighteenth-century author of "The Sot-Weed Factor."

3. Denham Sutcliffe, "Worth a Guilty Conscience," in *Critical Essays on John Barth*, ed. Joseph J. Waldmeir (Boston: G.K. Hall, 1980), 115.

4. Harris, *Passionate Virtuosity*, 57.

5. Jac Tharpe, *John Barth: The Comic Sublimity of Paradox* (Carbondale: Southern Illinois University Press, 1974), 51. In "Muse, Spare Me," *The Friday Book: Essays and Other Nonfiction* (New York: Putnam, 1984), 59, Barth comments on the advantage of using "historical or legendary material . . . in a farcical, even a comic, spirit." The way to handle the historical muse is not with "a long face," but with a "lighthearted approach." For Barth, all history is inevitably a fictionalization of our past, an inexhaustible source for tales. See Hayden White's explanation of this concept as "metahistory," in *Metahistory: The Historical Imagination in Nineteenth Century Europe* (Baltimore: Johns Hopkins University Press, 1979), 12. Alan Holder, " 'What Marvelous Plot . . . was Afoot?' " (Waldmeir 132), observes: "Ultimately, history exists in the book as a repository of details and plots that Barth wants to master and outdo, ending up as a literary John Coode or Henry Burlingame." Barth's "toying with history aims at our vital assumption that there are facts which can be indisputably established," observes Manfred Puetz in "John Barth's *The Sot-Weed Factor*: The Pitfalls of Mythopoesis" (Waldmeir 143).

6. See John Smith, *Travels and Works of Captain John Smith*, ed. Edward Arber with intro. by A. G. Bradley (Edinburgh: John Grant, 1910). References to the *Generall Historie* are to this edition.

7. Miguel de Cervantes, *Don Quixote*, ed. Kenneth Douglas and Joseph R. Jones (New York: Norton, 1981), 29.

8. John Barth, *Lost in the Funhouse* (1968; reprint, New York: Bantam, 1969), 94.

9. "Welcome to College—and My Books," *New York Times Book Review* (16 September, 1984): 37; see also the concluding line of *Chimera*: "The key to the treasure is the treasure" (56).

10. Richard Boyd Hauck, *A Cheerful Nihilism* (Bloomington: Indiana University Press, 1971), 228.

11. In "Welcome to College" (36), Barth explains that he regards *The Thousand and One Nights* "as a metaphor for the condition of narrative artists" and outlines the conditions of the parallel:

1. Scheherazade has to lose her innocence before she can begin to practice her art. Ebenezer Cooke did, too; so do most of us.
2. Her audience—the king—is also her absolute critic. It is "publish or perish" with a vengeance.
3. And her talent is always on the line. . . . she is only as good as her next piece. So are we all.

See also Barth's "Don't Count on It: A Note on the Number of the 1001 Nights" (1983), in *The Friday Book* 279.

12. John Leonard, "Books of the Times," *New York Times* (1 October 1979): C15.

13. Max Schulz, "Barth, *Letters*, and the Great Tradition," *Genre* 14 (1981): 113.

Notes

14. Harris, *Passionate Virtuosity,* 160.

15. Cotton Mather, *Magnalia Christi Americana,* bks. I and II, ed. Kenneth B. Murdock (Cambridge, Mass.: Harvard University Press, 1977), 101. See my discussion in chap. 1.

16. Earl Rovit, "The Novel as Parody: John Barth" (Waldmeir 122).

17. Campbell Tatham, "John Barth and the Aesthetics of Artifice" (Waldmeir 49), refers to the subordination but praises the artifice, nevertheless.

18. John J. Enck, "John Barth, An Interview," *Wisconsin Studies in Contemporary Literature* 6 (1965): 13.

19. Beverly Gross, "The Anti-Novels of John Barth" (Waldmeir 30).

20. Jay B. Hubbell's comments on Smith as legendary hero in "The Smith-Pocahontas Story in Literature," *Virginia Magazine* 65 (1957): 277; see also Philip Young's discussion of Pocahontas as "the most appealing of our saints": "The Mother of Us All: Pocahontas Reconsidered," *Kenyon Review* 24, no. 3 (1962): 391.

21. *Generall Historie* 2:530.

22. Compare the satiric tone in *Sot-Weed* with the reverent one in Smith's *Generall Historie* (2:395): "still defending himselfe [Smith] with the ayd of a Salvage his guid, whom he bound to his arme with his garters, and used him as a buckler, yet he was shot in his thigh a little, and had many arrowes that stucke in his cloathes but no great hurt, till at last they tooke him prisoner." Barth has explained: "This impulse to imagine alternatives to the world can become a driving impulse for writers. I confess that it is for me. So that really what you want to do is re-invent philosophy and the rest—make up your own whole history of the world" (Enck 8).

23. *Generall Historie* 2:531.

24. *Generall Historie* 2:400.

25. For further commentary on the Smith/Pocahontas story, see Jay Hubbell 277–78, 285–92, and Albert Keiser, *The Indian in American Literature* (New York: Oxford University Press, 1933), 70–74, 82–89. Critics have examined historical data to explain the significance of laying Captain Smith's head on a stone, ostensibly in preparation for beating out his brains. According to Philip Barbour, *The Three Worlds of Captain John Smith* (Boston: Houghton Mifflin, 1964), 441, this could have been an initiation rite set up by Emperor Powhatan to make Smith part of his tribe. Philip Young interprets the rescue as an "unorthodox and dramatic ceremony of marriage" (414).

26. Eric Bentley, "Farce," in *Comedy: Meaning and Form,* ed. Robert W. Corrigan (San Francisco: Chandler, 1965), 289. L. J. Potts, *Comedy* (London: Cheltenham Press, 1948), 151, observes that farce is "comedy with the meaning left out." See also Jessica Milner Davis, *Farce* (New York: Harper & Row, 1978), 1–24.

27. Richard Kostelanetz, "The New American Fiction," in *The New American Arts,* ed. R. Kostelanetz (New York: Horizon Press, 1965), 207, comments on "Barth's ability to mesh frustrated expectation, witty language, vivid description, timing, parody; so that, one kind of joke enhances another."

28. François Rabelais, *The Histories of Gargantua and Pantagruel,* trans. J. M. Cohen (Middlesex, England: Penguin, 1983), 74.

29. Smith's contemporaries W. Phettiplace and R. Pots, in rebutting slander against Smith, indicate that the historic Pocahontas craved John Smith as much as Barth's did: "Very oft shee came to our fort, with what shee could get for Captaine Smith. . . . If he would, he might have married her, or have done what him listed; for there was none that could have hindred his determination" (John Smith, *Works* 1:cxvii).

30. R.W.B. Lewis, *American Adam: Innocence, Tragedy and Tradition in the Nineteenth Century* (1955; reprint, Chicago: University of Chicago Press, 1971), 5. Eben is an Adam whose innocence is ridiculed. When Lord Baltimore (actually the disguised Henry Burlingame) hears him wish to "immortalize" the wonderful Maryland, he bursts into "a fit of laughing" and inquires, "Is't that you were born yesterday? Know you

naught of the true state o' the world?" (84–85). See Tharpe's comments on the theme of Adamic innocence (36); see also Holder 124–25.

31. As was mentioned earlier, however, the comparison also reflects ironically on the Whitmanesque persona, whose sheer idealism—advocating total freedom—could easily lead to anarchy and chaos.

32. Holder observes: "*The Sot-Weed Factor*'s own relation to the past would appear to be that of a Cosmic Lover . . . in the sense that the book refuses to commit itself to a particular conception of the past, of historical truth, but wants the freedom to embrace simultaneously a variety of possibilities" (130).

33. Tharpe 50.

34. Plato, *The Republic*, trans. Paul Shorey (Cambridge, Mass.: Harvard University Press, 1930–35), 514a–17a.

35. Plato, *The Republic*, 518d.

36. Henri Bergson, "Laughter," in *Comedy*, ed. Wylie Sypher (Garden City, N.Y.: Doubleday Anchor, 1956), 84.

37. See Aristotle's discussion of these terms in *The Poetics*, trans. William Hamilton Fyfe (Cambridge, Mass.: Harvard University Press, 1932), 1450b.

38. Russell H. Miller, "*The Sot-Weed Factor*: A Contemporary Mock Epic," *Critique* 8, no. 2 (1965–66): 94, cites this confrontation in which Eben uses "the language of romance and learning, Joan that of the street," as necessarily leading "only to misunderstanding" and to the "mock-epic" tone of the work.

39. Puetz observes that Eben "turns to the panacea of mythopoesis and creates fictional schemes and mythical worlds around himself" (136). Harris gives an optimistic argument for Eben's eventual change of myth: he exchanges "an inferior metaphor for a better one"—a "prelapsarian poet" for "postlapsarian man" (*Passionate Virtuosity* 76).

40. John Milton, *An Apology for Smectymnuus*, in *John Milton: Complete Poems and Major Prose*, ed. Merritt Y. Hughes (New York: Odyssey, 1957), 694.

41. Plato, *Symposium*, trans. W. R. M. Lamb (Cambridge, Mass.: Harvard University Press, 1925), 189c–93d.

42. Otto Rank, *Beyond Psychology* (1941; reprint, New York: Dover, 1958), 91.

43. Albert Camus, *The Myth of Sisyphus and Other Essays*, trans. Justin O'Brien (New York: Vintage, 1955), 37.

44. Ebenezer Cook, *The Sot-Weed Factor: Or, a Voyage to Maryland* (London: B. Bragg, 1708).

45. Robert Rogers, *A Psychoanalytic Study of the Double in Literature* (Detroit: Wayne State University Press, 1970), 130. It also can be said that the two women are doubles (Harris, *Passionate Virtuosity*, 81).

46. John V. Antush discusses the doubles Eben and Henry in "Allotropic Doubles in Barth's *Sot-Weed Factor*," *College Literature* 4 (1977): 71–79.

47. William Shakespeare, *Comedy of Errors*, in *The Complete Plays and Poems of William Shakespeare*, ed. William Allan Neilson and Charles Jarvis Hill (Cambridge, Mass.: Riverside Press, 1942), 5.1.332–34.

48. William Shakespeare, *Twelfth Night* 5.1.223–24.

49. Northrop Frye, *Anatomy of Criticism* (Princeton, N.J.: Princeton University Press, 1957), 167–70.

50. Barth is obviously aware of contemporary suspicions about the Pocahontas rescue. It is significant that Smith did not refer to the rescue in *A True Relation* (1608); he briefly mentioned it fourteen years later in the second edition of *New England Trials* (1622; Smith, *Works* 1:263) before writing the dramatic 1624 account in *The Generall Historie* (2:400). This account also includes a letter to Queen Anne (supposedly sent in 1616) that pays tribute to Pocahontas (2:531). E. Arber, in the Introduction to *The Works of Captain John Smith*, gives us a conventional answer to the problem: "The only

possible way of resisting the story is to regard Captain Smith as a confirmed liar, which is quite contrary to everything we know of him" (1:cxvi).

51. "A reverend Judge, who to the shame / Of all the Bench, cou'd write his Name" (Cook, *The Sot-Weed Factor,* lines 399–400).

52. J. A. Leo Lemay, *Men of Letters in Colonial Maryland* (Knoxville: University of Tennessee Press, 1972), 92, explains: "When Ebenezer Cook writes that 'In the County-Court of *Maryland,* very few of the Justices of the *Peace* can write or read,' he has crossed the boundary [of satire] and is burlesquing his English readers' notions of how ignorant and savage Americans are."

53. There has been debate over whether Cook's satire on the New World also ridicules the gullible persona and the British reader. Lawrence C. Wroth, *The Maryland Muse by Ebenezer Cooke: A Facsimile with an Introduction, American Antiquarian Society Proceedings,* n.s. 44 (1934): 280–81, states: "On account of the most unflattering picture of Maryland it presents it is read with indignation by those native sons who romanticize the history of their state." Lemay points out that the "account of New World manners [is] so distorted that it burlesques the ignorance and credulity of anyone believing such nonsense" (*Men of Letters* 92).

54. Puetz gives a more optimistic reading of Eben's pursuits at the close. The poet "abandons the false images [of perfection]. . . . He comes into his own, because he revokes all mythical preconceptions and deviates from the patterns of autistic creation." His "nasty work . . . heaps on Maryland the abuse it deserved all along" (Waldmeir 139).

55. Kenneth A. Thigpen, "Folkloristic Concerns in Barth's *The Sot-Weed Factor,*" *Southern Folklore Quarterly* 41 (1977): 237, explains that *Sot-Weed* moves "in a new direction" as the author "redefine[s] traditional notions about history and its transmission. We learn from *The Sot-Weed Factor* that any distinction between folklore and history must be subtle indeed."

56. Joseph Campbell, *The Hero with a Thousand Faces* (1949; reprint, New York: Meridian, 1956), 30.

57. Campbell 30.

58. Tharpe says: "Giles is less a tale of a hero's accomplishment than a tale of a hero's experiences" (57).

59. Robert Scholes, *Fabulation and Metafiction* (Urbana: University of Illinois Press, 1979), 75.

60. Pynchon and Gaddis also focus on age thirty-three: it is V.'s age when her deterioration has truly begun; and it is Wyatt's age when he chooses to "simplify" and live in the Spanish monastery. This shows the pervasiveness of Christianity as subject for ironic allusiveness in the comic epic novels.

61. Barth as scholar-teacher develops much of his humor by substituting academic terminology for biblical, as in the following examples:

Bible	Giles Goat-Boy
"Verily, verily, I say unto you, He that heareth my word, and believeth on him that sent me . . . is passed from death unto life." (John 5:24)	"Except ye believe in me, ye shall not pass." (391)
"A prophet is not without honor, but in his own country." (Mark 6:4)	"A proph-prof is never *cum laude* in his own quad." (690)
"For many be called, but few chosen." (Matt. 20:16)	"Many are Registered but few are Qualified." (296)

"Thou shalt love thy neighbor as thyself." (Matt. 22:39)	"Love thy classmate as thyself, or flunkèd be." (424)
"Whosoever shall not receive the kingdom of God as a little child, he shall not enter therein." (Mark 10:15)	"Except ye become as a kindergartener, ye shall not pass." (390)

See also James Gresham, *"Giles Goat-Boy:* Satyr, Satire, and Tragedy Twined" (Waldmeir 161), and his discussion of the pagan elements in the Spring Carnival party that George attends, where "Barth fuses tragedy and 'satire,' goat-song and 'satyr' " (161).

62. PAT is the acronym for Prenatal Aptitude Tests. When George is first fetched, he has his official PAT-card around his neck (104).

63. Richard Hauck observes that in George's first trial he "tries to divide humanity into elect and damned." Next, as a benevolent Christian, he decides to pass all: "absurd equalization." Finally aware of the comedy, he merely can "cheerfully and nihilistically . . . say both *yea* and *nay*" (*Cheerful Nihilism* 235–36).

64. Harris, *Passionate Virtuosity,* 94.

65. Harris, *Passionate Virtuosity,* 87.

66. Harris, *Passionate Virtuosity,* 88, 87.

67. Camus 10.

68. Enck, "Interview," 8.

69. See Josef A. Jungmann, *Public Worship,* trans. Clifford Howell, S. J. (Collegeville, Minn.: Liturgical Press, 1957), 73.

70. Barth comments: "The only way I could use it [tradition of the wandering hero] would be to make it comic, and there will be some of that in *Giles Goat-Boy*" (Enck, "Interview," 12). This figure is used with the permission of Random House, Inc., from its publication *Chimera,* by John Barth, New York, 1972. Copyright © 1972 by Random House, Inc.

71. See Joseph Campbell 245–46; Lord Raglan, *The Hero: A Study in Tradition, Myth and Drama* (London: Methuen, 1936), 179–80; and Campbell Tatham, "The Gilesian Monomyth: Some Remarks on the Structure of *Giles Goat-Boy*," *Genre* 3 (1970): 364–65.

72. Harris asserts that since " 'WESCAC's role had merely been that of an inseminatory instrument' . . . Giles is literally the son of man, a synthesis of 'studentdom's' various genes" (*Passionate Virtuosity* 92).

73. Tharpe 59.

74. Hauck, *Cheerful Nihilism,* 235.

75. Umberto Eco, "Innovation and Repetition: Between Modern and Post-Modern Aesthetics," *Daedalus* 114, no. 4 (1985): 171.

76. Alain Robbe-Grillet, *For a New Novel: Essays on Fiction,* trans. Richard Howard (1963; reprint, New York: Grove Press, 1965), 62, paraphrases Camus.

77. Claude J. Rawson, "Before the Professors Took Over," review of *A History of Modern Criticism: 1750–1950,* by René Wellek, *New York Times Book Review* (30 March 1986): 8, briefly remarks on "the production of a new poetry and prose that seem designed for classroom explication and cannot easily be decoded without it. . . . The massive fictions of what are called postmodern novelists are cases in point, not only in their difficulty, allusive density and simpering air of in-group donnishness, but also in their bulky appearance and learned showmanship, reminiscent of dissertations."

78. See Scholes, *Fabulation,* 82.

79. Enck, "Interview," 21.

80. For discussions of American and British academic novels, see John O. Lyons,

Notes

The College Novel in America (Carbondale: Southern Illinois University Press, 1962); and Mortimer R. Proctor, The English University Novel (1957; reprint, New York: Arno Press, 1977).

81. As Campbell Tatham, "The Gilesian Monomyth," 49, points out, it is a commonplace that "the 'key' to Giles Goat-Boy is simply the link between the universe and the university."

82. Visitors to the campus of Penn State often are shown particular landmarks mentioned in the novel.

83. Ralph Waldo Emerson, CW 1:53.

84. Emerson, CW 1:54.

85. Emerson, CW 1:59, 62.

86. Emerson, Early Lectures 2:195–204.

87. Emerson, Early Lectures 2:199, 202.

88. Mather, Magnalia 1:246; the account of Harvard College is in Magnalia 2:4.

89. Dr. Eierkopf's only involvement with the world is that of a voyeur. He uses his nightglass for such pleasures as watching a coed undress in her room a quarter mile away (Goat-Boy 364). Readers, however, are still tempted to work out the intricacies of Eierkopf's and Sear's scientific theories even though they ridicule the foolishness of these men. This is evident in James Gresham's lengthy analysis of how "the Tower Hall clockwork embodies Giles's dialectic principle" ("Giles Goat-Boy" 162).

90. Harris, Passionate Virtuosity, 93.

91. Sear and Eierkopf, always deep in thought, are mentally lost. They call to mind the mad astronomers in Swift's satire who "are so taken up with intense Speculations" that their Flappers must goad them to attention. This obsessive preoccupation is found as well in Swift's political projectors in the Grand Academy of Lagado, who are "wholly out of their Senses" and develop foolhardy "chimeras." Jonathan Swift, Gulliver's Travels, in The Prose Works of Jonathan Swift, ed. Herbert Davis (Oxford: Basil Blackwell, 1941), 11:143, 171.

92. For a serious interpretation of this maxim, see Scholes: "The mystery of the universe and the sphincter's riddle are the same because the genesis of the individual and the genesis of the cosmos are aspects of the same process. The proctoscope examining fundamental human anatomy will tell us the same thing as the lives of the saints: because saints, too, have fundaments, and because—though the place is the place for excrement—the mansions of love and creative power are indubitably there" (80).

93. The name of the college is particularly ironic because it is a blatant allusion to Tammany Hall in New York City: the prototype of mechanization and corruption of urban organization in the second half of the nineteenth century and on into a good part of the twentieth century.

94. Gresham 159.

95. Enck, "Interview," 21.

Chapter Five

1. Albert Camus, The Myth of Sisyphus and Other Essays, trans. Justin O'Brien (New York: Vintage, 1955), 37.

2. In "Black Humor: To Weep with Laughing," in Comedy: New Perspectives, ed. Maurice Charney (New York Literary Forum 1 [Spring 1978]: 42). Mathew Winston explains that black humorists "disorient us by their abuse of literary form, and they invite us to enjoy the joke." See the discussion of black humor in chap. 1 and its n. 30.

3. I use Pynchon's spelling for schlemihl throughout.

4. Morris Dickstein, "Black Humor and History: Fiction in the Sixties," Partisan Review 43, no. 2 (1976): 188.

5. Dickstein 188–89.

6. Walter Blair and Hamlin Hill, *America's Humor: From Poor Richard to Doonesbury* (New York: Oxford University Press, 1978), 226.

7. Walter Blair, *Tall Tale America: A Legendary History of Our Humorous Heroes* (1944; reprint, Chicago: University of Chicago Press, 1987), 71.

8. The frontier tales do have an underlying ominous aspect relating to the destruction of an Edenic wilderness as man kills nature's wildlife and cuts down its trees. However, as in "The Big Bear of Arkansas," the negative details are always ameliorated by scatalogical jokes and comic details.

9. The comments of Umberto Eco, "Innovation and Repetition: Between Modern and Post-Modern Aesthetics," *Daedalus* 114, no. 4 (1985), 161–84, have been helpful. See especially his discussion of the turbulent effect of ironic references in film (176–77). See also Wolfgang Kayser, *The Grotesque in Art and Literature*, trans. Ulrich Weisstein (New York: McGraw-Hill, 1966), esp. 173–75. This comical violence is a major strategy of Pynchon's social criticism.

10. This literary style of Pynchon's V. is also used in his *Gravity's Rainbow* and *The Crying of Lot 49*.

11. Because Pynchon often uses ellipses, brackets differentiate my ellipses from those in the text.

12. See Sanford Pinsker's discussion of Pynchon's urban adaptation of the tall tale, "The Urban Tall Tale: Frontier Humor in a Contemporary Key," in *Comic Relief: Humor in Contemporary American Literature*, ed. Sarah Blacher Cohen (University of Illinois Press, 1978), 261.

13. Blair and Hill 236.

14. Henri Bergson, "Laughter," in *Comedy*, ed. Wylie Sypher (Garden City, N.Y.: Doubleday Anchor, 1956), 84.

15. Pynchon's V. locks into earthly time instead of pointing to *kairos*, the providential time characterized by wholeness and fulfillment. It looks back to the riots in Florence in 1899, then to the destruction of natives in the German colony in South-West Africa in 1904, and to the repeated abuse and murder of the natives in 1922, and finally hints at World War II and the Holocaust.

16. Kayser 187–88.

17. Pynchon deals with the distressing content by reinterpreting it as a joke. In the process, the painful emotional energy is transformed and released in a humorous context. See Sigmund Freud, *Jokes and Their Relation to the Unconscious*, trans. James Strachey (New York: Norton, 1963), 51.

18. See *Gravity's Rainbow* 555. Samuel Eliot Morison discusses Thomas Pynchon's ancestor William, founder of the Springfield Colony, and the banning of Pynchon's book in "William Pynchon, Frontier Magistrate and Fur Trader," *Builders of the Bay Colony* (Boston: Northeastern University Press, 1981), 371–75; see also Ruth A. McIntyre, *William Pynchon: Merchant and Colonizer* (Springfield, Mass.: Connecticut Valley Historical Museum, 1961), 34.

19. The narrator's comments on Brenda serve as an ironic parallel to Michael Wigglesworth's message in his "Day of Doom," *The Day of Doom: or a Poetical Description of the Great and Last Judgment* (1662; reprint, New York: Spiral, 1929), 19, in which he urges the backsliding Puritans to renew their responsibilities and their faith: " 'Twas meet that ye should judged be, so that the world may spy / No cause of grudge, when as I Judge and deal impartially."

20. Pynchon's satire, however, is double-edged. He extends his ridicule to Puritanism itself, particularly in the stories about Slothrop's ancestry, in *Gravity's Rainbow*, where the author mocks the Puritans for their excessive control, which makes itself manifest in the twentieth century in the power of "They" over the new "preterite": people like Benny Profane.

21. Joseph W. Slade, *Thomas Pynchon* (New York: Warner, 1974), 111.

22. Camus 5. This absurdist concept gains much comic irony when considered in terms of Mircea Eliade's point that the religious man wishes to return to *"as it was in the beginning"* when man was closest to the sacred, and that man's desire to return takes the form of his yearning to "inhabit a space," a "dwelling." *The Sacred and the Profane: The Nature of Religion* (New York: Harcourt Brace Jovanovich, 1959), 65.

23. See Kesey, *Cuckoo's Nest,* 212.

24. William M. Plater, *The Grim Phoenix: Reconstructing Thomas Pynchon* (Bloomington: Indiana University Press, 1978), 226, writes that when Benny "receives messages—honest attempts at communication—from Rachel, Fina, and Paola, Profane invariably filters out anything human."

25. Though his actions are that of a schlemihl, Benny seems to make a travesty of Christian mysticism rather than Old Testament materials. Benny does, however, resemble the fool in Jewish literature in terms of his casual nature, his anti-intellectual stance, his lack of concern for society's riches. He affirms life, like them, but he continually speaks in terms of entropic decline instead of, like "Gimpel the Fool," showing a simple belief in God.

26. See Marghanita Laski, *Ecstasy: A Study of Some Secular and Religious Experiences* (Bloomington, Ind.: Indiana University Press, 1961), 341. Benny's shift from "yo-yoing" to experiencing excitement also parodies Evelyn Underhill's description of a mystic's "conversion" ,from restlessness and dissatisfaction to a contemplation of *"a hidden light"* and the experience of hearing "that which no tongue can express." *Mysticism: A Study in the Nature and Development of Man's Spiritual Consciousness* (New York: Dutton, 1930), 186–87.

27. Benny is an example of a *schlimmazel,* someone who has bad luck. As was mentioned in chap. 3, n. 12, the word is from the German *schlim* (bad) and the Hebrew *mazel* (luck).

28. They, like the rest of the Whole Sick Crew, are involved in yo-yoing, what Tanner calls "a pointless, destination-less moving around" (*Thomas Pynchon* 42–43).

29. See Underhill, 196, 232–33. Stencil's experience parodies the "awakening" of the mystic's consciousness, which Underhill describes as involving a break with the ordinary way of seeing things: "It was like entering into another world, a new state of existence" (191–92), one from which emerges a "deep intuitional knowledge of the 'secret plan' " (233), a perception that often is accompanied by a "Shining Brightness" (187). Laski describes the experience as causing "a loss of the normal sense of relationships" and a "regaining . . . in improved form" (*Ecstasy* 280).

30. W. T. Lhamon, "Pentecost, Promiscuity, and Pynchon's V.: From the Scaffold to the Impulsive," in *Mindful Pleasures: Essays on Thomas Pynchon,* ed. George Levine and David Leverenz (Boston: Little, Brown, 1976), 70, points out that "V. represents a mode in which the sacred and the profane are so profoundly mixed that an account which aims to experience the novel's primary subversions must attempt to discuss them together."

31. Tony Tanner, *Thomas Pynchon* (New York: Methuen, 1982), 44.

32. It has been commonplace in the twentieth century to refer to Wittgenstein: "The world is all that *is* the case" (italics added; Ludwig Wittgenstein, *Tractatus Logico-Philosophicus* [1921], trans. D. F. Pears and B. F. McGuinnes [New York: Humanities Press, 1974]). That Mondaugen's message is also derived from Wittgenstein adds to the humor. Barth also alludes to Wittgenstein in *Sot-Weed* when Ebenezer dismisses the possibility of viewing evil in the world in terms of the "fortunate fall" and God's grace: " 'Tis beyond me what it proves . . . I know only that the case is so" (657). See also *The End of the Road* in which the Doctor explains: *"The world is everything that is the case"* (81).

33. The scientific law has been used metaphorically to point to the decay in

physical, social, and spiritual aspects of our lives. Since society's "deterioration, decay, and dissolution are associated with the dissipation of energy," explains Stephen Brush, such degeneration "is the cultural counterpart" of the scientific law. "Thermodynamics and History," *Graduate Journal* 7, no. 2 (1967):481.

34. Henry Adams, *Degradation of the Democratic Dogma* (New York: Macmillan, 1919), 186–87.

35. Repercussions of the scientific law are developed in Pynchon's early short story "Entropy," *Kenyon Review* 22, no. 2 (1960): 277–92. The story indicates that the twentieth-century world is doomed to a "heat-death." Pynchon's character Callisto (using the third person, as he dictates to his girl friend) explains the ramifications of the Second Law of Thermodynamics: " 'As a young man at Princeton . . . Callisto had learned a mnemonic device for remembering the Laws of Thermodynamics: you can't win, things are going to get worse . . . who says they're going to get better' " (282). For Callisto, the "horrible significance of it all" is that "the isolated system—galaxy, engine, human being, culture, whatever—must evolve spontaneously toward the Condition of the More Probable" (282–83). Entropic decline would ultimately result in a universal leveling. This would lead to predictability, to the "More Probable," rather than the diversification and plenty that prevail in traditional American epic works such as "Song of Myself." Callisto is afraid that all would be like the endless party at Meatball Mulligan's apartment downstairs—where there is a breakdown of communication and a buildup of noise—or like the weather outside, which remains static, suggesting that equilibrium has already been reached. In his hermetically sealed apartment, Callisto tries to ward off the inevitable arrival of these moments of equilibrium, when "separate lives should resolve into a tonic of darkness and the final absence of all motion" (292). Thomas Pynchon, Introduction, *Slow Learner* (Boston: Little, Brown, 1984), 12–13, explains that "according to the OED the word [entropy] was coined in 1865 by Rudolf Clausius, on the model of the word 'energy,' which he took to be Greek for 'work-contents.' Entropy, or 'transformation-contents,' was introduced as a way of examining the changes a heat engine went through in a typical cycle, the transformation being heat into work. [. . . Eventually it was] given the cosmic moral twist it continues to enjoy in current usage."

36. Thomas Bangs Thorpe, "The Big Bear of Arkansas," in *Native American Humor*, ed. Walter Blair (New York: American Book, 1937), 347.

37. Blair and Hill 212.

38. J. A. Leo Lemay, "The Text, Tradition, and Themes of 'The Big Bear of Arkansas,' " *American Literature* 47 (1975): 342, writes of "Thorpe's portrayal of modern man, caught with his pants down, in the unthinking act of being human."

39. See Raymond M. Olderman, *Beyond the Wasteland: A Study of the American Novel in the Nineteen-Sixties* (New Haven, Conn.: Yale University Press, 1972), 124.

40. Dickstein 188.

41. Richard Slotkin, in *Regeneration through Violence: The Mythology of the American Frontier, 1600–1860* (Middletown, Conn.: Wesleyan University Press, 1973), and in *The Fatal Environment: The Myth of the Frontier in the Age of Industrialization, 1800–1890* (New York: Atheneum, 1985), analyzes the attitudes of those who experience a rebirth in committing atrocities and killing: "The trope of savage war . . . enriches the symbolic meaning of specific acts of war, transforming them into episodes of character building, moral vindication, and regeneration. At the same time it provides advance justification for a pressing of the war to the extreme point of extermination" (*The Fatal Environment* 61).

42. Tony Tanner, "The American Novelist as Entropologist," *London Magazine* 10 (October 1970): 11, observes that many contemporary American novelists "concentrate on people who precisely *are* turning themselves into 'isolated systems' . . . they take in a decreasing amount of information, sensory data, even food, with the result that

the sense of their own personal entropy is heightened and this sense is then projected over the world around them." Also helpful is Wylie Sypher's Freudian analysis of the "instinct . . . toward repeating or restating an earlier condition . . . [to move to the] untroubled security of not-being," the desire to extinguish "our individuality." *Loss of the Self in Modern Literature and Art* (New York: Random House, 1962), 75–76.

43. Slade observes that "V., in falling in 'love' with Mélanie, begins her career as a full fledged decadent." This episode, writes Slade, "marks her transformation into a goddess of death, a symbol of moribund Western culture" (*Thomas Pynchon* 72). Plater speaks of V.'s fetishism as showing her "drive to establish life only as a measure of decay' (148).

44. In 1922, as Vera Meroving (age forty-two), living in Foppl's baroque plantation house in South-West Africa, V. is identified by her glass eye, inside which are "the delicately-wrought wheels, springs, ratchets of a watch" (219). V., like the other people at Foppl's huge farm, is isolated from the massive slaughter of the Bondels, taking place nearby. Here, V. persists in questioning the elder Godolphin (now seventy-seven) about the shattering of his dream. "This," she says of the present destruction of the natives, "It's Vheissu. It's finally happened" (230). As she desires to hear about Vheissu, as seen through Godolphin's eyes, similarly she feels that she has experienced vicariously the killing of the natives in 1904 by General Lothar von Trotha and his men: "Lieutenant Weissmann and Herr Foppl have given me my 1904" (229).

45. Pynchon, like other black humorists, uses the comic to engage the reader in a novel that explores distressing problems in twentieth-century society. The historical details in *V.* disclose many worldwide and national problems: the corporate alliances, which have supported and controlled wars; the rise of mechanical energy, which has resulted in rocket programs; "nuclear weapons [which] multiply out of control" (Thomas Pynchon, "Is It O.K. To Be a Luddite?" *New York Times Book Review* [28 October 1984]: 40); the "racial sickness" in America and Europe, which causes riots and violence (Thomas Pynchon, "A Journey into the Mind of Watts," *New York Times Magazine* [12 June 1966]: 35).

46. From "The Ballad of Davy Crockett," *The Walt Disney Song Book* (New York: Golden Books, 1963), 91.

47. The hero Jim Doggett brags: "I once planted in those diggins a few potatoes and beets; they took a fine start, and after that an ox team couldn't have kept them from growing" (Thorpe 342).

48. Thorpe 339, 348.

49. See discussions of William Pynchon by Morison (371–75) and by McIntyre (34). Pynchon, in using Puritan themes, is in the tradition of American writers from colonial times to the present: Benjamin Franklin, Nathaniel Hawthorne, Herman Melville, and John Barth are obvious examples. Pynchon no doubt was influenced by his own personal Puritan heritage, having as ancestor William Pynchon, founder of the Springfield Colony. Later Puritan ancestors were Judge William Pyncheon (1723–98), who was a resident of Salem, and his extended family, who were described by Hawthorne in *The House of the Seven Gables.* Just as Slothrop's heritage ironically connects him to the Puritan past and so to "the origins of allegory in American culture" (Maureen Quilligan, *The Language of Allegory: Defining the Genre* [Ithaca, N.Y.: Cornell University Press, 1979], 205), so do the Puritan allusions and the jeremiad form of *Gravity's Rainbow* connect the epic novel to America's earlier literature. Richard Poirier discusses the "cultural inundation" in Pynchon's "distinctly American" fiction, "The Importance of Thomas Pynchon" (Levine and Leverenz 29).

50. Edward Mendelson, "Gravity's Encyclopedia" (Levine and Leverenz 166).

51. Perry Miller, *The New England Mind: From Colony to Province* (Cambridge, Mass.: Harvard University Press, 1953), 27; Miller explains that from the jeremiad

sermons "men arose with new strength and courage: having acknowledged what was amiss, the populace could . . . [return] trusting that a covenanted Jehovah would remember His bond" (51); see also Sacvan Bercovitch, *The American Jeremiad* (Madison: University of Wisconsin Press, 1978), 9–11, and *The Puritan Origins of the American Self* (New Haven, Conn.: Yale University Press, 1975), 115. See Marcus Smith and Khachig Tololyan's discussion of Pynchon's reworking of the Puritan jeremiad in "The New Jeremiad: *Gravity's Rainbow*," in *Critical Essays on Thomas Pynchon*, ed. Richard Pearce (Boston: G. K. Hall, 1981), 169.

52. Samuel Danforth, *A Brief Recognition of New England's Errand into the Wilderness* (1670), in *The Wall and the Garden: Selected Massachusetts Election Sermons 1670–1775*, ed. A. William Plumstead (Minneapolis: University of Minnesota Press, 1968), 63.

53. Danforth 64–65, 74.

54. Danforth 73, 75.

55. See Smith and Tololyan 172. See Michael Seidel, "The Satiric Plots of *Gravity's Rainbow*," in *Pynchon: A Collection of Critical Essays*, ed. Edward Mendelson (Englewood Cliffs, N. J.: Prentice-Hall, 1978), 193–212. Richard Poirier, in *The Performing Self: Compositions and Decompositions in the Languages of Contemporary Life* (New York: Oxford University Press, 1971), 27–28, writes that literature of "self-parody . . . makes fun of itself *as it goes along*" and "calls into question not any particular literary structure so much as the enterprise, the activity itself of creating any literary form." Charles Harris, in *Contemporary American Novelists of the Absurd* (New Haven, Conn.: College and University Press, 1971), 23, observes that contemporary writers "reject traditional forms and styles while at the same time continuing to use these forms and styles." The ironic imitation "becomes a comment upon the artificiality not only of art, but of life as it is usually lived . . . of all things which prevent the realization that life is absurd."

56. Readings of *Gravity's Rainbow* and *V.* range from the nihilistic to the qualified positive view. At one end of the scale are Josephine Hendin, "What Is Thomas Pynchon Telling Us? *V.* and *Gravity's Rainbow*" (Pearce 48), discussing Pynchon as revealing "death at the heart of all experience"; Tony Tanner, in "*V.* and *V-2*" (Mendelson 22), identifying "the most inclusive theme of the book . . . [as the fact] that twentieth-century man seems to be dedicating himself to the annihilation of all animateness"; Michael Seidel, "Satiric Plots," focusing on entropic disintegration; Roger Henkle, "Pynchon's Tapestries on the Western Wall" (Mendelson 100), tracing patterns that connect "the fall of western culture with the debasement of religious and poetic myths"; Plater, writing that "the entire backdrop of the novel is essentially the aftermath of Hitler's dream" (113). Others are more positive but still voice qualifications: George Levine, "Risking the Moment" (Levine and Leverenz 135), emphasizes the need to "risk action and loss by penetrating the moment . . . as Pynchon does, terrified but lovingly, for the risk is the possibility"; Seidel underlines the vision of paranoia leading to meaning. W. T. Lhamon, "Pentecost, Promiscuity, and Pynchon's *V*.: From the Scaffold to the Impulsive" (Levine and Leverenz 70), stresses the ambivalence of Pynchon's view: "Entropy . . . describes the ultimate collapse into material, Pentecost . . . an ultimate ascent into the spiritual." Pynchon's perspective is "entropic but it is also Pentecostal . . . it is promising terribly and also terribly promising" (Lhamon 84–85).

57. See Eco's discussion of this method (170).

58. See Blair and Hill's discussion of black humor (501).

59. John M. Krafft, " 'And How Far Fallen': Puritan Themes in *Gravity's Rainbow*," *Critique* 18, no. 3 (1977): 55, discusses how "New England and New England's Puritanism . . . constitute a major thematic element in . . . *Gravity's Rainbow*."

60. Eco discusses a *"post-modern aesthetics*, which is revisiting the very concepts of repetition and iteration under a different profile" (166).

61. See Richard Pearce, *The Novel in Motion* (Columbus: Ohio State University Press, 1984), 96.

62. See also Slade: "As Pynchon sees it, an older order is passing in apocalypse.... The rocket, a system itself, will dominate them all" (*Thomas Pynchon* 178).

63. At the opening a dreaming, sleeping body is identified as Prentice: "*But it is already light.* [...] His name is Capt. Geoffrey ('Pirate') Prentice" (3–5).

64. *PL* II.622-25. *Paradise Lost* is the premier example of a Puritan world view to which Pynchon, as an absurdist, poses a dark contrast in his novel about hell on earth.

65. *PL* I.63.

66. See Steven Weisenburger, "The End of History? Thomas Pynchon and the Uses of the Past" (Pearce 145).

67. Blicero's troubled thoughts link him to Satan's "Which way I fly is Hell; myself am Hell; / And in the lowest deep a lower deep / Still threat'ning to devour me opens wide" (*PL* IV.75–77).

68. Lhamon 74.

69. Slade reads this church episode as positive: "Mexico can be excited by a beautiful Christmas night scene in a Kentish church, a rare night of possibility which seems to 'banish the Adversary' " (*Thomas Pynchon* 214–15). But I believe there is an absurd contrast between Roger Mexico's desire for "the *possibility* of another night that could actually ... banish the Adversary" and the fact that this night cannot obliterate evil or Mexico's being "alone in the dark" (*Gravity's Rainbow*, 135–36; italics added).

70. Frank D. McConnell, *Four Postwar American Novelists: Bellow, Mailer, Barth and Pynchon* (Chicago: University of Chicago Press, 1977), 187.

71. Smith and Tololyan 171.

72. For a different view of Pynchon, see Edward Mendelson, "The Sacred, the Profane, and *The Crying of Lot 49*" (Mendelson 144–45), who believes that *Gravity's Rainbow*, like *V.*, is concerned with "the possibility of a transcendent coherence and connectedness," that both Pynchon's first and third novels are concerned with " 'real' connectedness ... [that] the book's final coherence, like that of the earlier book, is religious."

73. Dante Alighieri, "Letter to Can Grande," in *The Literary Criticism of Dante Alighieri*, trans. and ed. Robert S. Haller (Lincoln: University of Nebraska Press, 1973), 99.

74. Introduction (Levine and Leverenz 10).

75. The scene gives an interesting twist to Slothrop's sensitivity to things in the sky. It is possible to say that Slothrop's vision of the rainbow has moved him to a more organic life. He has lost the identities given him by his Puritan family and by the war. He seems to be disentangled from the system. He neither connects to the Puritan God nor to the man-made V-2 machine, but to a rainbow, as he reacts freely.

76. As Melvin Maddocks explains, "Slothrop figures as Pynchon's hellish parody on manipulated—that is modernly damned—man.... Gradually Slothrop becomes his own myth, his own abstraction, finally known only as Rocketman." "Paleface Takeover," *Atlantic Monthly* 231 (March 1973): 99–100.

Chapter Six

1. William Gaddis, "The Rush for Second Place," *Harper's* (April 1981): 36.

2. Nikolai Gogol, *Dead Souls*, trans. Andrew R. MacAndrew, Foreword by Frank O'Connor (New York: New American Library, 1961), 236. References to *Dead Souls* are to this edition.

3. William Gaddis, "Why I Write," lecture at the University of Delaware, 1 May 1985.

4. Gaddis, University of Delaware, 1 May 1985. Malcolm Bradbury, "The House That Gaddis Built," review of *Carpenter's Gothic*, by William Gaddis, *Washington Post Book World* (7 July 1985): 1, has called *The Recognitions* "the starting place for a whole new direction in contemporary American fictional experiment, opening the path for Thomas Pynchon and the modern labyrinthine novel." Cynthia Ozick, "Fakery and Stony Truths," review of *Carpenter's Gothic*, by William Gaddis, *New York Times Book Review* (7 July 1985): 1, calls William Gaddis "new coinage: an American original." At the same time, however, she points out that such a claim would "fall into his own comedy," for "originality is exactly what he has made absurd; unrecognizable." Tony Tanner, *City of Words: American Fiction, 1950–1970* (New York: Harper & Row, 1971), 393, praises "this amazing one-thousand-page work" for being "immensely rich and funny" and for ushering in a "new period of American fiction in which the theme of fictions/recognitions has come to occupy the forefront of the American writer's consciousness"; Steven Moore, Introduction, *A Reader's Guide to William Gaddis's "The Recognitions"* (Lincoln: University of Nebraska Press, 1982), 3, calls *The Recognitions* "a precursor of what in later years may be considered one of the most creative periods in American literature."

5. Gogol taunts the reader for being unwilling to have the "Christian humility" to ask himself: "Am I not, even slightly, somewhat of a Chichikov" (276).

6. Gogol 115–16.

7. René Wellek, Introduction, *Dead Souls*, Nikolai Gogol, trans. Bernard Guilbert Guerney (New York: Holt, Rinehart, and Winston, 1961) xiii. See also Philip Rahv, *Literature and the Sixth Sense* (Boston: Houghton Mifflin, 1969), 197, who points out that *Dead Souls* moves from "levity to despair."

8. Gogol 14.

9. Gogol 160. See also Donald Fanger's discussion of the novel's paradox: "Living people and dead ones may be clearly distinguished in the action, but the cumulative sense of the text denies this distinction." *"Dead Souls:* The Mirror and the Road," in Nikolai Gogol, *Dead Souls*, ed. George Gibian, trans. George Reavey (New York: Norton, 1985), 471.

10. "Rush" 36.

11. Gogol 253.

12. Lloyd Grove, "Gaddis and the Cosmic Babble: Fiction Rich with the Darkly Funny Voices of America," *Style, the Washington Post* (23 August 1985): B10, observes that Gaddis satirically emphasizes the confrontation between the desire in twentieth-century America to reestablish the values of the nation's heritage, on the one hand, and, on the other, the inclination to "grasp at mere counterfeits."

13. See Umberto Eco, "Innovation and Repetition: Between Modern and Post-Modern Aesthetics," *Daedalus* 114, no. 4 (1985):170.

14. Scramble the letters of *The Recognitions*, and you can come up with titles such as "I CHOSE ROTTEN GIN," "OI CHITTERING ONES," "THE R I COONS IGNITE," "THE ONION CREST G I," "TEN ECHOES RIOTING" (*JR* 515).

15. See *Book Review Digest* (1955) for excerpts from the original reviews of *The Recognitions*, which include statements from Milton Rugoff (*JR*'s Milton R. Goth), the *New York Herald Tribune Book Review* (13 March 1955); Granville Hicks (Glandvil Hix); Maxwell Geismar (M Axswill Gummer); and *Kirkus* (*Kricket Reviews*).

16. Brackets are used to distinguish editorial ellipses from those in *The Recognitions*. Frederick Karl, *American Fictions 1940/1980* (New York: Harper & Row, 1983), 183, points out that "Gaddis's aim is clearly to defamiliarize the familiar so as to force us to experience it freshly." Thomas LeClair, "William Gaddis, *JR*, and the Art of Excess," *Modern Fiction Studies* 27 (1981–82): 590, calls this method a "mimetic aesthetic." He emphasizes that "Gaddis was suggesting that art must admit its imitation of other art to free itself from unknowing copying and to restore the full being of its

subjects." Gaddis's novels provide "a new vision of contemporary reality"; John Leverence, "Gaddis Anagnorisis," in *In Recognition of William Gaddis,* ed. John Kuehl and Steven Moore (Syracuse, N.Y.: Syracuse University Press, 1984), 39, comments on the novel's "aesthetic theme of recognition, that is, originality is not invention but a sense of recall, a recognition of patterns that are already there."

17. Oxford English Dictionary.

18. Quoted in Cindy Smith, "William Gaddis Rails Against Misrepresentation" [University of Delaware], *The Review* (30 April 1985): 18.

19. From Ralph Waldo Emerson, "Old Age," *Essays of Ralph Waldo Emerson* (Garden City, N.Y.: Blue Ribbon Books, 1941), 548.

20. Ralph Waldo Emerson, "Nature," *CW* 1:13.

21. See Odell Shepard, *Pedlar's Progress: The Life of Bronson Alcott* (Boston: Little, Brown, 1937), 246–61; for further discussion of the content of some of the conversations, see Lawrence Buell, *Literary Transcendentalism: Style and Vision in the American Renaissance* (Ithaca, N.Y.: Cornell University Press, 1973), 82–89.

22. Kathleen L. Lathrop, "Comic-Ironic Parallels in William Gaddis's *The Recognitions,*" *Review of Contemporary Fiction* 2 (1982): 32, points out that "the author/ prophet sounds far more like Milton Berle than Jeremiah."

23. Erwin Panofsky, *Early Netherlandish Painting* (Cambridge, Mass.: Harvard University Press, 1966), I:2, refers to this alleged remark by Michelangelo.

24. *Recognitions of Clement, The Ante-Nicene Fathers,* ed. Alexander Roberts and James Donaldson (New York: Scribner, 1903), vol. 8; hereafter referred to parenthetically in the text as *Clem. R.* This third-century work is actually a pseudo-Clementine tract. Saint Clement of Rome, the follower of Saint Peter, lived in the first century A.D. For information about the text see the Introductory Notice. Basilius Valentinus, *The Triumphal Chariot of Antimony,* trans. Arthur Edward Waite (London: Vincent Stuart Ltd., 1962); see also Basilius Valentinus, "Practica," in *The Hermetic Museum,* ed. Arthur Edward Waite (London: John M. Watkins, 1953), vol. 1: 311–57; hereafter referred to parenthetically in the text as *HM*.

25. See Eco's analysis of the way such an author invites the reader "to play upon his encyclopedic competence" (171).

26. Albert Camus, *The Myth of Sisyphus and Other Essays,* trans. Justin O'Brien (New York: Vintage, 1955), 11.

27. Wyatt indicates that he is thirty-three when he speculates on his life in relation to Christ's: "Why, two thousand years ago, thirty-three was old, and time to die" (876).

28. That Camilla Gwyon died thirty years prior to Wyatt's visit to San Zwingli indicates that Wyatt was three at her death. This squares with the fact that "Wyatt was four years old when his father returned alone from Spain" (18) after traveling for several months following Camilla's death.

29. John Seelye, "Dryad in a Dead Oak Tree: The Incognito in *The Recognitions*" (Kuehl and Moore 79), observes: "The ritual of the Eucharist, as in a Black Mass, becomes an obscenity."

30. In the early part of *The Recognitions,* the protagonist is referred to as "Wyatt." In the middle, he is not referred to by name, and toward the end he is called "Stephen." On a literal level, we realize that the change to Stephen arises from Wyatt's assuming the identity of Stephan Asche, from the Swiss passport that Mr. Sinisterra/Yák forges for him. On a symbolic level, we appreciate that Wyatt finally has taken on the name of Stephen, first Christian martyr, the name his parents originally designated for him (27). Perhaps Gaddis wishes to call attention to the literal and symbolic levels by using the different spellings Stephan/Stephen. Bernard Benstock, "On William Gaddis: In Recognition of James Joyce," *Contemporary Literature* 6 (1965): 181, observes that "Stephen" is "the name Gaddis goes on to use for him, returning him full circle to the Stephen he should have been." Frederick Karl, "Gaddis: A Tribune of the Fifties" (Kuehl

and Moore 180), comments on "the paradoxes and ironies" of the name, for after burning his paintings, turning them to ashes, Wyatt assumes the name Stephan Asche: "He is the first Christian martyr, born out of the ashes of his own work." See also Steven Weisenburger, "Paper Currencies: Reading William Gaddis" (Kuehl and Moore 149–50), for a discussion of names in the novel.

31. Henri Bergson, "Laughter," in *Comedy*, ed. Wylie Sypher (Garden City: Doubleday Anchor, 1956), 84.

32. See John Leverence's discussion of links with alchemy in the novel. "Gaddis" (Kuehl and Moore 42). See also Moore, who discusses the importance of alchemy "in unifying the symbolic elements . . . and in providing a spiritual 'plot' to complement (and justify) the narrative of the novel" (*Reader's Guide* 10).

33. Leverence, "Gaddis" (Kuehl and Moore 40).

34. *HM* 1:316.

35. See John Read, *Prelude to Chemistry: An Outline of Alchemy* (1936; reprint, Cambridge, Mass.: M.I.T. Press, 1966), 183. Basilius Valentinus could have been a charlatan alchemist like the one whom Chaucer describes in the "Canon's Yeoman's Tale."

36. A typical alchemical laboratory had furnaces, odorous vapors arising from boiling liquids, various vessels with matter in different stages of change, emitting a variety of colors in the process. Usually sulphur, mercury, copper, lead, and, occasionally, antimony were dissolved, separated, and reunited. They often were combined with organic substances, such as eggs, blood, and excrement. Very important in the laboratory was a book of prayers, for the worker would appeal for divine help as he carried out his process. See Wayne Shumaker, "Alchemy," *The Occult Sciences in the Renaissance* (Berkeley: University of California Press, 1972) 170–75. See also Moore, who observes that the "secularization of salvation . . . takes the form of the redemptive power of art" (*Reader's Guide* 18).

37. In regard to color changes, the alchemist Cremer observes: "When the mixture is still black it is called the Black Raven. As it turns white, it is named the Virgin's Milk, or the Bone of the Whale. In its red stage, it is the Red Lion. When it is blue, it is called the Blue Lion. When it is all colours, the Sages name it Rainbow" (*HM* 2:77). Basilius Valentinus explained that the alchemist using antimony "can colour it red or yellow, white or black, according to the way in which he regulates the fire" (*Triumphal Chariot* 48). For a discussion of the "seasons" or "states" of the alchemical process, see also Martinus Rulandus, *A Lexicon of Alchemy* [1612], trans. A. E. Waite (1893; reprint London: John M. Watkins, 1964), 421–22; and Titus Burckhardt, *Alchemy*, trans. William Stoddart (1960; reprint, Baltimore: Penguin, 1974), esp. 182–95.

38. Gaddis states (in his notes): "The process of art is the artist's working out of his own redemption." Peter Koenig, " 'Splinters from the Yew Tree': A Critical Study of William Gaddis's *The Recognitions*" (Ph.D. diss., New York University, 1971), 90.

39. The alchemist Raymond Lully explains the process: "In our art, the thing that is unjustly defiled by the one will be absolved, cleansed and delivered from that foulness by another that is contrary to it" (*Recognitions* 222).

40. Tanner, *City of Words*, 398; see also David Madden, "William Gaddis's *The Recognitions*," in *Rediscoveries*, ed. David Madden (New York: Crown, 1971), 304: "The achievement of the orchestration of Gaddis's technical devices is the creation . . . [of a] perhaps spiritual, state of recognition." Grace Eckley, "Exorcising the Demon Forgery, or the Forging of Pure Gold in Gaddis's *Recognitions*," in *Literature and the Occult*, ed. Luanne Frank (Arlington, Tex.: University of Texas Press, 1977), 128, says that the occult serves as the "unifying force" in the novel, developing the anticipatory pattern of details pointing to Wyatt's redemption. For Peter William Koenig, "Recognizing Gaddis's *Recognitions*," *Contemporary Literature* 16 (1975): 71, "the novel offers no final answers to the questions it raises, but . . . the very suggestiveness and structure of his questioning constitutes a partial answer."

41. Karl comments that Stanley's death "while his . . . work soars in atonement, is a perfect expression of Henry Adams's virgin and dynamo: the machine crushes, the Virgin saves" (*American Fictions* 186); Christopher Knight, "Flemish Art and Wyatt's Quest for Redemption in William Gaddis's *The Recognitions*" (Kuehl and Moore 65–68), writes that Gaddis points out "the failure of not only Wyatt's but also his own quest for redemption through art. . . . Scraping the paint off the El Greco canvas in the monastery is symbolic of his recognition of this limitation. Truth must finally be sought beyond art's boundaries." On the other hand, Joseph S. Salemi, "To Soar in Atonement: Art as Expiation in Gaddis's *The Recognitions*," *Novel* 10, no. 2 (1977): 136, argues: "Stanley's work expiates the falsity of Wyatt's and that same work is the instrument of his martyrdom." For Salemi, "Art is the ultimate expiation, for through it . . . falsehood which lies at the core of existence is transfigured beyond the pettiness and sordidness of its context and origins." It is the frustrated desire to affirm this view, I think, that develops the black humor of the absurd in *The Recognitions*.

42. The leg incident becomes the source of farce when it is stolen, carried about town, and finally left in a train where it causes a commotion when "a shabby old man had found something" (340; see also 317, 325–26). This "coincidentally" happens in the same car in which Stanley is riding.

43. Johann Wolfgang von Goethe, *Faust: A Tragedy*, trans. Bayard Taylor (New York: Macmillan, 1930), II.ii.6834–35. Further references to *Faust* are listed parenthetically in the text; page numbers are to Taylor's edition, and line numbers have been added in brackets.

44. See Eco 170.

45. Johann Wolfgang von Goethe, *Conversations of Goethe with Eckermann and Soret*, trans. John Oxenford (London: Smith, Elder, 1850), 2: 400.

46. Emil Staiger, "On the 'Great Lacuna' and the Pact Scene," *Faust: A Tragedy*, trans. Walter Arndt and ed. Cyrus Hamlin (New York: Norton, 1976), 515–16, emphasizes the celebration of "incessant endeavor, striving and accomplishment" in Faust, the "symbol of the German soul." He also, however, thinks that Goethe, though seeing this as "spiritually justifiable behavior," would condemn this "eternal unrest . . . as tragic madness."

47. See, e.g., Wagner's imitation of Faust in the "Laboratory" scene in which Wagner is unaware of Mephistophelean magic in the creation of Homunculus (297 [II.ii.6820–7004]).

48. Moore points out that "Wyatt's asides to the dog during the preceding pages parallel those of Faust to the poodle Mephistopheles" (*Reader's Guide* 127). But, neither Moore nor anyone else, to the best of my knowledge, has closely examined these connections.

49. Leverence argues that there is an "alchemical parallel" to Wyatt's giving up the world and planning to simplify his life: "Wyatt has found wisdom through simplicity, even as the minor opus finds its completion with the simple purity and symbolic wisdom of silver." "Gaddis" (Kuehl and Moore 42).

50. Many critics see Wyatt's act as more promising than I do and stress his comment, "It's only the living it through that redeems it" (898). Miriam Fuchs, " 'il miglior fabbro': Gaddis' Debt to T. S. Eliot" (Kuehl and Moore 103), explains that each person "is punished for someone else's [sin] and atones for someone else's, just as that person does for him." Knight observes: "Gaddis defiantly argues for the reality of sin and, in turn, the possibility, through love, of redemption" (68). David [Peter] Koenig, "The Writing of *The Recognitions*" (Kuehl and Moore 31), writes: "Wyatt still has at least the possibility of finding redemption." However, Koenig does point out that Gaddis "deliberately reduced Wyatt's visible means of salvation" in the novel as compared to Gaddis's plans in the notes.

Notes

51. Harold Jantz, *The Form of Faust* (Baltimore: Johns Hopkins University Press, 1978), 83, describes our last vision of Faust as a movement from darkness to light, "death and resurrection, an end situation followed by a promise of continuity . . . a condemnation followed by a vindication." This is the pattern in the drama as a whole. Neil M. Flax, "The Presence of the Sign in Goethe's *Faust*," *PMLA* 98 (1983): 192, discusses the rainbow at the close as "a symbol provided by a divinely ordered nature"; Stuart Atkins, *Goethe's Faust: A Literary Analysis* (Cambridge, Mass.: Harvard University Press, 1958), 272–74, also stresses the sense of a regularly ordered design in *Faust*.

52. Koenig explains: "The hope that Gaddis extinguished in his plot he rekindled through parody." "The Writing" (Kuehl and Moore 31).

Chapter Seven

1. Commentators have faulted *Sometimes a Great Notion* for having "quirky and hallucinatory" images (Irving Malin, "Ken Kesey, *Sometimes a Great Notion*," *Books Abroad* 39 [Spring 1965]: 218), characters who engage in a "self-defeating struggle" (Kingsley Widmer, "The Post-Modernist Art of Protest: Kesey and Mailer as American Expressions of Rebellion," *Centennial Review* 19 [1975]: 124), and—in general—for being too diffuse, for having no central unity. Leslie Fiedler, "Making It with a Little Shazam," *Book Week* 2 (August 1964): 10, argues that the novel lacks unity. For a more positive view, see Barry Leeds, *Ken Kesey* (New York: Frederick Ungar, 1981), 55, who states that *Notion* "is a far more artistically impressive work [than *Cuckoo's Nest*] on several levels. In terms of structure, point of view, and theme, it is more ambitious, more experimental, and ultimately more successful." See also Stephen Tanner, *Ken Kesey* (Boston: Twayne, 1983), 142, who praises Kesey's "technical inventiveness": his "manipulation of point of view and experimentation with narrative technique."

The material in this chapter is taken in part from my article "The Absurd Quest and Black Humor in Ken Kesey's *Sometimes a Great Notion*," *Critique* 24, (1983): 228–40. It is used with the permission of the Helen Dwight Reid Educational Foundation. Published by Heldref Publications, 4000 Albemarle St., N.W., Washington, D.C., 20016. Copyright © 1983.

2. Martin Esslin, *The Theatre of the Absurd* (New York: Doubleday Anchor, 1969), 6. See my discussion in chap. 1 and its n. 29.

3. See *Cuckoo's Nest* 254. This seems to be what Kesey was referring to when he told interviewer Gordon Lish that in *Notion* he was "fooling around with reality and what reality can be." Gordon Lish, "What the Hell You Looking in Here for, Daisy Mae? An Interview with Ken Kesey," *Genesis West* 2 (1963): 23.

4. James F. Knapp, "Tangled in the Language of the Past: Ken Kesey and Cultural Revolution," *Midwest Quarterly* 19 (Summer 1978): 402.

5. Fiedler observes: "This vulgar gesture of contempt [seems] . . . the true symbol of his book's noblest and funniest meaning." However, Fiedler criticizes Kesey for not being able to hold it "long enough or heroically enough or comically enough" to sustain the novel ("Making It" 11).

6. Stephen Tanner points out that Kesey's writing embodies "the tension between nostalgia for the values and myths of the western frontier experience and rejection of the past in favor of radical social-cultural change" (Preface i).

7. W. D. Sherman, "The Novels of Ken Kesey," *Journal of American Studies* 5, no. 2 (August 1971): 195–96, argues: "This had been Hank's philosophy: laughter in the face of absurdity. . . . Had Joby not laughed, he may have been saved."

8. Kesey uses this term to emphasize the absurd.

9. Albert Camus, *The Myth of Sisyphus and Other Essays*, trans. Justin O'Brien (New York: Vintage, 1955), 11.

Notes

10. James E. Miller, *Quests Surd and Absurd* (Chicago: University of Chicago Press, 1967), 26.

11. For convenience, I have numbered Kesey's eleven chapters. Chapter 10 includes pages 505–46.

12. Camus 21.

13. Camus 37.

14. Camus 5.

15. The epigraph from *Sometimes a Great Notion* is from the song "Good Night, Irene." The sense of the absurd, however, does not vitiate the positive forces in the novel. M. Gilbert Porter, *The Art of Grit: Ken Kesey's Fiction* (Columbia: University of Missouri Press, 1982), 77, argues: "What prevails . . . is the indomitable human spirit to fight back against all odds, to struggle most fiercely for life when its back is against the wall, to show in every test true old-fashioned guts."

16. Porter comments on Lee's "Oedipal loss of mother love and concomitant loss of self esteem" (60); Leeds points out that Lee's lovemaking with Viv signifies being with the "wife of his symbolic father" and also, because of connections between Viv and Myra, repossessing "his mother sexually, apparently resolving his own classically Oedipal conflict" (85).

17. Kesey seems to have combined Freud's emphasis of a boy's Oedipal desire for the mother and Adler's "masculine goal" theory, which stresses the quest for power. See Sigmund Freud, *Three Contributions to the Theory of Sex. The Basic Writings of Sigmund Freud*, trans. A. A. Brill (New York: Modern Library, 1965), 533–629; and Patrick Mullahy, "The Theories of Alfred Adler," *Oedipus: Myth and Complex* (New York: Grove Press, 1955), 114.

18. Sigmund Freud, "The 'Uncanny,' " *Collected Papers*, trans. Alix Strachey (New York: Basic Books, 1959), 4:390–91.

19. Fiedler calls Lee an "impotent and envious witness" ("Making It" 10).

20. One is reminded of Sartre's Antoine Roquentin, who continually tries to control the physical nausea caused by the "fundamental absurdity" he experiences. Jean-Paul Sartre, *Nausea*, trans. Lloyd Alexander (New York: New Directions, 1964), 129.

21. Wolfgang Kayser, *The Grotesque in Art and Literature*, trans. Ulrich Weisstein (New York: McGraw-Hill, 1963), 186, observes: "Tragedy opens precisely within the sphere of the meaningless and the absurd the possibility of a deeper meaning—in fate, which is ordained by the gods, and in the greatness of the tragic hero."

22. See Stephen Tanner 68.

23. Whether Hank actually knows that Lee has seen him with Myra is debatable. His words to Lee—"If you wasn't a kid and I found out what you'd been" (40)—seem to refer to Lee's pretending to be sick so that his mother will take him to the East. However, it could refer to Lee's watching Hank and Myra through the hole in the wall. Similarly, Lee's later conclusion is ambiguous: "So *that's* how he used to know I was watching; my room would cast a corresponding beam into the next-door dimness which went out when interrupted by something solid, like my head" (500). Here, again, it seems that Lee's statement is not conclusive evidence. Hank was probably too engrossed in lovemaking to be looking at the bedroom wall, while Lee, focusing always on his effect on Hank, looks around and views the scene "with academic detachment" (500).

24. Joseph Heller, *Catch-22* (1955; reprint, New York: Dell, 1970), 270–72.

25. Henri Bergson, "Laughter," in *Comedy*, ed. Wylie Sypher (New York: Doubleday Anchor, 1956), 84, 97–98. Thomas Hobbes, *The Elements of Law, Natural and Politic*, ed. Ferdinand Tönnies (Cambridge: Cambridge University Press, 1928), 32.

26. John Ruskin, "Grotesque Renaissance," *The Stones of Venice*, chap. 3, *The Works of John Ruskin*, ed. E. T. Cook and Alexander Wedderburn (London: George Allen, 1904), 11:151; Ruskin observes: "The grotesque is, in almost all cases, composed of two elements, one ludicrous, the other fearful"; Kayser 187–88; Annie Reich, "The

Notes

Structure of the Grotesque-Comic Sublimation," *Bulletin of the Menninger Clinic* 13, no. 5 (1949): 166.

27. What really matters at the conclusion is not whether or not Lee and Hank will succeed in their logging mission but that they, like Sisyphus, are striving. In this sense, each "is superior to his fate" just as Sisyphus "is stronger than his rock" (Camus 89). Therefore, critics have pointed out that "Kesey's focus is on gains, not losses" (Porter 72); that Hank and Lee, in their fistfight and merger, "complete their fusion, a union of East and West, urbane and countrified, cerebral and physical" (Leeds 57).

28. Bruce Jay Friedman, *Stern* (1962; reprint, New York: Pocket Books, 1970), 43.

29. Irving Malin says this about Kesey's first novel in "Ken Kesey, *One Flew Over the Cuckoo's Nest*," in *Ken Kesey: One Flew Over the Cuckoo's Nest,* ed. John Clark Pratt (New York: Viking, 1973), 434. See also Joseph J. Waldmeir, "Two Novelists of the Absurd: Heller and Kesey" (Pratt 401–11); James E. Miller, "The Humor in the Horror" (Pratt 397–400); and Terry G. Sherwood, "*One Flew Over the Cuckoo's Nest* and the Comic Strip" (Pratt 382–96).

30. See Tom Wolfe, *The Electric Kool-Aid Acid Test* (New York: Bantam, 1969), 35.

31. Wolfe 352.

32. Sherwood 383.

33. Leslie Fiedler, *The Return of the Vanishing American* (New York: Stein and Day, 1969), 178.

34. Fiedler, *Return,* 181, says that this is Bromden's view of McMurphy.

35. Sherwood 383.

36. Camus 91.

Chapter Eight

1. For further discussion of the intermixing of styles, see Peter Mercer, "The Rhetoric of *Giles Goat-Boy,*" *Novel* 4, no. 2 (Winter 1971): 147–51.

2. See Homer Goldberg, *The Art of Joseph Andrews* (Chicago: University of Chicago Press, 1969). See also Martin Battestin, who writes that "in *Joseph Andrews* character and action were made to imply a dimension of meaning larger than their literal reality: the twin heroes . . . [are] representatives of the cardinal Christian virtues of chastity and charity." *The Providence of Wit: Aspects of Form in Augustan Literature and the Arts* (Oxford: Clarendon, 1974), 11. See also Martin C. Battestin, *The Moral Basis of Fielding's Art* (Middletown, Conn.: Wesleyan University Press, 1959), 30–43.

3. See E.M.W. Tillyard, *The Epic Strain in the English Novel* (London: Chatto & Windus, 1958), 24; Barbara Kiefer Lewalski, *'Paradise Lost' and the Rhetoric of Literary Forms* (Princeton, N.J.: Princeton University Press, 1985), 45, points out that traditional epics have been described as a composite of literary types.

4. See Hugh Kenner's discussion of Joyce's "Protean text," *The Stoic Comedians: Flaubert, Joyce and Beckett* (Berkeley: University of California Press, 1972), 50–54. See also Umberto Eco, *The Aesthetics of Chaosmos: The Middle Ages of James Joyce,* trans. Ellen Esrock (Tulsa, Okla.: University of Tulsa Press, 1982), 33, who calls *Ulysses* "an encyclopedia and a literary *summa.*"

5. Kenner, *Stoic Comedians,* 59, says this of *Ulysses.*

6. James Joyce, *Ulysses: The Corrected Text,* ed. Hans Walter Gabler (New York: Vintage Books, 1986), 161. As was mentioned earlier, this line is added in the "Corrected Text."

7. See Frank Kermode's discussion of the readers' expectation for fulfillment, their desire for *kairos*—eternal, providential time. *The Sense of an Ending* (1967; reprint, New York: Oxford University Press, 1968), 48.

8. See Umberto Eco, "Innovation and Repetition: Between Modern and Post-Modern Aesthetics," *Daedalus* 114, no. 4 (1985): 170.

9. Michael Seidel, "The Satiric Plots of *Gravity's Rainbow*," *Pynchon: A Collection of Critical Essays,* ed. Edward Mendelson (Englewood Cliffs, N.J.: Prentice-Hall, 1978), 196.

10. Cotton Mather, *Magnalia Christi Americana,* ed. Kenneth B. Murdock (Cambridge, Mass.: Harvard University Press, 1977), 101, makes this point.

11. Jorge Luis Borges, *Labyrinths,* ed. Donald A. Yates and James E. Irby (New York: New Directions, 1964), 18.

12. Hugh Kenner, *The Counterfeiters* (New York: Doubleday Anchor, 1973), 5.

13. Malcolm Bradbury, review of *Moscow 2042,* by Vladimir Voinovich, *New York Times Book Review* (7 June 1987): 1.

SELECTED
BIBLIOGRAPHY

Adams, Henry. *The Degradation of the Democratic Dogma*. New York: Macmillan, 1919.
———. *The Education of Henry Adams*. Boston: Houghton Mifflin, 1918.
Allen, Gay Wilson. *The New Walt Whitman Handbook*. New York: New York University Press, 1975. [*New Handbook*]
———. *Walt Whitman Handbook*. Chicago: Packard, 1946. [*Handbook*]
Alter, Robert. *After the Tradition*. New York: Dutton, 1969.
———. "The New American Novel." *Commentary* 60 (November 1975): 44–51.
———. *Partial Magic*. Berkeley: University of California Press, 1975.
Antush, John V. "Allotropic Doubles in Barth's *Sot-Weed Factor*." *College Literature* 4 (1977): 71–79.
Arber, Edward, ed. *Travels and Works of Captain John Smith*. By John Smith. Edinburgh: John Grant, 1910.
Archives of Maryland. Vol. 5. *Proceedings of the Council of Maryland 1667–87*. Edited by William Hand Browne. Baltimore: Maryland Historical Society.
Aristotle. *The Poetics*. Translated by William Hamilton Fyfe. Cambridge, Mass.: Harvard University Press, 1932.
Arnheim, Rudolf. *Entropy and Art*. Berkeley: University of California Press, 1971.
Atkins, Stuart. *Goethe's Faust: A Literary Analysis*. Cambridge, Mass.: Harvard University Press, 1958.
Ayrton, Michael. Introduction. In *Art Themes and Variations*. By K. E. Maison. New York: Harry N. Abrams, 1960.
Bakhtin, M. M. *The Dialogic Imagination*. Edited by Michael Holquist and translated by Caryl Emerson and Michael Holquist. Austin: University of Texas Press, 1981.
———. *Rabelais and His World*. Translated by Helene Iswolsky. Bloomington: Indiana University Press, 1984.
Barbour, Philip L. *The Three Worlds of Captain John Smith*. Boston: Houghton Mifflin, 1964.
Barth, John. *Chimera*. New York: Random House, 1972.
———. *The End of the Road*. New York: Doubleday, 1958. Revised edition, 1967. Reprint. New York: Bantam, 1969.
———. *The Friday Book: Essays and Other Nonfiction*. New York: Putnam, 1984.
———. *Giles Goat-Boy or, The Revised New Syllabus*. New York: Doubleday, 1966. Reprint. Greenwich, Conn.: Fawcett Crest, 1968.

193

Bibliography

———. "John Barth: An Interview." With John J. Enck. *Wisconsin Studies in Contemporary Literature* 6 (1965): 3–14.

———. *Letters: A Novel*. New York: Putnam, 1979.

———. "The Literature of Exhaustion." *Atlantic Monthly* (August 1967): 29–34.

———. "The Literature of Replenishment." *Atlantic Monthly* (January 1980): 65–71.

———. *Lost in the Funhouse*. New York: Doubleday, 1968. Reprint. New York: Bantam, 1969.

———. "Muse Spare Me." In *The Friday Book: Essays and Other Nonfiction*, 55–59. New York: Putnam, 1984.

———. *Sabbatical: A Romance*. New York: Putnam, 1982.

———. *The Sot-Weed Factor*. New York: Doubleday, 1960. Revised edition, 1967. Reprint. New York: Bantam, 1975.

———. "Welcome to College—and My Books." *New York Times Book Review* (16 September 1984): 1+.

Basilius Valentinus. "Practica." *The Hermetic Museum*. Translated by Arthur Edward Waite. 1678. London: John M. Watkins, 1953. 1:307–57. [HM 1]

———. *The Triumphal Chariot of Antimony*. Translated by Arthur Edward Waite. London: Vincent Stuart, 1962.

Battestin, Martin C., ed. *Joseph Andrews*. By Henry Fielding. Middletown, Conn.: Wesleyan University Press, 1967.

———. *The Moral Basis of Fielding's Art*. Middletown, Conn.: Wesleyan University Press, 1959.

———. *The Providence of Wit: Aspects of Form in Augustan Literature and the Arts*. Oxford: Clarendon, 1974.

Beasley, Jerry C. *Novels of the 1740's*. Athens: University of Georgia Press, 1982.

Behrendt, Stephen C. "The Best Criticism: Imitation as Criticism in the Eighteenth Century." *Eighteenth Century* 24 (1983): 3–22.

Bellow, Saul. "Some Notes on Recent American Fiction." In *The World of Black Humor*, edited by Douglas M. Davis, 329–37. New York: Dutton, 1967.

Benstock, Bernard. "On William Gaddis: In Recognition of James Joyce." *Contemporary Literature* 6 (1965): 177–89.

Bentley, Eric. "Farce." *Comedy: Meaning and Form*, edited by Robert W. Corrigan, 279–303. San Francisco: Chandler, 1965.

Bercovitch, Sacvan. *The American Jeremiad*. Madison: University of Wisconsin Press, 1978.

———, ed. *The American Puritan Imagination*. London: Cambridge University Press, 1974.

———. "Cotton Mather." *Major Writers of Early American Literature*. Edited by Everett Emerson. Madison: University of Wisconsin Press, 1972.

———. " 'Nehemias Americanus': Cotton Mather and the Concept of the Representative American." *Early American Literature* 8 (1974): 220–38.

———. "New England Epic: Cotton Mather's *Magnalia Christi Americana*." *ELH* 33 (1966): 337–50.

———. *The Puritan Origins of the American Self*. New Haven, Conn.: Yale University Press, 1975.

———. "Rhetoric and History in Early New England: The Puritan Errand Reassessed." *Toward a New American Literary History: Essays in Honor of Arlin Turner*, edited by Louis J. Budds et al., 54–68. Durham, N.C.: Duke University Press, 1980.

———. *Typology and Early American Literature*. Amherst: University of Massachusetts Press, 1972.

———. "The Typology of America's Mission." *American Quarterly* 30 (Summer 1978): 135–55.

Bibliography

Bergson, Henri. "Laughter." In *Comedy*. Edited by Wylie Sypher. Garden City, N.Y.: Doubleday Anchor, 1956.

Berkeley, George. "Verses on the Prospect of Planting Arts and Learning in America." In *A Collection of English Poems 1660–1800*, edited by Ronald S. Crane, 340. New York: Harper, 1932.

Black, Joel Dana. "The Paper Empires and Empirical Fictions of William Gaddis." In *In Recognition of William Gaddis*, edited by John Kuehl and Steven Moore, 162–73. Syracuse, N.Y.: Syracuse University Press, 1984.

Blair, Walter. *Tall Tale America: A Legendary History of Our Humorous Heroes*. 1944. Reprint. Chicago: University of Chicago Press, 1987.

———, ed. *Native American Humor*. New York: American Book, 1937.

———, and Hamlin Hill. *America's Humor: From Poor Richard to Doonesbury*. New York: Oxford University Press, 1978.

Bloom, Harold. *A Map of Misreading*. New York: Oxford University Press, 1975.

Borges, Jorge Luis. *Labyrinths*. Edited by Donald A. Yates and James E. Irby. New York: New Directions, 1964.

Bradbury, Malcolm. "The House That Gaddis Built." Review of *Carpenter's Gothic*, by William Gaddis. *Washington Post* (7 July 1985): 1+.

———. *The Modern American Novel*. New York: Oxford University Press, 1983.

———. Review of *Moscow 2042*, by Vladimir Voinovich. *New York Times Book Review* (7 June 1987): 1, +.

Bradford, William. *History of Plymouth Plantation, 1620–1647*. 2 vols. Edited by Worthington Chauncey Ford. Boston: Houghton Mifflin, 1912. [Ford]

———. *Of Plymouth Plantation, 1620–1647*. Edited by Samuel E. Morison, New York: Knopf, 1952.

Bradley, Sculley, and Harold W. Blodgett, eds. *Walt Whitman: Leaves of Grass*. New York: Norton, 1973.

Brennan, William. "Milton's *Of Education* and the Translatio Studii." *Milton Q* 15 (1981): 55–59.

Bridenbaugh, Carl, ed. *The Pynchon Papers*. Boston: Colonial Society of Massachusetts, 1982.

Brower, Reuben Arthur. *Alexander Pope: The Poetry of Allusion*. Oxford: Clarendon, 1959.

Brumm, Ursula. *American Thought and Religious Typology*. Translated by John Hooglund. New Brunswick, N.J.: Rutgers University Press, 1970.

———. "Did the Pilgrims Fall upon Their Knees When They Arrived in the New World? Art and History in the Ninth Chapter, Book One, of Bradford's History *Of Plymouth Plantation*." *Early American Literature* 12 (Spring 1977): 25–35.

Brush, Stephen G. "Thermodynamics and History." *Graduate Journal* 7, no. 2 (1967): 477–565.

Buell, Lawrence. *Literary Transcendentalism: Style and Vision in the American Renaissance*. Ithaca, N.Y.: Cornell University Press, 1973.

———. "Transcendentalist Catalogue Rhetoric: Vision Versus Form." *American Literature* 40 (1968): 325–39.

Burckhardt, Titus. *Alchemy*. Translated by William Stoddart. 1960. Reprint. Baltimore: Penguin, 1974.

Burns, Edward McNall. *The American Idea of Mission: Concepts of National Purpose and Destiny*. New Brunswick, N.J.: Rutgers University Press, 1957.

Byington, Ezra Hoyt. *The Puritan in England and New England*. New York: Burt Franklin, 1972.

Campbell, Joseph. *The Hero with a Thousand Faces*. 1949. Reprint. New York: Meridian, 1956.

Camus, Albert. *The Myth of Sisyphus and Other Essays.* Translated by Justin O'Brien. New York: Vintage, 1955.

Cervantes, Miguel de. *Don Quixote.* Edited by Kenneth Douglas and Joseph R. Jones. New York: Norton, 1981.

Charney, Maurice. *Comedy High and Low.* New York: Oxford University Press, 1978.

Clementine Recognitions. See *Recognitions of Clement.*

Cochrane, Rexmond C. "Bishop Berkeley and the Progress of Arts and Learning: Notes on a Literary Convention." *Huntington Library Quarterly* 17 (May 1954): 229–49.

Cohen, Sarah Blacher, ed. Introduction. *Comic Relief: Humor in Contemporary American Literature.* Urbana: University of Illinois Press, 1978.

———. *Jewish Wry.* Bloomington: Indiana University Press, 1987.

Cook, Ebenezer. *The Sot-Weed Factor: Or, a Voyage to Maryland.* London: B. Bragg, 1708.

Cooper, Peter L. *Signs and Symptoms: Thomas Pynchon and the Contemporary World.* Berkeley: University of California Press, 1983.

Cowart, David. *Thomas Pynchon: The Art of Allusion.* Carbondale: Southern Illinois University Press, 1980.

Cowley, Malcolm, ed. *The Complete Poetry and Prose of Walt Whitman.* New York: Pellegrini & Cudahy, 1948.

Cox, Roger L. "The Structure of Comedy." *Thought* 50 (1975): 67–83.

Dannenfeldt, Karl H. "The Renaissance and the Pre-Classical Civilizations." *JHI* 13 (1952): 435–49.

Danforth, Samuel. *A Brief Recognition of New England's Errand into the Wilderness* (1670), in *The Wall and the Garden: Selected Massachusetts Election Sermons 1660–1775,* edited by A. William Plumstead, 47–77. Minneapolis: University of Minnesota Press, 1968.

Dante Alighieri. "Letter to Can Grande." *The Literary Criticism of Dante Alighieri.* Translated and edited by Robert S. Haller. Lincoln: University of Nebraska Press, 1973.

Davenant, Sir William. "Preface to *Gondibert.*" *Critical Essays of the Seventeenth Century.* Edited by J. E. Spingarn. 1908. Reprint. Illinois: Interstate Printers, 1957.

Davis, Douglas M. Introduction. *The World of Black Humor.* New York: Dutton, 1967.

Davis, Jessica Milner. *Farce.* New York: Harper & Row, 1978.

Demott, Benjamin. "Did the 1960's Damage Fiction?" *New York Times Book Review* (8 July 1984): 1+.

Dickstein, Morris. "Black Humor and History: Fiction in the Sixties." *Partisan Review* 43, no. 2 (1976): 185–211.

Dundes, Alan, and Thomas Hauschild. "Auschwitz Jokes." *Western Folklore* 42, no. 4 (October 1983): 249–60.

Dürrenmatt, Friedrich. *Problems of the Theatre* and *The Marriage of Mr. Mississippi.* Translated by Gerhard Nellhaus. New York: Grove Press, [1965].

Eckley, Grace. "Exorcising the Demon Forgery, or the Forging of Pure Gold in Gaddis's *Recognitions.*" In *Literature and the Occult,* edited by Luanne Frank, 125–36. Arlington, Tex.: University of Texas Press, 1977.

Eco, Umberto. "Innovation and Repetition: Between Modern and Post-Modern Aesthetics." *Daedalus* 114, no. 4 (1985): 161–84.

———. *The Aesthetics of Chaosmos: The Middle Ages of James Joyce.* Translated by Ellen Esrock. Tulsa, Okla.: University of Tulsa Press, 1982.

Eliade, Mircea. *The Sacred and the Profane.* Translated by Willard R. Trask. New York: Harcourt Brace Jovanovich, 1959.

Eliot, T. S. "Tradition and the Individual Talent." In *The Sacred Wood,* 47–59. 1920. Reprint. London: Methuen, 1967.

Ellmann, Richard. Preface. *Ulysses: The Corrected Text*. By James Joyce. Edited by Hans Walter Gabler. New York: Vintage Books, 1986.

Emerson, Ralph Waldo. "Address on Education." In *The Early Lectures of Ralph Waldo Emerson*. 3 vols. Edited by Stephen E. Whicher, Robert E. Spiller, and Wallace E. Williams, 2:195–204. Cambridge, Mass.: Harvard University Press, 1964.

———. *Collected Works*. 3 vols. Edited by Alfred R. Ferguson et al. Cambridge, Mass.: Harvard University Press, Belknap Press, 1971–83. Citations are to volume and page. [CW]

———. *The Early Lectures of Ralph Waldo Emerson*. 3 vols. Edited by Stephen E. Whicher, Robert E. Spiller, and Wallace E. Williams. Cambridge, Mass.: Harvard University Press, 1959–72.

———. "Old Age." In *Essays of Ralph Waldo Emerson*, 542–49. Garden City, N.Y.: Blue Ribbon Books, 1941.

Enck, John J. "John Barth, An Interview." *Wisconsin Studies in Contemporary Literature* 6 (1965): 3–14.

Esslin, Martin. *The Theatre of the Absurd*. New York: Doubleday Anchor, 1969.

Farwell, Harold. "John Barth's Tenuous Affirmation: 'The Absurd, Unending Possibility of Love.' " In *Critical Essays on John Barth*, edited by Joseph J. Waldmeir, 55–67. Boston: G. K. Hall, 1980.

Feldman, Burton. "Anatomy of Black Humor." In *The American Novel Since World War II*, edited by Marcus Klein, 224–28. New York: Fawcett, 1969.

Fiedler, Leslie A. "Making It with a Little Shazam." *Book Week* (2 August 1964): 1+.

———. *The Return of the Vanishing American*. New York: Stein and Day, 1969.

Fielding, Henry. *Joseph Andrews*. Edited by Martin C. Battestin. Middletown, Conn.: Wesleyan University Press, 1967.

Fielding, Sarah. *The Adventures of David Simple*. 1744. New York: Oxford University Press, 1969.

Flax, Neil M. "The Presence of the Sign in Goethe's *Faust*." *PMLA* 98 (1983): 183–203.

Foster, Frank Hugh. *A Genetic History of the New England Theology*. New York: Russell & Russell, 1963.

Freud, Sigmund. *Three Contributions to the Theory of Sex*. In *The Basic Writings of Sigmund Freud*, 553–629. Translated by A. A. Brill. New York: Modern Library, 1965.

———. "The 'Uncanny.' " Translated by Alix Strachey. *Collected Papers*, 4:368–407. New York: Basic Books, 1959.

Friedman, Bruce Jay. Foreword. *Black Humor*. New York: Bantam, 1965.

———. *Stern*. 1962. New York: Pocket Books, 1976.

Frothingham, Octavius B. *Transcendentalism in New England*. Boston: American Unitarian Association, [1876].

Frye, Northrop. *Anatomy of Criticism*. Princeton, N.J.: Princeton University Press, 1957.

Fuchs, Miriam. " 'il miglior fabbro': Gaddis' Debt to T. S. Eliot." In *In Recognition of William Gaddis*, edited by John Kuehl and Steven Moore, 92–105. Syracuse, N.Y.: Syracuse University Press, 1984.

Gabler, Hans Walter, ed. *Ulysses: The Corrected Text*. By James Joyce. New York: Vintage Books, 1986.

Gaddis, William. *JR*. New York: Knopf, 1975.

———. *The Recognitions*. New York: Harcourt, 1955.

———. "The Rush for Second Place." *Harper's* (April 1981): 31–39.

———. "Why I Write." Lecture at the University of Delaware, 1 May 1985.

Galloway, David. *The Absurd Hero in American Fiction*. 2d ed. Austin: University of Texas Press, 1981.

Gardner, John. *On Moral Fiction*. New York: Basic Books, 1978.

———. "The Sound and Fury Over Fiction." With Stephen Singular. *New York Times*

Magazine (8 July 1979): 12+.

Gay, Peter. *A Loss of Mastery: Puritan Historians in Colonial America*. Berkeley: University of California Press, 1966.

Goethe, Johann Wolfgang von. *Conversations of Goethe with Eckermann and Soret*. 2 vols. Translated by John Oxenford. London: Smith, Elder, 1850.

———. *Faust: A Tragedy*. Translated by Walter Arndt and edited by Cyrus Hamlin. New York: Norton, 1976.

———. *Faust: A Tragedy*. Translated by Bayard Taylor. New York: Macmillan, 1930.

Gogol, Nikolai. *Dead Souls*. Edited by George Gibian and translated by George Reavey. New York: W. W. Norton, 1985.

———. *Dead Souls*. Translated by Bernard Guilbert Guerney with Introduction by René Wellek. New York: Holt, Rinehart and Winston, 1961.

———. *Dead Souls*. Translated by Andrew R. MacAndrew and Foreword by Frank O'Connor. New York: New American Library, 1961.

———. *Letters of Nikolai Gogol*. Edited by Carl R. Proffer and translated by Carl R. Proffer with Vera Krivoshein. Ann Arbor: University of Michigan Press, 1967.

Goldberg, Homer. *The Art of Joseph Andrews*. Chicago: University of Chicago Press, 1969.

Gresham, James. "*Giles Goat-Boy:* Satyr, Satire and Tragedy Twined." In *Critical Essays on John Barth*, edited by Joseph J. Waldmeir, 157–71. Boston: G. K. Hall, 1980.

Griffith, John. "*Of Plymouth Plantation* As a Mercantile Epic." *Arizona Quarterly* 28 (1972): 231–42.

Gross, Beverly. "The Anti-Novels of John Barth." In *Critical Essays on John Barth*, edited by Joseph J. Waldmeir, 30–42. Boston: G. K. Hall, 1980.

Grove, Lloyd. "Gaddis and the Cosmic Babble: Fiction Rich With the Darkly Funny Voices of America." *Washington Post* (23 August 1985): B1+.

Gurewitch, Morton. *Comedy: The Irrational Vision*. Ithaca, N.Y.: Cornell University Press, 1975.

Haller, Robert S., trans. and ed. "The *Letter to Can Grande*." In *Literary Criticism of Dante Alighieri*. Lincoln: University of Nebraska Press, 1973.

Hanford, James Holly, and James G. Taaffe. *A Milton Handbook*. New York: Appleton-Century-Crofts, 1970.

Harris, Charles B. *Contemporary American Novelists of the Absurd*. New Haven, Conn.: College and University Press, 1971.

———. *Passionate Virtuosity: The Fiction of John Barth*. Urbana: University of Illinois Press, 1983.

[Harvard]. See Cotton Mather.

Hassan, Ihab. "Laughter in the Dark: The New Voice in American Fiction." *American Scholar* 33 (1964): 636–40.

Hauck, Richard Boyd. *A Cheerful Nihilism*. Bloomington, Ind.: Indiana University Press, 1971.

Hawthorne, Nathaniel. *The English Notebooks*. Edited by Randall Stewart. New York: MLA of America, 1941.

Heimert, Alan. *Religion and the American Mind*. 1966. Reprint. Cambridge, Mass.: Harvard University Press, 1968.

Heller, Joseph. *Catch-22*. 1955. Reprint. New York: Dell, 1970.

Hendin, Josephine. "What Is Thomas Pynchon Telling Us? *V*. and *Gravity's Rainbow*." In *Critical Essays on Thomas Pynchon*, edited by Richard Pearce, 42–50. Boston: G. K. Hall, 1981.

Henkle, Roger B. "Pynchon's Tapestries on the Western Wall." In *Pynchon: A Collection of Critical Essays*, edited by Edward Mendelson, 97–111. Englewood Cliffs, N.J.: Prentice-Hall, 1978.

Herbert, George. "The Church Militant." *The Works of George Herbert*. Edited by

Bibliography

F. E. Hutchinson. Oxford: Clarendon, 1970.

Hill, Hamlin. "Black Humor: Its Cause and Cure." *Colorado Quarterly* 17 (1968): 57–64.

Hobbes, Thomas. *The Elements of Law, Natural and Politic.* Edited by Ferdinand Tonnies. Cambridge, Mass.: Cambridge University Press, 1928.

Holder, Alan. " 'What Marvelous Plot . . . Was Afoot?': John Barth's *The Sot-Weed Factor.*" In *Critical Essays on John Barth*, edited by Joseph J. Waldmeir, 123–33. Boston: G. K. Hall, 1980.

Howard, Leon. *Literature and the American Tradition.* New York: Doubleday, 1960.

Howe, Irving, ed. *Literary Modernism.* Greenwich, Conn.: Fawcett, 1967.

Hubbell, Jay B. "The Smith-Pocahontas Story in Literature." *Virginia Magazine* 65 (1957): 275–300.

Hughes, Merritt, ed. *John Milton: Complete Poems and Major Prose.* New York: Odyssey, 1957.

Hunt, John W. "Comic Escape and Anti-Vision: *V.* and *The Crying of Lot 49.*" In *Critical Essays on Thomas Pynchon*, edited by Richard Pearce, 32–41. Boston: G. K. Hall, 1981.

Hunter, G. K. *Paradise Lost.* Boston: George Allen & Unwin, 1980.

Jantz, Harold S. *The Form of Faust.* Baltimore: Johns Hopkins University Press, 1978.

———. "The Myths about America: Origins and Extensions." *Deutschlands literarisches Amerikabild*, edited by Alexander Ritter, 37–49. Hildesheim, N.Y.: Georg Olms, 1977.

Johnson, Samuel. *The Idler* 22 (9 September, 1758). In *Samuel Johnson*, edited by Donald Greene. New York: Oxford University Press, 1984.

Johnson, W. R. *Darkness Visible: A Study of Vergil's* Aeneid. Berkeley: University of California Press, 1976.

Jones, Howard Mumford. *Ideas in America.* Cambridge, Mass.: Harvard University Press, 1944.

Jordy, William. *Henry Adams: Scientific Historian.* New Haven, Conn.: Yale University Press, 1952.

Joyce, James. *Ulysses: The Corrected Text.* Edited by Hans Walter Gabler. New York: Vintage, 1986.

Jungmann, Josef A. *Public Worship.* Translated by Clifford Howell, S. J. Collegeville, Minn.: Liturgical Press, 1957.

Kaplan, Justin. *Walt Whitman: A Life.* New York: Simon & Schuster, 1980.

Karl, Frederick. *American Fictions 1940/1980.* New York: Harper & Row, 1983.

———. "Gaddis: A Tribune of the Fifties." In *In Recognition of William Gaddis*, edited by John Kuehl and Steven Moore, 174–98. Syracuse, N.Y.: Syracuse University Press, 1984.

———. *Research Notes. Chronicle of Higher Education* (9 January 1985): 5–6.

Kayser, Wolfgang. *The Grotesque in Art and Literature.* Translated by Ulrich Weisstein. New York: McGraw-Hill, 1966.

Keiser, Albert. *The Indian in American Literature.* New York: Oxford University Press, 1933.

Kendrick, Walter. Review of *The Friday Book* by John Barth. *New York Times Book Review* (18 November 1984): 15.

Kenner, Hugh. *The Counterfeiters.* 1968. New York: Doubleday Anchor, 1973.

———. *Joyce's Voices.* Berkeley: University of California Press, 1978.

———. *The Stoic Comedians: Flaubert, Joyce and Beckett.* 1962. Reprint. Berkeley: University of California Press, 1974.

Kermode, Frank. *The Sense of an Ending.* 1967. Reprint. New York: Oxford University Press, 1968.

Kesey, Ken. *One Flew Over the Cuckoo's Nest.* New York: Signet, 1962.

———. *Sometimes a Great Notion.* New York: Viking, 1964. Reprint. New York: Bantam, 1969.

Kittel, Gerhard, ed. *Theological Dictionary of the New Testament.* Translated and edited by Geoffrey W. Bromiley. Grand Rapids, Mich.: Eerdmans, 1964–67.

Klinkowitz, Jerome. *Literary Disruptions: The Making of a Post-Contemporary American Fiction.* Urbana: University of Illinois Press, 1975.

Knapp, James F. "Tangled in the Language of the Past: Ken Kesey and Cultural Revolution." *Midwest Quarterly* 19 (Summer 1978): 398–412.

Knickerbocker, Conrad. "Humor with a Mortal Sting." In *The World of Black Humor,* edited by Douglas M. Davis, 299–305. New York: Dutton, 1967.

Knight, Christopher."Flemish Art and Wyatt's Quest for Redemption in William Gaddis's *The Recognitions.*" In *In Redemption of William Gaddis,* edited by John Kuehl and Steven Moore, 58–69. Syracuse, N.Y.: Syracuse University Press, 1984.

Koenig, David [Peter]. "The Writing of *The Recognitions.*" In *In Recognition of William Gaddis,* edited by John Kuehl and Steven Moore, 20–31. Syracuse, N.Y.: Syracuse University Press, 1984.

Koenig, Peter W. "Recognizing Gaddis's *Recognitions.*" *Contemporary Literature* 16 (1975): 61–72.

———. " 'Splinters from the Yew Tree': A Critical Study of William Gaddis's *The Recognitions.*" Ph.D. diss., New York University, 1971.

Kostelanetz, Richard, "The American Absurd Novel." In *The World of Black Humor,* edited by Douglas M. Davis, 306–13. New York: Dutton, 1967.

———. "The New-American Fiction." In *The New American Arts,* edited by R. Kostelanetz, 194–236. New York: Horizon Press, 1965.

Krafft, John M. " 'And How Far-Fallen': Puritan Themes in *Gravity's Rainbow.*" *Critique* 18, no. 3 (1977): 55–73.

Kuehl, John, and Steven Moore, eds. *In Recognition of William Gaddis.* Syracuse, N.Y.: Syracuse University Press, 1984.

Laski, Marghanita. *Ecstasy: A Study of Some Secular and Religious Experiences.* Bloomington, Ind.: Indiana University Press, 1961.

LeClair, Thomas. "William Gaddis, *JR,* & the Art of Excess." *Modern Fiction Studies* 27 (1981–82): 587–600.

Leeds, Barry H. *Ken Kesey.* New York: Frederick Ungar, 1981.

Lehrer, Tom. *That Was the Year That Was.* Reprise Records 6179.

Lemay, J. A. Leo. "The Frontiersman from Lout to Hero." *Proceedings of the American Antiquarian Society* 88 (1979): 187–223.

———. *Men of Letters in Colonial Maryland.* Knoxville: University of Tennessee Press, 1972.

———. "The Text, Tradition, and Themes of 'The Big Bear of Arkansas.' " *American Literature* 47 (1975): 321–42.

Leonard, John. "Books of the Times." *New York Times* (1 October 1979): C15.

Leverence, John. "Gaddis Anagnorisis." In *In Recognition of William Gaddis,* edited by John Kuehl and Steven Moore, 32–45. Syracuse, N.Y.: Syracuse University Press, 1984.

Levine, George. "Risking the Moment: Anarchy and Possibility in Pynchon's Fiction." In *Mindful Pleasures: Essays on Thomas Pynchon,* edited by George Levine and David Leverenz, 113–36. Boston: Little, Brown, 1976.

———. "V-2." In *Pynchon: A Collection of Critical Essays,* edited by Edward Mendelson, 178–91. Englewood Cliffs: Prentice-Hall, 1978.

———, and David Leverenz, eds. Introduction. *Mindful Pleasures: Essays on Thomas Pynchon.* Boston: Little, Brown, 1976.

Lewalski, Barbara Kiefer. Paradise Lost *and the Rhetoric of Literary Forms.* Princeton,

N.J.: Princeton University Press, 1985.

Lewis, C. S. *A Preface to* Paradise Lost. 1942. Reprint. London: Oxford University Press, 1979.

Lewis, R.W.B. *The American Adam: Innocence, Tragedy and Tradition in the Nineteenth Century.* 1955. Reprint. Chicago: University of Chicago Press, 1971.

———. *The Picaresque Saint.* Philadelphia: Lippincott, 1959.

Lhamon, W. T. "Pentecost, Promiscuity, and Pynchon's *V.:* From the Scaffold to the Impulsive." In *Mindful Pleasures: Essays on Thomas Pynchon,* edited by George Levine and David Leverenz, 69–86. Boston: Little, Brown, 1976.

Lish, Gordon. "What the Hell You Looking in Here for, Daisy Mae? An Interview with Ken Kesey." *Genesis West* 2 (1963): 17–29.

Lodge, David. *The Modes of Modern Writing.* Ithaca, N.Y.: Cornell University Press, 1977.

———. *Working with Structuralism.* Boston: Routledge & Kegan Paul, 1981.

Lowance, Mason I. *The Language of Canaan: Metaphor and Symbol in New England from the Puritans to the Transcendentalists.* Cambridge, Mass.: Harvard University Press, 1980.

Lynen, John F. *The Design of the Present: Essays on Time and Form in American Literature.* New Haven, Conn.: Yale University Press, 1969.

Lyons, John O. *The College Novel in America.* Carbondale, Ill.: Southern Illinois University Press, 1962.

McConnell, Frank D. *Four Postwar American Novelists: Bellow, Mailer, Barth and Pynchon.* Chicago: University of Chicago Press, 1977.

McFadden, George. *Discovering the Comic.* Princeton, N.J.: Princeton University Press, 1982.

McIntyre, Ruth A. *William Pynchon: Merchant and Colonizer 1590–1662,* Springfield, Mass.: Connecticut Valley Historical Museum, 1961.

Madden, David. "William Gaddis's *The Recognitions.*" In *Rediscoveries,* edited by David Madden, 291–304. New York: Crown, 1971.

Maddocks, Melvin. "Paleface Takeover." *Atlantic Monthly* 231 (March 1973): 98–101.

Malin, Irving. "Ken Kesey, *One Flew Over the Cuckoo's Nest.*" In *Ken Kesey: One Flew Over the Cuckoo's Nest,* edited by John Clark Pratt, 429–34. New York: Viking, 1973.

———. "Ken Kesey, *Sometimes a Great Notion.*" *Books Abroad* 39 (Spring 1965): 218.

Malvern, Marjorie M. "The Parody of Medieval Saints' Lives in John Barth's *Giles Goat-Boy or, The Revised New Syllabus.*" *Studies in Medievalism* 2 (1982): 59–76.

Manierre, William R. "Cotton Mather and the Biographical Parallel." *American Quarterly* 13 (1961): 153–60.

Martin, Ronald E. *American Literature and the Universe of Force.* Durham, N.C.: Duke University Press, 1981.

Mather, Cotton. *Magnalia Christi Americana.* Books I and II. Edited by Kenneth B. Murdock. Cambridge, Mass.: Harvard University Press, 1977. [Harvard]

———. *Magnalia Christi Americana.* London, 1702. Reprint. 2 vols. Edited by Thomas Robbins. Hartford: Silas Andrus and Son, 1853. Photo-litho reprint. Pennsylvania: Banner of Truth Trust, 1979.

Mather, Samuel. *The Figures or Types of the Old Testament.* New York: Johnson Reprint Corporation, 1969.

Mell, Donald C. "Dryden and the Transformation of the Classical." *Papers on Language and Literature* 17, no. 2 (1981): 146–63.

Melville, Herman. *The Confidence-Man: His Masquerade.* Edited by Harrison Hayford, Hershel Parker, and G. Thomas Tanselle. Evanston, Ill.: Northwestern University Press, 1984.

————. *Moby-Dick*. Edited by Harrison Hayford and Hershel Parker. New York: Norton, 1967.

Mendelson, Edward. "Gravity's Encyclopedia." In *Mindful Pleasures: Essays on Thomas Pynchon*, edited by George Levine and David Leverenz, 161–95. Boston: Little, Brown, 1976.

————. "The Sacred, the Profane, and *The Crying of Lot 49*." In *Pynchon: A Collection of Critical Essays*, edited by Edward Mendelson, 112–46. Englewood Cliffs, N.J.: Prentice-Hall, 1978.

————, ed. *Pynchon: A Collection of Critical Essays*. Englewood Cliffs, N.J.: Prentice-Hall, 1978.

Mercer, Peter. "The Rhetoric of *Giles Goat-Boy*." *Novel* 4, no. 2 (Winter 1971): 147–58.

Merchant, Paul. *The Epic*. London: Methuen, 1977.

Miller, George. "Archetype and History." *Modern Language Studies* 10, no. 3 (Fall 1980): 12–21.

Miller, James E. *The American Quest for a Supreme Fiction: Whitman's Legacy in the Personal Epic*. Chicago: University of Chicago Press, 1979.

————. *A Critical Guide to* Leaves of Grass. Chicago: University of Chicago Press, 1957.

————. "The Humor in the Horror." In *Ken Kesey: One Flew Over the Cuckoo's Nest*, edited by John Clark Pratt, 397–400. New York: Viking, 1973.

————. *Quests Surd and Absurd*. Chicago: University of Chicago Press, 1967.

Miller, Perry. *Errand into the Wilderness*. Cambridge, Mass.: Harvard University Press, Belknap Press, 1956.

————. *Nature's Nation*. Cambridge, Mass.: Harvard University Press, 1967.

————. *The New England Mind: From Colony to Province*. Cambridge, Mass.: Harvard University Press, 1953.

Miller, Russell H. "*The Sot-Weed Factor:* A Contemporary Mock Epic." *Critique* 8, no. 2 (1965–66): 88–100.

Milton, John. *An Apology for Smectymnuus*. In *John Milton: Complete Poems and Major Prose*, edited by Merritt Y. Hughes, 690–95. New York: Odyssey, 1957.

————. *Areopagitica*. In *John Milton: Complete Poems and Major Prose*, edited by Merritt Y. Hughes, 716–49. New York: Odyssey, 1957.

————. *Paradise Lost*. In *John Milton: Complete Poems and Major Prose*, edited by Merritt Y. Hughes, 207–469. New York: Odyssey, 1957.

————. *The Reason of Church Government Urged against Prelaty*. In *John Milton: Complete Poems and Major Prose*, edited by Merritt Y. Hughes, 640–89. New York: Odyssey, 1957.

Moore, Steven, and John Kuehl, eds. *In Recognition of William Gaddis*. Syracuse, N.Y.: Syracuse University Press, 1984.

————. *A Reader's Guide to William Gaddis's* The Recognitions. Lincoln: University of Nebraska Press, 1982.

Morgan, Speer. "*Gravity's Rainbow:* What's the Big Idea?" In *Critical Essays on Thomas Pynchon*, edited by Richard Pearce, 82–98. Boston: G.K. Hall, 1981.

Morison, Samuel Eliot. "William Pynchon, Frontier Magistrate and Fur Trader." In *Builders of the Bay Colony*, 337–75. Boston: Northeastern University Press, 1981.

————. "William Pynchon: The Founder of Springfield." *Proceedings of the Massachusetts Historical Society* 64 (1932): 66–109.

Morrell, David. *John Barth: An Introduction*. University Park: Pennsylvania State University Press, 1976.

Mullahy, Patrick. *Oedipus: Myth and Complex*. New York: Grove Press, 1955.

Murdock, Kenneth B. "Clio in the Wilderness: History and Biography in Puritan New England." *Church History* 24 (1955): 221–38.

————, ed. *Magnalia Christi Americana*. Books I and II. By Cotton Mather. Cambridge, Mass.: Harvard University Press, 1977. [Harvard]

Bibliography

Nabokov, Vladimir. *Lolita*. 1955. Reprint. New York: Berkley Medallion, 1970.

O'Donnell, Patrick. *Passionate Doubts: Designs of Interpretation in Contemporary American Fiction*. Iowa City: University of Iowa Press, 1986.

Olderman, Raymond M. *Beyond the Wasteland: A Study of the American Novel in the Nineteen-Sixties*. New Haven, Conn.: Yale University Press, 1972.

Ortega y Gasset, José. "Decline of the Novel." Translated by Helene Weyl. 1925. In *The Dehumanization of Art and Other Essays on Art, Culture, and Literature*, 57–60. Princeton, N.J.: Princeton University Press, 1968.

Ozick, Cynthia. "Fakery and Stony Truths." Review of *Carpenter's Gothic*, by William Gaddis. *New York Times Book Review* (7 July 1985): 1.

Panofsky, Erwin. *Early Netherlandish Painting*. Vol. 1. Cambridge, Mass.: Harvard University Press, 1966.

Parrington, Vernon. *Main Currents in American Thought*. 3 vols. New York: Harcourt, Brace, 1930.

Pearce, Richard, ed. *Critical Essays on Thomas Pynchon*. Boston: G. K. Hall, 1981.

————. *The Novel in Motion*. Columbus: Ohio State University Press, 1983.

Pearce, Roy Harvey. *The Continuity of American Poetry*. Princeton, N.J.: Princeton University Press, 1961.

Perl, Jeffrey M. *The Tradition of Return: The Implicit History of Modern Literature*. Princeton, N.J.: Princeton University Press, 1984.

Perri, Carmela. "On Alluding." *Poetics* 7 (1978): 289–307.

Perry, Bliss. *The Praise of Folly and Other Papers*. Boston: Houghton Mifflin, 1923.

Pinsker, Sanford. "The Urban Tall Tale: Frontier Humor in a Contemporary Key." In *Comic Relief*, edited by Sarah Blacher Cohen, 249–62. Urbana: University of Illinois Press, 1978.

Plater, William M. *The Grim Phoenix: Reconstructing Thomas Pynchon*. Bloomington: Indiana University Press, 1978.

Plato. *The Republic*. 2 vols. Translated by Paul Shorey. Cambridge, Mass.: Harvard University Press, 1930–35.

————. *Symposium*. Translated by W.R.M. Lamb. Cambridge, Mass.: Harvard University Press, 1925.

Poirier, Richard. "The Importance of Thomas Pynchon." In *Mindful Pleasures: Essays on Thomas Pynchon*, edited by George Levine and David Leverenz, 15–29. Boston: Little, Brown, 1976.

————. *The Performing Self: Compositions and Decompositions in the Languages of Contemporary Life*. New York: Oxford University Press, 1971.

Porter, M. Gilbert. *The Art of Grit: Ken Kesey's Fiction*. Columbia: University of Missouri Press, 1982.

Porush, David. *The Soft Machine: Cybernetic Fiction*. New York: Methuen, 1985.

Potts, Leonard J. *Comedy*. London: Cheltenham Press, 1948.

Pratt, John Clark, ed. *Ken Kesey: One Flew Over the Cuckoo's Nest*. New York: Viking, 1973.

Prince, Alan. "An Interview with John Barth." *Prism* [Sir George Williams University] (Spring 1968): 42–62.

Proctor, Mortimer R. *The English University Novel*. 1957. Reprint. New York: Arno Press, 1977.

Puetz, Manfred. "John Barth's *The Sot-Weed Factor*: The Pitfalls of Mythopoesis." In *Critical Essays on John Barth*, edited by Joseph J. Waldmeir, 134–45. Boston: G. K. Hall, 1980.

Pynchon, Thomas. *The Crying of Lot 49*. Philadelphia: Lippincott, 1966.

————. "Entropy." *Kenyon Review* 22, no. 2 (1960): 277–92.

————. *Gravity's Rainbow*. New York: Viking, 1973.

————. "Is It O.K. to Be a Luddite?" *New York Times Book Review* (28 October

1984): 1+.
————. "A Journey into the Mind of Watts." *New York Times Magazine* (12 June 1966): 34+.
————. *Slow Learner.* Boston: Little, Brown, 1984.
————. *V.* Philadelphia: Lippincott. 1963. Reprint. New York: Bantam, 1968.
Quilligan, Maureen. *The Language of Allegory: Defining the Genre.* Ithaca, N.Y.: Cornell University Press, 1979.
Rabelais, François. *The Histories of Gargantua and Pantagruel.* Translated by J. M. Cohen. Middlesex, England: Penguin Books, 1983.
Raglan, Lord. *The Hero: A Study in Tradition, Myth and Drama.* London: Methuen, 1936.
Rahv, Philip. *Literature and the Sixth Sense.* Boston: Houghton Mifflin, 1969.
Rank, Otto. *Beyond Psychology.* 1941. New York: Dover, 1958.
Rawson, Claude J. "Before the Professors Took Over." Review of *A History of Modern Criticism: 1750–1950,* by René Wellek. *New York Times Book Review* (30 March 1986): 8–9.
————. "The Character of Swift's Satire." In *Focus: Swift,* edited by C. J. Rawson. London: Sphere Books, 1971.
Read, John. *Prelude to Chemistry: An Outline of Alchemy.* 1936. Cambridge, Mass.: MIT Press, 1966.
Recognitions of Clement. Translated with an Introduction by Thomas Smith. In *The Ante-Nicene Fathers.* 10 vols. Edited by Alexander Roberts and James Donaldson, 8:75–211. New York: Scribner, 1903.
Reich, Annie. "The Structure of the Grotesque-Comic Sublimation." *Bulletin of the Menninger Clinic* 13, no. 5 (1949): 160–71.
Research Notes. By Frederick Karl. *Chronicle of Higher Education* (9 January 1985): 5–6.
Ricks, Christopher. "Allusion: The Poet as Heir." In *Studies in the Eighteenth Century,* edited by R. F. Brissenden and J. C. Eade, 209–40. Toronto: University of Toronto Press, 1976.
Robbe-Grillet, Alain. *For a New Novel: Essays on Fiction.* Translated by Richard Howard. 1963. New York: Grove Press, 1965.
Robbins, Thomas, ed. *Magnalia Christi Americana.* 2 vols. By Cotton Mather. Hartford: Silas Andrus and Son, 1853; Photo-litho reprint. Pennsylvania: Banner of Truth Trust, 1979.
Roberts, Alexander, and James Donaldson. *Recognitions of Clement.* In *The Ante-Nicene Fathers.* 10 vols. 8: 75–214. New York: Scribner, 1903.
Rogers, Robert. *A Psychoanalytic Study of the Double in Literature.* Detroit: Wayne State University Press, 1970.
Rosenmeier, Jesper. " 'With My Owne Eyes': William Bradford's *Of Plymouth Plantation.* " In *Typology and Early American Literature,* edited by Sacvan Bercovitch, 69–105. Amherst, Mass.: University of Massachusetts Press, 1972.
Rovit, Earl. "The Novel as Parody: John Barth." In *Critical Essays on John Barth,* edited by Joseph J. Waldmeir, 116–22. Boston: G. K. Hall, 1980.
Rulandus, Martinus. *A Lexicon of Alchemy.* 1612. Translated by A. E. Waite. 1893. Reprint. London: John M. Watkins, 1964.
Ruskin, John. "Grotesque Renaissance." *The Stones of Venice,* chapter 3. In *The Works of John Ruskin,* edited by E. T. Cook and Alexander Wedderburn, 11:135–95. London: George Allen, 1904.
Safer, Elaine B. "The Allusive Mode and Black Humor in Barth's *Giles Goat-Boy* and Pynchon's *Gravity's Rainbow.*" *Renascence* 32 (1980): 89–104.
————. "The Allusive Mode and Black Humor in Barth's *Sot-Weed Factor.*" *Studies in the Novel* 13 (1981): 424–38.

204

———. "The Allusive Mode, the Absurd and Black Humor in William Gaddis's *The Recognitions.*" *Studies in American Humor* 1 [n.s.], no. 2 (1982): 103–18.

———. "The Essay as Aesthetic Mirror: John Barth's 'Exhaustion' and 'Replenishment.'" *Studies in American Fiction* 15, no. 1 (1987): 109–17.

Salemi, Joseph S. "To Soar in Atonement: Art as Expiation in Gaddis's *The Recognitions.*" *Novel* 10, no. 2 (1977): 127–36.

Sanders, Scott. "Pynchon's Paranoid History." In *Mindful Pleasures: Essays on Thomas Pynchon,* edited by George Levine and David Leverenz, 139–59. Boston: Little, Brown, 1976.

Sartre, Jean-Paul. *Nausea.* Translated by Lloyd Alexander. New York: New Directions, 1964.

———. "Existentialism Is a Humanism." In *Existentialism from Dostoevsky to Sartre,* edited by Walter Kaufmann, 345–69. New York: New American Library, 1975.

Schaub, Thomas H. *Pynchon: The Voice of Ambiguity.* Urbana: University of Illinois Press, 1981.

Scholes, Robert. *Fabulation and Metafiction.* Urbana: University of Illinois Press, 1979.

Schulz, Max F. "Barth, *Letters,* and the Great Tradition." *Genre* 14, no. 1 (Spring 1981): 95–115.

———. *Black Humor Fiction of the Sixties.* Athens, Ohio: Ohio University Press, 1973.

Seelye, John. "Dryad in a Dead Oak Tree: The Incognito in *The Recognitions.*" In *In Recognition of William Gaddis,* edited by John Kuehl and Steven Moore, 70–80. Syracuse, N.Y.: Syracuse University Press, 1984.

———. *Prophetic Waters: The River in Early American Life and Literature.* New York: Oxford University Press, 1977.

Seidel, Michael. "The Satiric Plots of *Gravity's Rainbow.*" In *Pynchon: A Collection of Critical Essays,* edited by Edward Mendelson, 193–212. Englewood Cliffs, N.J.: Prentice-Hall, 1978.

Sensabaugh, George F. *Milton in Early America.* Princeton, N.J.: Princeton University Press, 1964.

Shakespeare, William. *The Complete Plays and Poems of William Shakespeare.* Edited by William Allan Neilson and Charles Jarvis Hill. Cambridge, Mass.: Riverside Press, 1942.

Shepard, Odell. *Pedlar's Progress: The Life of Bronson Alcott.* Boston: Little, Brown, 1937.

Sherman, W. D. "The Novels of Ken Kesey." *Journal of American Studies* 5, no. 2 (August 1971): 185–96.

Sherwood, Terry G. "*One Flew Over the Cuckoo's Nest* and the Comic Strip." In *Ken Kesey: One Flew Over the Cuckoo's Nest,* edited by John Clark Pratt, 382–96. New York: Viking, 1973.

Shumaker, Wayne. "Alchemy." *The Occult Sciences in the Renaissance,* chapter 4, pp. 160–200. Berkeley: University of California Press, 1972.

Siegel, Mark Richard. *Pynchon: Creative Paranoia in* Gravity's Rainbow. Port Washington, N.Y.: Kennikat Press, 1978.

Silverman, Kenneth. *The Life and Times of Cotton Mather.* New York: Harper & Row, 1984.

Slade, Joseph W. " 'Entropy' and Other Calamities." In *Pynchon: A Collection of Critical Essays,* edited by Edward Mendelson, 69–86. Englewood Cliffs, N.J.: Prentice-Hall, 1978.

———. *Thomas Pynchon.* New York: Warner, 1974.

Slotkin, Richard. *The Fatal Environment: The Myth of the Frontier in the Age of Industrialization, 1800–1890.* New York: Atheneum, 1985.

———. *Regeneration through Violence: The Mythology of the American Frontier, 1600–1860.* Middletown, Conn.: Wesleyan University Press, 1973.

Smith, Cindy. "William Gaddis Rails against Misrepresentation." *The* (University of Delaware) *Review* (30 April 1985): 18.

Smith, John. *Travels and Works of Captain John Smith.* Edited by Edward Arber with an Introduction by A. G. Bradley. Edinburgh: John Grant, 1910.

Smith, Marcus, and Khachig Tololyan. "The New Jeremiad: *Gravity's Rainbow.*" In *Critical Essays on Thomas Pynchon,* edited by Richard Pearce, 169–86. Boston: G. K. Hall, 1981.

Staiger, Emil. "On the 'Great Lacuna' and the Pact Scene." In *Faust: A Tragedy,* translated by Walter Arndt and edited by Cyrus Hamlin, 504–18. New York: Norton, 1976.

Stark, John O. *The Literature of Exhaustion: Borges, Nabokov, and Barth.* Durham, N.C.: Duke University Press, 1974.

———. *Pynchon's Fictions: Thomas Pynchon and the Literature of Information.* Athens: Ohio University Press, 1980.

Stuart, Dabney. "A Service to the University." In *Critical Essays on John Barth,* edited by Joseph J. Waldmeir, 150–53. Boston: G. K. Hall, 1980.

Summers, Joseph. *The Muse's Method: An Introduction to* Paradise Lost. Cambridge, Mass.: Harvard University Press, 1962.

Sutcliffe, Denham. "Worth a Guilty Conscience." In *Critical Essays on John Barth,* edited by Joseph J. Waldmeir, 113–15. Boston: G. K. Hall, 1980.

Sutton, Walter. "Apocalyptic History and the American Epic: Cotton Mather and Joel Barlow." In *Toward a New American Literary History,* edited by Louis J. Budd et al., 69–83. Durham, N.C.: Duke University Press, 1980.

Swearingen, James. "Philosophical Hermeneutics and the Renewal of Tradition." *The Eighteenth Century: Theory and Interpretation* 22 (1981): 195–221.

Swift, Jonathan. *Gulliver's Travels.* In *The Prose Works of Jonathan Swift,* edited by Herbert Davis, vol. 11. Oxford: Basil Blackwell, 1941.

———. "Letter to Pope 29 Sept. 1725." In *The Correspondence of Jonathan Swift,* edited by Sir Harold Williams, vol. 3. Oxford: Clarendon Press, 1965.

Sypher, Wylie. *Loss of the Self in Modern Literature and Art.* New York: Random House, 1962.

———. "The Meanings of Comedy." In *Comedy,* edited by Wylie Sypher. New York: Doubleday, 1956.

Tanner, Stephen. *Ken Kesey.* Boston: Twayne, 1983.

Tanner, Tony. "The American Novelist as Entropologist." *London Magazine* 10 (October 1970): 5–18.

———. "Caries and Cabals." In *Mindful Pleasures: Essays on Thomas Pynchon,* edited by George Levine and David Leverenz, 49–67. Boston: Little, Brown, 1976.

———. *City of Words: American Fiction, 1950–1970.* New York: Harper & Row, 1971.

———. *Thomas Pynchon.* New York: Methuen, 1982.

———. "V. and V-2." In *Pynchon: A Collection of Critical Essays,* edited by Edward Mendelson, 16–55. Englewood Cliffs, N.J.: Prentice-Hall, 1978.

Tatham, Campbell. "The Gilesian Monomyth: Some Remarks on the Structure of *Giles Goat-Boy.*" *Genre* 3, no. 4 (1970): 364–75.

———. "John Barth and the Aesthetics of Artifice." In *Critical Essays on John Barth,* edited by Joseph J. Waldmeir, 43–54. Boston: G. K. Hall, 1980.

Tayler, Edward W. *Milton's Poetry: Its Development in Time.* Pittsburgh: Duquesne University Press, 1979.

Taylor, Bayard, ed. *Faust: A Tragedy.* By Johann Wolfgang von Goethe. New York: Macmillan, 1930.

Tharpe, Jac. *John Barth: The Comic Sublimity of Paradox.* Carbondale: Southern Illinois University Press, 1974.

Bibliography

Thigpen, Kenneth A. "Folkloristic Concerns in Barth's *The Sot-Weed Factor.*" *Southern Folklore Quarterly* 41 (1977): 225–37.

Thoreau, Henry David. *Walden and Civil Disobedience.* Edited by Owen Thomas. New York: Norton, 1966.

Thorpe, Thomas Bangs. "The Big Bear of Arkansas." In *Native American Humor,* edited by Walter Blair, 337–48. New York: American Book, 1937.

Tillyard, E.M.W. *The Epic Strain in the English Novel.* London: Chatto & Windus, 1958.

Tilton, John. "*Giles Goat-Boy:* An Interpretation." *Bucknell Review* 18, no. 1 (1970): 92–119.

Tocqueville, Alexis de. *Democracy in America.* Edited by J. P. Mayer and Max Lerner and translated by George Lawrence. New York: Harper & Row, 1966.

Tololyan, Khachig, and Marcus Smith. "The New Jeremiad: *Gravity's Rainbow.*" In *Critical Essays on Thomas Pynchon,* edited by Richard Pearce, 169–86. Boston: G. K. Hall, 1981.

Torrance, Robert M. *The Comic Hero.* Cambridge, Mass. Harvard University Press, 1978.

Tyler, Moses Coit. *A History of American Literature, 1607–1765.* Ithaca, N.Y.: Cornell University Press, 1949.

Underhill, Evelyn. *Mysticism: A Study in the Nature and Development of Man's Spiritual Consciousness.* New York: Dutton, 1930.

Valentinus, Basilius. "Practica." *The Hermetic Museum.* Vol. 1. Edited by Arthur Edward Waite. London: John M. Watkins, 1953. [*HM*]

———. *The Triumphal Chariot of Antimony.* Translated by Arthur Edward Waite. London: Vincent Stuart, 1962.

Van Cromphout, Gustaaf. "Cotton Mather as Plutarchan Biographer." *American Literature* 46 (1974–75): 465–81.

Virgil. *Aeneid.* Translated by H. Rushton Fairclough. Cambridge, Mass.: Harvard University Press, 1978.

von Braun, Werner. See Tom Lehrer.

Waggoner, Hyatt H. *American Poets: From the Puritans to the Present.* 1968. Reprint. Baton Rouge, La.: Louisiana State University Press, 1984.

Waldmeir, Joseph J., ed. *Critical Essays on John Barth.* Boston: G. K. Hall, 1980.

———. "Two Novelists of the Absurd: Heller and Kesey." In *Ken Kesey: One Flew Over the Cuckoo's Nest,* edited by John Clark Pratt, 401–18. New York: Viking, 1973.

Warren, Austin. "Grandfather Mather and His Wonder Book." *Sewanee Review* 72 (1964): 96–116.

Watters, David H. "The Spectral Identity of Sir William Phips." *Early American Literature* 18 (Winter 1983–84): 219–32.

Watters, R. E. "Biographical Technique in Cotton Mather's *Magnalia.*" *WMQ* 3rd series, no. 2 (1945): 154–63.

Weber, Brom. "The Mode of 'Black Humor.'" In *The Comic Imagination in American Literature,* edited by Louis D. Rubin, 361–71. New Brunswick, N.J.: Rutgers University Press, 1973.

Weisenburger, Steven. "The End of History? Thomas Pynchon and the Uses of the Past." In *Critical Essays on Thomas Pynchon,* edited by Richard Pearce, 140–56. Boston: G. K. Hall, 1981.

———. "Paper Currencies: Reading William Gaddis." In *In Recognition of William Gaddis,* edited by John Kuehl and Steven Moore, 147–61. Syracuse, N.Y.: Syracuse University Press, 1984.

Weixlmann, Joseph N. *John Barth: A Bibliography.* New York: Garland, 1976.

Wellek, René. Introduction. *Dead Souls.* By Nikolai Gogol. Translated by Bernard Guilbert Guerney. New York: Holt, Rinehart and Winston, 1961.

Bibliography

Wendell, Barrett. *Cotton Mather: The Puritan Priest.* 1891. New York: Harcourt, 1963.

Wenska, Walter P. "Bradford's Two Histories: Pattern and Paradigm in *Of Plymouth Plantation.*" *Early American Literature* 13 (Fall 1978): 151–64.

White, Hayden. *Metahistory: The Historical Imagination in Nineteenth-Century Europe.* Baltimore: Johns Hopkins University Press, 1979.

Whitman, Walt. *Democratic Vistas.* In *Prose Works 1892.* 2 vols. Edited by Floyd Stovall, 2:361–426. New York: New York University Press, 1964.

————. *Leaves of Grass.* Edited by Sculley Bradley and Harold W. Blodgett. 1965. Reprint. New York: Norton, 1973.

Widmer, Kingsley. "The Post-Modernist Art of Protest: Kesey and Mailer as American Expressions of Rebellion." *Centennial Review* 19, no. 3 (Summer 1975): 121–35.

Wigglesworth, Michael. *The Day of Doom: Or a Poetical Description of the Great and Last Judgment.* 1662. New York: Spiral, 1929.

Winston, Mathew."Black Humor: To Weep with Laughing." In *Comedy: New Perspectives,* edited by Maurice Charney, 31–43. (*New York Literary Forum* 1 [Spring 1978].)

————. "Humour Noir and Black Humor." In *Veins of Humor,* edited by Harry Levin, 269–84. Harvard English Studies 3. Cambridge, Mass.: Harvard University Press, 1972.

————. "The Quest for Pynchon." In *Mindful Pleasures: Essays on Thomas Pynchon,* edited by George Levine and David Leverenz, 251–63. Boston: Little, Brown, 1976.

Winthrop, John. "A Model of Christian Charity." *Old South Leaflets,* no. 207. Boston: Directors of the Old South Work, 1883.

Wittgenstein, Ludwig. *Tractatus Logico-Philosophicus.* 1921. Translated by D. F. Pears and B. F. McGuinnes. New York: Humanities Press, 1974.

Wittreich, Joseph Anthony. *Visionary Poetics.* San Marino, Calif.: Huntington Library, 1979.

Wolfe, Tom. *The Electric Kool-Aid Acid Test.* New York: Bantam, 1969.

Wolfley, Lawrence. "Repression's Rainbow: The Presence of Norman O. Brown in Pynchon's Big Novel." In *Critical Essays on Thomas Pynchon,* edited by Richard Pearce, 99–123. Boston: G. K. Hall, 1981.

Wright, Thomas Goddard. *Literary Culture in Early New England, 1620–1730.* New York: Russell & Russell, 1966.

Wroth, Lawrence C. *"The Maryland Muse* by Ebenezer Cooke: A Facsimile with an Introduction." *American Antiquarian Society Proceedings,* n.s. 44 (1934): 267–335.

Young, Philip. "The Mother of Us All: Pocahontas Reconsidered." *Kenyon Review* 24, no. 3 (1962): 391–415.

INDEX

Note: Works by John Barth, William Gaddis, Ken Kesey, Cotton Mather, Thomas Pynchon, and Walt Whitman are indexed under the authors.

Index

Index